Management Issues in Ch

The rapid pace of economic development in China in the 'reform' period since 1979 has brought with it a host of new problems associated with the management of change. As China simultaneously integrates itself into the world economy for the first time, introduces technology which is often a quantum leap from that which it replaces, and decentralizes control over its industries, with the possibility in prospect of the ultimate dismantling of socialism, China's managers are challenged as never before. This book discusses their successes and failures.

The editors have brought together contributions from more than a dozen specialists in Chinese management practice. Initially, the reform process is introduced, compared with that of the former Soviet Union and Eastern Europe, and the nature of the new enterprise culture is discussed. A section on decision making follows, looking at the impact of decentralization, the role of politics and culture, and similarities in practice between Chinese and Western approaches. Some of the challenges facing Chinese enterprises are then examined, especially the evolution of township enterprises and the organization of production and research. Finally, the management and development of people is considered, the human resource in China's modernization, along with the current provision for management education.

The perspectives offered in this book are the result of the most up-to-date research in China by experts who, in many cases, have been associated with China throughout the entire period of reform. Together they represent a comprehensive picture of the current stage of the Chinese reform process as it affects management.

Published in conjunction with *Management Issues in China: Volume II: International Enterprises* (edited by John Child and Yuan Lu), this volume will provide an invaluable compendium of the most authoritative information available to management students and practitioners alike on the current situation for business in China.

David H. Brown is Chair of the University China Group and is a Senior Lecturer in the Department of Management Science at Lancaster University.
Robin Porter is Head of the China Business Centre at Keele University.

Management Issues in China: Volume I

Domestic Enterprises

Edited by David H. Brown
and Robin Porter

London and New York

First published 1996
by Routledge
11 New Fetter Lane, London EC4P 4EE

Simultaneously published in the USA and Canada
by Routledge
29 West 35th Street, New York, NY 10001

Typeset in Times Ten by Florencetype, Stoodleigh, Devon
Printed and bound in Great Britain by
Clays Ltd, St Ives PLC

British Library Cataloguing in Publication Data
A catalogue record for this book is available from the
British Library

Library of Congress Cataloguing in Publication Data
A catalogue record for this book has been requested

ISBN 0–415–13001–8 (hbk)
ISBN 0–415–13002–6 (pbk)

Contents

Illustrations

Notes on contributors

Max Boisot is Professor of Strategic Management at ESADE, Barcelona and Senior Associate of the Judge Institute of Management Studies, University of Cambridge. From 1984 to 1988 he was Dean and Director of the China–Europe Management Institute in Beijing. His research focuses on the interface between information, technology and culture with special reference to complex systems.

Mohamed Branine is Lecturer of Human Resource Management at the Department of Management and Organisation, University of Stirling. His research interests are in comparative and international HRM. Until recently he was in the Department of Behaviour in Organisations at Lancaster University, where he was a substantial contributor to a major UNDP-funded management education and development project in China's foreign trade sector.

David H. Brown is a Senior Lecturer in the Department of Management Science at the University of Lancaster and is Chair of the University's China Group. He has taught and researched in China since 1985. Most recently he was the UK co-ordinator of a major international United Nations Development Programme into management education and development. His research interests are in the areas of management decisions processes and strategy formulation.

Nigel Campbell founded the China Research Unit at Manchester Business School in 1986 and is Senior Lecturer in Strategic Management. He is currently researching the role of foreign business in China's industrial development. He is series editor of the multi-volume *Advances in Chinese Industrial Studies* (JAI Press) and has written extensively about aspects of Chinese Management.

M. W. Luke Chan is the Director of Management Education in China and Director of the International Programmes at the Michael G. DeGroote School of Business at McMaster University in Hamilton, Ontario, Canada. He is also a Professor of Finance and Business Economics at the School.

His research interest is in the area of financial economics and economic and business development in China.

Ha-Joon Chang is Assistant Director of Research, Faculty of Economics and Politics, Cambridge University. He is author of *The Political Economy of Industrial Policy*, and co-editor with Peter Nolan of *The Transformation of the Communist Economies* (Macmillan 1995).

John Child is the Guinness Professor of Management Studies at the Judge Institute of Management Studies, University of Cambridge. He was Dean and Director of the China–Europe Management Institute, Beijing in 1989 and 1990. His research interests are in the general field of organization, and in the management of joint ventures in China and other emerging economies. He is the author of *Management in China during the Age of Reform* (Cambridge 1994).

Mark Easterby-Smith is Head of the Department of Management Learning at Lancaster University. He has maintained close academic links with China since 1983. His research interests include international comparisons of managing and learning in organizations, and the methodological problems of conducting such research collaboratively.

Paul Forrester is Lecturer in Production Management in the Department of Management at Keele University, Staffordshire. He previously held research posts at Aston Business School and Wolverhampton Polytechnic, following seven years management experience in industry. He is co-author of the book *Market-focused Production Systems: Design and Implementation* (Prentice-Hall 1993). In recent years his research interests have been in Eastern Europe, South-East Asia and China.

Gao Junshan is Associate Professor of Management at Beijing University of Science and Technology. He has been a visiting scholar at the universities of Stanford and Lancaster. His research specializes in decision making and in adapting Western models and practices to Chinese needs.

Charles Quan Li is Asia Pacific Economist at NatWest Markets. He graduated from Beijing Institute of Technology in 1985. His PhD research on technology policy in China was conducted at Aston Business School and completed in 1991.

Hong Liu is the Director of the China Research Unit at Manchester Business School and a Lecturer in International Marketing. His current research interests are foreign business marketing strategies and marketing channel management in joint ventures in China.

Yuan Lu was awarded a PhD by Aston University in Birmingham, UK for research in decision making in Chinese enterprises. He was previously awarded an MBA by the China–Europe Management Institute (CEMI). From 1991 to 1992, he was Research Officer at the University of Lancaster working on an ESRC-funded project comparing decision making in British and Chinese enterprises. In 1993 he joined the Judge Institute of Management Studies at the University of Cambridge, where his work focuses on management in China, cross-cultural management and international business.

Peter Nolan is a Lecturer in the Faculty of Economics and Politics and Fellow of Jesus College, Cambridge University. Publications include *China's Rise, Russia's Fall* (Macmillan 1995) and his co-edited book with Chang *The Transformation of the Communist Economies* (Macmillan 1995). He is editor of the Macmillan series on *Studies in the Chinese Economy*.

Robin Porter is Head of the China Business Centre at Keele University, Staffordshire. Originally a specialist in the history and politics of China, in the 1980s he became the British automotive industry's adviser on China. His publications include work on the Chinese news media, China's early industrial development, and China's foreign trade practices.

Fred Steward is Senior Lecturer in the Strategic Management group at Aston Business School. He heads the Technology Policy Unit which conducts research on the management of innovation and science and technology policy. He has visited the People's Republic of China on several occasions since 1987.

Malcolm Warner is Fellow of Wolson College, Cambridge, and a member of the Judge Institute of Management Studies, University of Cambridge. He has previously taught and researched at Stanford and Columbia Universities and the London Business School. He has published a wide range of books and articles including *How Chinese Managers Learn* (Macmillan 1992) and *The Management of Human Resources in Chinese Industry* (Macmillan 1995).

Wang Yanzhong is a researcher in the Institute of Industrial Economics, Chinese Academy of Social Science. His research focuses on the development of rural industry in China.

Lu Zheng is a Research Fellow and the Deputy Director of the Institute of Industrial Economics, Chinese Academy of Social Science. He researches China's industrial development.

Introduction

David H. Brown and Robin Porter

It is now fifteen extraordinary years since China embarked on its programme of economic reform. That decision, taken in 1978, represented a sea change in the direction of Chinese society in general and in the role and importance of Chinese managers in particular. First announced by Deng Xiaoping just two years after the death of Mao and the end of the Great Proletarian Cultural Revolution, the new policy of reform undoubtedly had a complex set of motivations behind it. The party needed to engender loyalty in the population following a long period of political instability. There had been an almost complete collapse in the credibility of moral incentives among the younger generation, and a tangible improvement in the standard of life was urgently needed. There was too a desire to make China a great and respected nation through modernization. There was also a growing recognition of the cost in technological progress of international isolation, and before that of wholesale reliance on often obsolete Soviet technology and equipment.

There is a good case for saying that the reform programme was not thought through at the beginning, or even that it has not been thought through in any comprehensive way since. The slogan 'the four modernizations' – of industry, agriculture, science and technology and national defence – was reminiscent in style of slogans used in the campaigns of the Cultural Revolution, all encompassing, but leaving the detail to be worked out later. The appeal to national sentiment that it implied could elicit loyalty across the spectrum of the party leadership, whereas a set of policy prescriptions could invite factional conflict.

In the event, the new techniques which are at the heart of market reform in China have been introduced unevenly and often quite tentatively in different parts of the country and across different sectors of the economy, sometimes led by local initiative or with the support of only a part of the leadership. Among the milestones have been the re-emergence of private production and free markets in agriculture, beginning in Sichuan in 1979, the implementation of the contract responsibility system in certain industries and the practice of director responsibility in certain factories in the early 1980s. The devolution of authority in the state sector beginning in the mid-1980s was accompanied by the growth of wholly private commercial enterprise.

These developments have occurred within a framework of growing institutional and legal provision for foreign investment, to attract the enabling finance and technology for China's economic growth which she could not provide herself. This has included the creation of the Special Economic Zones for trade and investment which began in 1984, the elaboration of a growing body of trade and investment law, the designation of development zones, and even the creation of the Shanghai stock exchange.

All of these developments have been the subject of controversy at the highest levels of the party, and almost all have in consequence suffered some degree of reversal or obstruction in practice. Despite these difficulties the economic outcome is not a matter of dispute. The combination of market, enterprise, legal and fiscal reform had delivered a decade of GDP growth averaging 9 per cent per year. Into the 1990s the early setback resulting from the Tiananmen Square incident of 4 June 1989 was soon overcome. By the end of 1994 annual growth had reached 13 per cent, foreign trade volumes had exceeded US$235 billion and China returned to a trade surplus of US$5 billion. A remarkable 50,000 new foreign projects were approved during 1994 involving a direct investment of US$35 billion, making China the most sought after developing country for foreign investors (*China Britain Trade Review*, CBTE, London, March 1995). But such conspicuous success has brought a litany of taxing economic and social problems. Inflation at 24 per cent in 1994 and corruption continue to be the major concerns and were central themes of the 1995 National People's Congress. Urban unemployment standing at 5 million at the end of 1994 and an estimated further 30 million under-used workers pose growing difficulties for the state and for enterprise managers. Finally, excessive fixed asset investments, poor organization structures in industry and the ailing state owned enterprises with over a third of the main 100,000 organizations in receipt of subsidies exemplify further the mistakes made and the problems yet to be tackled. (*China Britain Trade Review*, CBTE, London, January 1995).

This then is the context within which Chinese managers have had to manage. Seen from their perspective there has been a bewildering range of experiments, initiatives and directives. These range from the very early reforms dealing with profit retention, through a plurality of systems dealing with enterprise, contract management and director responsibilities, to the current developments reinforcing enterprise autonomy and financial accountability, and further separating politics from management. All of these changes have been complemented by parallel reforms aimed at opening up the domestic markets. As a result a completely different mind set and range of competences is being demanded of China's managers. In short their traditional focus on how to meet targets has been replaced with 'What are the targets, both now and in the future?' And then, 'How can we meet them and be profitable?'

For Western researchers and managers to gain insight into these questions is to traverse the slow and difficult learning curve that is Chinese management. The importance and relevance of doing so, however, becomes readily apparent from the economic outline of China in the 1990s described earlier in the introduction. Fortunately, as Mark Easterby-Smith has observed, the climate and opportunities for learning about China have changed significantly and for the better over the past few years. This is particularly so in business and management. Whereas previously, independent research, whether by Chinese or non-Chinese, was seen as threatening to established priorities and practice, and in some cases to be positively subversive, in the 1990s the value of research in management has been much more widely accepted. Joint ventures, newly autonomous enterprises, and even large state owned industries in the throes of reform have come to see research collaboration with outsiders as a way of gaining valuable feedback on their management practice. This change has been built on acceptance of the need for Western-style management courses at a number of universities in the 1980s, courses frequently implemented with foreign assistance.

In practical terms, this change in climate has meant that it has been increasingly possible for independent research teams to spend time living close to functioning enterprises, interviewing staff, becoming familiar with their operations and facilities, and generally observing them on a day to day basis. Questionnaires may be put to staff now with the reasonable expectation of a response. Managers are more willing to discuss details of organization or production which might previously have been considered state secrets. It is now quite accepted for plants to welcome foreign researchers; they are seen and used as advisers in the effort to modernize management practice and make the plant more competitive. Of course, many problems remain. The sheer difficulty of getting around, the language barrier for most Western researchers and, of course, the cost of research in China and the need to fund it externally are all significant obstacles. Less tangible but possibly more problematic are the continuing conceptual and cultural barriers, especially those which may call into question the suitability of certain analytical constructs and approaches widely used in the West.

All the contributors to this book are researchers who have overcome (with varying degrees of success) the many difficulties, and have taken advantage of the new openness. Their experience is both personal and recent. At St John's College, Cambridge in 1994 the third major conference on China management (following those at Manchester in 1987 and Leuven in 1989) was held.[1]

The conference, Management Challenges for China in the 1990s: Domestic and Foreign-Funded Enterprises, brought together researchers from Britain, China, Europe and North America. From the many contributions, two books, this one on domestic enterprises and a sister volume by John Child and Yuan Lu on foreign funded enterprises, have been

produced. Many books, articles and column inches have been written
about the economic and management changes in China, especially macro
level economic and political analyses. Indeed, beyond analysis speculation
about China is a favoured journalistic pastime. In terms of understanding
China in the age of reform Child's 1994 book of this title is a major and
authoritative contribution. Our aim in creating this book is to take our
understanding of the challenges facing China's managers further, especially in the area of domestic enterprises where engaging at the individual
firm level is both difficult and yet a requirement.

From the many papers given at the conference we have selected, and
revised with the authors, eleven which we believe offer an insight both
into the inner workings and difficulties in Chinese enterprises and the
wider context in which they operate. The material covered in this book
is broad in scope and we have organized it into four parts. Each part
tackles a distinct theme: the reform process, decision making, enterprise
challenges and managing and developing people.

PART I: REFLECTIONS ON REFORM

Virtually all the contributions in this book refer to the reforms, but
typically within a particular context such as decision making or managing
people. However, in the two chapters which introduce this book a much
broader perspective is taken. Chang and Nolan are concerned with
explaining the outcomes from different reform processes on a comparative basis. Their focus is the contrast between the 'European' and 'Asian'
communist economies, in which Asia, and in particular China, emerges as
the most significant achiever. They recognize that there is no simple explanation. Relevant elements in their comprehensive analysis include the pre-
reform conditions, economic policy and the political setting. Chang and
Nolan note that China to date has preserved a supervisory role for central
authority and that this has 'sustained and controlled moves towards a
market economy', and contained conflict.

Boisot and Child in their chapter take as a starting point the absolute
and comparative success of the Chinese economy and seek to question in
a fundamental way our interpretation of this success. The authors reflect
on the nature of the market institutions and conceptualize the contractual relations which have grown up in this new enterprise culture. They
find in China a lack of conformity with Western capitalist market models
in the area of property rights and in the way transactions are organized,
as well as in the role of government.

Taken together the two chapters underline the pragmatic, incremental
and experimental approach that has characterized the reform process in
China. For the enterprise managers it has meant a 15-year agenda of
change which looks set to continue, but with the added uncertainties
arising from the accelerating withdrawal of state support.

PART II: DECISION MAKING

Decision making in Chinese enterprises has been a particular focus of UK management research in China. Not only have the new reforms made it the responsibility of individual enterprises to make decisions themselves on a broad range of matters previously determined by the central authority, residual political structures and patterns of interaction, and widely differing skill levels among managers have made decision making processes fertile material for researchers in recent years. There has, moreover, been the opportunity to compare and contrast practice with that in the former Soviet Union and in Eastern European countries.

Child and Lu in their chapter 'Decentralization of decision making in China's state enterprises', examine decision making in six state enterprises, and find the state has sought to compensate for loss of direct control through decentralization by applying regulatory measures and controlling infrastructure to govern economic relations. The result is a hybrid economy, in which enterprise decisions in the state sector reflect a greater autonomy over the eight years of their study, 1985 to 1993, but are still subject to 'soft' budgetary constraints imposed from above, and to other factors arising from the partial nature of the market. Moreover decentralization has been accompanied by the progressive arrogation to top managers within individual enterprises of powers previously the prerogative of work groups and middle managers. In this way, the growth in responsibility for strategic decision making within enterprises, it is suggested, contributes to the emergence of a new professional management class.

Easterby-Smith and Gao, in their chapter 'Vision, mechanism and logic in investment decision making' compare three Chinese and three British companies. They find much in common in the process of decision making on investment, identifying the requirement for budget planning, strategy review procedures, approval from higher authority, and a gestation period before a decision is formally dealt with, for example. Moreover, both in the UK and in China multiple criteria are employed; apart from financial considerations, company strategy, the nature of the technology to be used, and the likely public image of an investment project are all important factors in the final decision.

The third chapter in this section, Porter's 'Politics, culture and decision making in China', stands in contrast to some degree with that of Easterby-Smith and Gao. Porter seeks to emphasize the particular political and cultural factors which still affect decision making in Chinese organizations, and which in his view continue to render decision processes less rational in organizational terms than they might otherwise be. Porter looks at three decision sequences in different types of organizations with which he was professionally involved in China, and traces the impact of extraneous factors on each decision. He finds that the context for management of

enterprises in transitional China may be such as to undermine expectations of Western-style decision making.

Finally, within the section on decision making as a whole several sub-
themes are apparent. The crucial importance of accurate information to
informed decision making is apparent throughout, especially in a society
where in recent decades facts have been difficult to establish. Another
sub-theme is the evident and growing need for commitment to the
management tasks at hand, in organizations where there has until the past
few years been no real requirement to do much other than carry out
orders. A third characteristic of decision making is detailed by the amassed
evidence in each chapter of the continued influence of the communist
party on decision processes, even if at one remove. Taken as a whole,
decision making illustrates in microcosm the contradictions across the
range of management tasks in China in the present day.

PART III: ENTERPRISE CHALLENGES

Since enterprises are at the core of the economic transition the chapters
in this book have been selected to illustrate the sheer variety of issues
that enterprises face. The paper by Liu, Campbell and colleagues is particularly welcome. Although township enterprises have been hugely
important in China's growth, and will continue to be so, there has been
a dearth of information and analysis. The authors trace their rise and highlight the advantages that they have over their state owned counterparts.
These include greater flexibility, a market awareness and, especially for
those in the coastal regions, an export and international orientation.
Importantly, however, Liu and Campbell also identify their problems,
which can be considerable, and include poor resourcing, technology and
management. Given the importance within the economy placed on such
enterprises, coping with these problems will be critical. Since many are
small, management development, technology acquisition and the need to
collaborate are likely to emerge as the key strategic issues for township
enterprises.

In contrast, Forrester's chapter looks at the classical impact of the
reforms on the manufacturing industry in the state sector. Divorced from
the market for so long many still lack the market and strategic awareness
necessary for effective operation. Technology led production aimed at
optimizing performance with respect to cost and productivity remains a
priority for many firms. Similarly, design as a concept is poorly understood and quality is seen as a problem of conformity, rather than an
integral part of the broad manufacturing operation.

Finally, in the area of production planning and control the legacy of
the central planning system in China has resulted in many conflicts at the
planning and control levels within factories. High levels of raw materials,
work-in-progress and finished goods stocks are common. Forrester

concludes that whilst Chinese managers are anxious to adopt best practice this is inhibited by the wider context within which manufacturing management decisions are made.

The third chapter in this section by Steward and Li, looks at technical innovation which is a relevant concern for both state and township enterprises. China's current science and technology development policy combines elements of both market competition and state control. The authors analyse in detail the changing pattern of collaboration between the research institutes, universities and enterprises. Commercialization of research activities is identified as a highly significant development and directly affects the access that enterprises have to institute expertise. Enterprise managers are now confronted with R&D policy issues (including whether or not to develop in-house capability), which simply did not exist before the science and technology awards of the mid-1980s.

Linking all these contributions is the reality of a state receding from the affairs of the enterprise, state owned or private. For many this is welcome but for others, especially those in the state sector, the prospect is threatening. Such tensions are growing and pose immense difficulties. We return to these in our concluding remarks.

PART IV: MANAGING AND DEVELOPING PEOPLE

In the concluding part of the book our focus is people – managers and workers who together are trying to cope with the continual change. In the first chapter Brown and Branine, in a study of the foreign trade corporations, look at changing personnel and management practices and to what extent Western HRM styled developments are in evidence. Their research suggests that in this sector flexibility in employment practices, the development of the individual and a growing strategic awareness of the human resource is a reality. However, they find little evidence that the traditional importance of the personnel function is declining, or that the nature of worker representation has undergone any major change. Brown and Branine conclude that in this sector what appears to be happening is 'adaptive personnel management', rather than the set of practices and policies that collectively characterize HRM.

Warner, in his chapter, focuses on labour reform in the state owned enterprises in north-east China. In his study of 10 such pilot enterprises he shows the variability in the implementation of the state labour reforms, and in particular labour contracts. In his analysis he finds that 'Western style' practices in the areas of personnel, rewards and social insurance have been grafted on to status-quo characteristics, rather than replacing them. Nevertheless, despite the evidence of organization inertia in adopting and internalizing the reforms in the pilot sites the pressure to make firms fully responsible for their profit and losses will ensure the widespread extension of the policy. Together the Brown and Branine chapter and Warner's chapter illustrate clearly the growing differences that are emerging in China's management practices as a contingent response to regional and sectorial developments.

The final chapter in this part and, indeed in the book, is Chan's 'Management education in the People's Republic of China'. This is appropriate given that the key determinant of China's continued modernization will be the ability to develop a sufficient number of effective and competent managers. Chan traces the development of management education during the reform. His account deals with domestic and foreign assisted programmes and concludes that in the main their benefits are now being realized. The author recognizes, however, that an expression of the management education activity in both numbers and scope is required and that there are considerable difficulties in achieving this, especially funding.

Overall, at the culmination of a process of selecting, reviewing and exchanging ideas with contributors we were conscious of a major theme running as a subtext through this book: namely, *China's relentless movement from homogeneity to heterogeneity*. The People's Republic of China, like any state founded on Leninist principles, was from 1949 to the first impact of reform in 1979 both rigid and hierarchical in its structures and methods of organization. Communist party structures paralleled those of the state from the highest level to the grass roots, forming and supervising the implementation of policy. Almost all economic activity took place within the state sector, and interactions between organizations and individuals were often highly routinized and formalistic. Production, conditioned by social need rather than by market forces, revolved about the fulfilling of quotas for items chosen by central authority. There was no business environment in the Western sense of the term. The implication of this situation was a very high degree of homogeneity in approaches and procedures internalized throughout China.

It was perhaps inevitable that the decision first taken in 1978 to modernize China, and to do so by importing foreign technology and assistance, would completely undermine this homogeneity, bringing widespread regional, sectoral and organizational variations in the way the productive economy was run. China has over the past decade and a half permitted a diversity of responses to the newly emergent market forces in her economy. Campbell and Liu, Forrester, and Steward and Quan illustrate the wide variety of approaches adopted in meeting the challenges of the new situation, notably in developing the township enterprises, in managing production in China's factories, and in elaborating new patterns of collaboration in research. Warner, and Brown and Branine show the starkly different employment practices now obtaining in China across sectors and regions. Luke Chan's chapter provides evidence of the range of new postgraduate management programmes from a variety of foreign sources introduced in Chinese universities in the 1980s, further

diversifying management technique downstream in the factories and enterprises. This diversity would scarcely have been imagined only a decade
and a half ago.

For the future two developments appear critical. The first is the continuing withdrawal of financial support for loss making state owned enterprises. The second is the gradual decoupling of their social and welfare
responsibilities, leaving the state firms to increasingly concentrate their
scarce resources on productive capability. All the chapters in this book
offer evidence of the often acute organizational and individual tensions
generated during this extraordinary period of rapid change and these
developments will accelerate such tensions. It will be for China and
China's managers to find ways of resolving or diffusing these tensions
within this decade, or face the consequences.

Finally, the aim of this book, and its sister volume, is to disseminate
quickly and effectively our many different findings and insights about
China and the management challenges it faces. The potential advantage
of a collected work, over the lone heroic researcher, is the scope of
research which is possible and the different perspectives and disciplines
which can deepen the insights. Our responsibility as editors is to realize
that potential. We hope we have achieved this and that researchers and
managers interested in the management issues in China will find this book
furthers their understanding.

NOTE

1 The first two international conferences on management in China have been
  reported in the JAI series on *Advances in Chinese Industrial Studies*, Greenwich,
  Conn.: JAI Press. See Child, J. and Lockett, M. (eds) (1990) *Reform Policy
  and the Chinese Enterprises* Vol. 1 Part A. Campbell, N. and Henley, J. (eds)
  (1990) *Joint Ventures and Industrial Change in China* Vol. 1 Part B. Campbell,
  N., Plaschaert, S. and Brown, D. (eds) (1991) *The Changing Nature of
  Management in China*.

Part I
Reflections on reform

1 Structural inheritance or policy choice?

Explaining the results of post-Stalinist reform in Europe and Asia

Ha-Joon Chang and Peter Nolan

ABSTRACT

In this chapter, the authors seek to explore the reasons for the success of economic reform in China through an analysis of factors which may be similar to or different from the experience of the Soviet Union and former Eastern European countries on one hand, and the non-Chinese communist Asian countries on the other.

While all the former Stalinist countries shared a common systemic inheritance, the choice of economic policies and the political context for reform in the case of China and certain other Asian countries were distinct. A destructive phase did not precede reform, and a programme of economic shock therapy was found to be unnecessary. Moreover, success was achieved despite apparently inadequate economic and political institutions. As China possessed no obvious advantages over the Soviet Union and Eastern Europe, the rapid-change policies of 'capitalist triumphalism' implemented in those countries may simply have been wrong; the strong state, with a self-reforming communist party, may be the 'least bad vehicle' with which to achieve a successful transition away from a communist economy.

INTRODUCTION

The reform efforts in the European and the Asian communist economies have produced most remarkably different outcomes. This chapter argues that there was a wide range of common systemic factors which placed the former Stalinist countries in a position in which they might advance extremely rapidly, and asks why then was the outcome so dramatically different. It is argued that, while there were some important differences in the set of initial conditions affecting the capacity of the Stalinist countries to respond to the reform challenge, it is not clear that these were to the net advantage of the Asian countries. The key elements affecting their capacity to respond were both the choice of economic policies and the political setting within which reform occurred. This article argues that, whatever the historical forces that led to the contrast in approach, in hindsight it is clear that the Asian path offered a vastly better prospect for successful economic results from reforming the Stalinist system.

CONTRASTING RESULTS

China

In the first decade or so of reform, China's economic performance was much better than under Maoist policies. The rate of growth of net national output was arguably the fastest in the world (Table 1.1). China's authoritarian political system enabled it to control population growth, although obviously with considerable human costs. And in per capita terms the annual growth rate of net national output more than doubled compared to the Maoist period. Although the overall industrial growth rate changed little, there were important changes in the efficiency of resource use. In state run industry, there was a sharp reversal of the long-run decline in productivity which China had experienced in the Maoist years. Moreover, the typical Stalinist relationship between the growth rate of heavy and light industry was reversed with explosive growth of light industry. The agricultural growth rate accelerated far ahead of that achieved during the Maoist period, and with much more economy in resource use. The growth rate of commerce and transport increased sharply compared to the Maoist years. Moreover, it remained relatively unburdened by foreign debt and achieved fast growth with relatively low inflation. As a result, a remarkable improvement occurred in the Chinese population's standard of living. A huge increase occurred in the consumption of food, clothing, and consumer durable goods. Housing space per person more than doubled over the course of a decade. Large improvements took place in the availability of professional health care. A massive transformation occurred in the number and variety of services available. The reported improvement in the already exceptional figures for life expectancy and mortality rates (Table 1.1) suggests that the growth in living standards affected most social strata, even if there was greater inequality in consumption than under the extreme egalitarianism of Maoism.

Non-Chinese Asian Communist Countries

In almost all the Asian communist countries, the communist party, as in China, remained in power, so that today a species of communist one-party state still exists in North Korea, Laos, Mongolia, Vietnam and Burma. The influence of the Chinese road to reform in the region has been enormous. Except North Korea, which has still hardly altered its Stalinist system, and Mongolia, which initially pursued a 'big bang' strategy, the

Table 1.1 Comparative economic performance of the Chinese economy in the 1980s

	China	India	Low income countries*	Middle income countries
Average annual growth rate, 1980/89(%)				
GDP	9.7	5.3	3.4	2.9
Agriculture	6.3	2.9	2.5	2.6
Industry	12.6	6.9	3.1	3.0
Services	9.3	6.5	4.4	2.8
Average annual real growth rate of exports. 1980/89 (%)	11.5	5.8	0.8	5.5
Average annual growth rate of population, 1980/89(%)	1.4	2.1	2.7	2.1
Average annual rate of inflation, 1980/89(%)	5.8	7.7	14.9	73.0
Debt service as % of exports of goods and services				
1980	4.6	9.1	11.4	26.1
1989	9.8	26.4	27.4	23.1
Index of average p.c. food consumption, 1987/89 (1979/81=100)	128	113	103	101
Daily calorie intake p.c.				
1965	1,931	2,103	1,960	2,482
1988	2,632	2,104	2,182	2,834
Crude death rate (no/1000)				
1965	10	20	21	13
1989	7	11	13	8
Infant mortality rate (no/1000)				
1981	71	121	124	81
1989	30	95	94	51
Life expectancy at birth (years)				
1981	67	52	50	60
1989	70	59	55	66

Source: World Bank 1983 and 1991

Note: * Excluding India and China

others all explicitly adopted a Chinese style incremental economic reform programme under continued authoritarian rule by the communist party. There is already plenty of evidence that they are beginning to enter Chinese-type growth paths. For example, Vietnam is reported to have attained a growth rate of real GDP of over 8 per cent per annum from 1989 to 1992, and to be currently growing at a rate in excess of this (*Financial Times* 30 November 1993).

USSR

Soviet economic performance under Gorbachev was extremely poor. Since the collapse of the communist government a poor performance has turned into a disaster (Table 1.2). The consequences of the collapse are not just economic, but also involve the deepest sense of national humiliation in a country which for most of the twentieth century was used to considering itself as the leader of the world's socialist nations. Bare statistics fail to capture the massive extent of the dislocation and suffering for a large proportion of the population. The consequences include the disintegration of the health service and the large increases in crime. Partly as a consequence of these, there has been an alarming rise in death rates to a level which was about one-quarter above the levels of the late 1980s and was possibly behind the middle income countries (Ellman, 1994). Moreover, alongside the spiralling collapse has gone a massive redistribution of wealth. A new 'aristocracy', often building on the old positions of power under the communist party, is being created at high speed under a wide process of 'primitive capitalist accumulation'.

Table 1.2 Selected economic indicators for the former USSR (all data are at constant prices except where indication is to the contrary)

	1989	1990	1991	1992	1993
Net material product	100	96.0	80.7	64.5*	58.1
Gross industrial output	100	98.9	90.9	77.3	68.0
Gross agricultural output	100	97.7	87.9	80.0*	75.2
Retail trade turnover	100	110.4	99.4	59.6*	53.6
Gross fixed investment	100	101.0	89.2	49.1	–
Volume of foreign trade					
Exports	100	86.9	85.2	63.0*	
Imports	100	98.6	90.8	70.8*	
Foreign trade in current US$					
Exports	100	94.8	71.5	53.5	–
Imports	–	100	64.1	57.5	
Foreign debt	60	61	65	76	
Consumer prices (change on previous year)	50	8.0	150	2,500*	1,000

Source: Economist Intelligence Unit, *Country Report*, CIS (formerly USSR) 4, 1992; and United Nations, Economic Commission for Europe, 1993

Notes:* Estimates, for Russia only

Table 1.3 Output performance in Eastern Europe

	Index of real net material product, 1991 (1988=100)	Index of real industrial output 1992, (1988=100)
Bulgaria	68	46
Romania	72	48
Czechoslovakia	78	60
Hungary	89	68
Poland	79	68
Albania	49	42

Source: Economist Intelligence Unit, *Country Reports*, various issues; and *Economist* 13 March 1993

Table 1.4 Consumer price inflation in Eastern Europe

	1989	1990 %	1991
Bulgaria	6.2	19	334
Romania	0.8	4.2	175
Czechoslovakia	1.4	10.0	54
Hungary	17	29	35
Poland	251	585	70

Source: Economist Intelligence Unit, *Country Reports*, various issues

Eastern Europe

The performance of Eastern Europe since 1988 in terms of most key socio-economic indicators also has been extremely poor. Between 1989 and 1991 national income in the Central and Eastern European countries as a whole dropped by an average of about 15–20 per cent and industrial output fell by about 25–30 per cent (*Transition* 3(11): 12–13) (also see Table 1.3). Initial inflation, often hyper-inflation (Table 1.4), has been brought down but far from defeated. Hopelessly small amounts of foreign direct investment have been attracted into the region. Moreover, two-thirds of this has gone to a single country, Hungary (*Transition* 4(1): 5). Even in the least badly hit economies, the initial surge in employment in the private sector was unable to absorb the large decline in employment in the state sector. One of the most remarkably candid assessments of the prospects for Eastern Europe was made by John Flemming, the chief economist at the European Bank for Reconstruction and Development:

It will take thirty-five years for eastern European income levels to reach even half of average western incomes under current predictions about economic growth.... 'What is needed to close the gap is the growth we have seen in the Pacific Rim', said Mr Flemming, citing

China's growth rate of 10 per cent, 'but no-one is predicting that type of growth in eastern Europe'. . . Little fall is predicted in inflation levels, which run from the low 'teens' in the 'success stories' such as Poland to 1,000 per cent in Russia. . . . As a result . . . the punitively high levels of effective marginal labour and capital tax rates create 'dismal prospects for private investment . . . that have not been widely appreciated'.

(*Financial Times* 22 September 1993)

COMMON POTENTIALITIES IN STALINIST ECONOMIES FOR IMPROVED ECONOMIC PERFORMANCE

The planned economies at the end of the Stalinist phase presented a special case of 'catch up'. Despite large and well-documented problems, in certain respects the Stalinist economies had made great progress. This left them with important common strengths which could form the basis of rapid progress, provided suitable policies could be devised to harness them. Far more than in previous 'catch up' experiences, the reforming Stalinist economies could rely on making better use of existing capacities rather than having to create new physical and human capital. Relatively simple institutional changes could release a large advance in economic performance provided they were put into effect in the correct political–economic setting.

Underused Human Capacities

A consequence of the socialist ideals of the communist systems is that there was a high degree of equality of access to primary and secondary education. Equally importantly, rationing and price controls on basic items of consumption, in addition to a high commitment to low price (or even free provision) of mass health facilities, ensured generally high achievements in life expectancy relative to income level.[1] However, the human capacities thus created were not fully utilized under the Stalinist system for well-known institutional reasons, such as the high level of job security, large incentives for enterprises to hoard labour, erratic production schedules due to fluctuating intermediate input supplies, and an absence of management incentives to push workers to maintain high quality. Thus, a huge reservoir of surplus labour power was waiting to be tapped if a suitable structure of incentives could be found, which might enable increased work intensity to be rewarded with increased income.

Entrepreneurial potential

It is usually thought that entrepreneurship was squashed completely in the communist countries. In fact, there was a huge area of parallel 'black' and 'grey' markets alongside the formal system of state controlled allocation.[2] While it is not clear whether this kind of 'equilibriating' (or Marshallian) entrepreneurship provides the right type of raw material for the 'innovating' (or Schumpeterian) entrepreneurship required for dynamic growth of the economy, it is undeniable that a substantial proportion of the population was exposed to some kind of 'entrepreneurial' activities.

Industry

There existed many ways in which industrial performance in the Stalinist economies might improve through the introduction of relatively simple reforms, as long as the economies were not immediately exposed to the full force of international competition.

It is well known that the communist economies suffered from poor product quality, excessive hoarding of physical and labour inputs, and stagnating technical progress. While there were other reasons (such as the inferior capital stock), these were largely the consequences of lack of competition and profit motives. The introduction of domestic competition and profit motives without full privatization or wholesale trade liberalization, as in the case of China, could eliminate most of these problems and thus provide room for improvement in industrial performance.

Another way in which industrial performance could be improved was to reorganize production. Under communism, a heavy emphasis was given to scale economy considerations and many gigantic plants were created (Erlich 1985). While this had its own benefits, there were also problems associated with excessive vertical integration and managerial diseconomies. Moreover, this meant that the communist economies were not able to benefit from the economies of scope associated with reduced transaction costs involved in the transfer of goods and services from one operating unit to another – related to marketing, research and development, installation of equipment, credit provision to customers and after-sales service and repair (Chandler 1990: 200). Thus seen, spinning off certain in-house operations as independent units and 'creating firms from ministries and plants' would have improved the industrial performance.

Agriculture

There are deep problems with the collective and state farm method of farm organization due mainly to the peculiar difficulty of labour supervision in agriculture, which caused large managerial diseconomies of scale (measured by the number of workers, not the amount of capital) in most aspects of the direct tasks of cultivation (Nolan 1988). However, there still exists large scope for economies of scale, and hence benefit from co-operation, in the ancillary aspects of the farm process, such as research, irrigation, crop spraying, processing, and marketing – as indeed is practised in many capitalist economies.

Given these conditions, relatively simple institutional changes had the potential to produce large, if once-and-for-all, improvements in efficiency, and to release labour and investible resources for employment elsewhere in the economy. In addition, it might have had beneficial balance of payments effects through reducing food and raw material imports. The most important and simplest institutional change is contracting farmland out to individual households, allowing households to take the main decisions about organizing the means of production. This 'land reform' alone should be able to reverse the profound managerial diseconomies of scale associated with collective agriculture and state farms, and, when combined with the introduction of co-operative managements in ancillary activities, could have radically improved peasant incentives.[3]

POSSIBLE EXPLANATIONS FOR THE CONTRAST IN RESULTS

Despite the presence of some important common potentialities for a rapid improvement in economic performance, the results of post-Stalinist reform were strikingly different in the Far East and in Eastern Europe and Russia. Comparing Europe and Asia is, of course, problematic since the countries within each region are so diverse. However, we believe there is a sufficiently striking contrast between the outcomes of post-Stalinist reform in the two regions to justify some attempt to understand this process as an integrated whole. There is no simple explanation for the contrast. This section simply presents a number of possible hypotheses.

Initial conditions

Cultural differences

China is the birthplace of Confucianism, which appears to have been a powerful vehicle of industrialization elsewhere. The fact that many star performers of post-war capitalist development happened to be Confucian countries revived theories linking culture and economic development, long neglected after Max Weber's attempt to explain the rise of capitalism in Western Europe by the Protestant ethic. It is tempting to add China to the list of countries whose growth can be explained by Confucianism. However, this is a problematic argument.

Far from promoting modern economic growth, the Chinese variety of Confucianism has frequently been accused of holding the country back. For example, Morishima (1982) has argued that Japan modernized while China failed to do so, because, unlike the Chinese or the Korean variety, Japanese Confucianism emphasized hierarchy and loyalty over individual edification. A long scholarly tradition also argues that China's variety of Confucianism constitutes a large handicap to economic development, due to long-ingrained habits of familism, nepotism and corruption (e.g., Levy 1949). However, its Confucian legacy did not prevent China from industrializing later. The point is that 'culture' is not a given factor, but is continually being reconstructed either consciously or unconsciously (Hobsbawm and Ranger 1983). What needs to be explained is why and how the old culture of Confucianism could be reconstructed in Japan and elsewhere in East Asia in a form amenable to industrial development.

It has also been argued that China had a large advantage over the USSR and Eastern Europe because of its entrepreneurial tradition. It is argued that at least some parts of China had a substantial entrepreneurial culture dating back many centuries (see e.g., Wu *et al.* forthcoming). Moreover, capitalism flourished in some parts of China in the twentieth century before the revolution (Bergere 1986), allowing Chinese people in the reform period to build on a strong memory of capitalism.

However, much of Eastern Europe did have substantial pre-revolutionary capitalist experience, which was just as recent and often much more sophisticated than that of pre-communist China (especially in the cases of Czechoslovakia and the GDR). Moreover, the large growth of capitalism in pre-1914 Russia is not consistent with a popular thesis of cultural incompatibility between Russianness and capitalism (Guroff and Carstenson 1983; Gattrell 1986). Moreover, given the fact that a lot of people in Eastern Europe under socialism were involved in black and grey market activities, it is clear that entrepreneurial culture was not killed in these countries. In fact, few socialist countries have gone so far as China did under Mao Zedong in attempting to obliterate entrepreneurship entirely: capitalism was likened to 'a dog in the water to be beaten and drowned'.

Advantages of the latecomer

When China started its reform it was much poorer than Eastern Europe and Russia. And given that there are well-known advantages that a latecomer country has over the early developers, it has frequently been argued that China's better performance can largely be explained by a greater scope for catch-up accorded by its greater backwardness. Sachs and Woo have presented the most coherent such argument to date. They argue: 'It was neither gradualism nor experimentation, but rather China's economic structure, that proved so felicitous to reform. China began reform as a peasant agricultural society, EEFSU[4] as urban and overindustrialized. . . . In Gerschenkron's famous phrase [China] had the 'advantage of backwardness' (Sachs and Woo, 1994: 102–104).

However, there are many problems with this argument. Countries which catch up successfully need to possess a certain level of 'social capability' in order to be able to exploit the technology of advanced countries

(Abramovitz 1986). When China's reform began, it was much closer to the latter stage than were the Eastern European economies, which had completed the minimum necessary institution building process. Indeed, within Eastern Europe those countries that have done least badly since the end of Stalinism have been those that were most advanced at the end of the communist period. It is 'sophisticated' Hungary and Czechoslovakia, not impoverished Albania or Romania that have done the best (or, rather, done the least badly) since 1989 (see Tables 1.3 and 1.4). As of the late 1970s, even the latter countries were vastly more advanced than was China.

Having a large proportion of national output and employment generated in agriculture is not necessarily an advantage, as some argue. Indeed, many economists have argued that a main factor explaining the success of the East Asian Four Little Tigers was precisely the fact that each had a relatively small farm sector at the start of their phase of accelerated growth (Little 1979: 450). Moreover, the capital needs for expanding agriculture often are extremely large, especially in a densely populated economy such as China's. Finally, the idea that China's economy was agriculture-led throughout the reform period and therefore the implication that being more agrarian provided China with an important advantage is incorrect. In the early stages of the reform, the growth rate of farm output was extremely high, at almost the same figure as that for national income. However, in the latter phase, the growth rate of farm output fell sharply to less than one half the growth rate of national income, which remained high despite the drop in the growth rate of farm output.

Conjunctural factors in the world economy

In the late 1970s when China began its reforms, only a small number of countries that formerly had followed the so-called 'inward looking' strategies had undergone substantial policy change towards export promotion. By the early 1990s, not only had almost all the former communist countries undertaken massive liberalization programmes, but so too had a wide range of developing countries. This meant that there was much greater competition for access to the markets of the advanced capitalist countries among reforming economies. The fact that the world economy went into recession simultaneously with the overthrow of communism in Eastern Europe and the USSR, it is frequently argued, also damaged the export potentialities of the reforming economies in the region.

However, at a comparable period in China's economic reforms in the early 1980s, the world economy also faced problems as severe as those of the early 1990s. The World Bank summed up the situation in its 1983 Report as the following: 'The recession that had started in 1980 thus continued for a third year, making it the longest since the depression of the 1930s' (World Bank 1983: 7). Thus, it is not possible to argue that

China set upon its course of reform in a world economic environment which was more favourable than that which Eastern Europe and the USSR faced at the start of their reform.

Also, it needs to be pointed out that a recession within the advanced capitalist countries may also have positive effects on the less developed countries undergoing large structural change. During recessions the capital goods industries suffer an especially severe decline in demand, so that these are advantageous times for buying capital goods from producers, many of whom are situated in the advanced economies (a notable case in point was the USSR during the Great Depression). Moreover, a recession in the advanced capitalist countries means that more capital is available than might otherwise have been: the long swing of capital export related to business cycles in the advanced capitalist countries is well known. However, the reforming countries of Eastern Europe and Russia mostly were extremely unsuccessful in attracting foreign investment even during this period (for reasons discussed below), whereas China and Vietnam were extremely successful in this regard.[5]

Geo-political location

China is located in the most dynamic part of the world economy, that is, East Asia. In sharp contrast, the reforming countries of Eastern Europe are located next to a region with large structural problems and slow growth rates, namely, Western Europe. Moreover, the fast growing economies of Japan and the East Asian NICs started experiencing acute labour short-ages, large trade surpluses and appreciating exchange rates in the 1980s, coinciding with China's economic reform. These economies were extremely keen to invest in foreign countries with lower labour costs in less technologically complex lines of manufacturing. China was a major beneficiary from this process.

The degree of importance of immediate geographical location can easily be exaggerated. The fact that neighbouring economies have fast growth rates may not be as important as it at first sight appears to be. While Western Europe is growing relatively slowly, the income levels in the region are still far above those in most of East Asia, and the absolute levels of trade are extremely large.[6] The US economy also grew relatively slowly in the 1990s. However, this was the most important market upon which the export success of the East Asian NICs rested, and it became increasingly important for China in the 1980s.

Physical location *per se* is unimportant in determining international capital movements. Moreover, East Asia itself is brimming with countries wanting to and able to attract foreign investments. The Chinese (and, latterly, the Vietnamese) reform package had to prove itself and gain credibility amongst foreign investors. Moreover, the successful achieve-ment of rapid growth behind high protectionist barriers made China attractive as a potentially huge market both for consumer durables and capital goods, thereby inducing investments by foreign companies in a wider range of industries than simply those for which low labour costs are most critical (for example, steel joint venture with Korea's POSCO, or joint ventures with Japanese and European automobile producers).

China did undoubtedly enjoy an advantage over much of the rest of the reforming communist world in that there is a large amount of capital in the hands of the Chinese diaspora. However, it is very easy to exaggerate its role. First, foreign capital, 'overseas Chinese' or not, still occupies only a small position in the Chinese economy, albeit it is now growing very fast.[7] Second, the really large inflows of private foreign direct investment did not get under way until relatively late in the reform process. Third, a diaspora alone is neither sufficient nor necessary to guarantee inward investment flows.[8]

At the start of their reforms, Eastern European countries also had the potential to become attractive investment sites. Their proximity to Western Europe, which was to become the largest single market in the world in 1992, was potentially an important attraction. They also possessed a labour force which was much better educated and more skilled as well as a much larger pool of well-trained scientific personnel than China. Moreover, their infrastructure was much more developed than that of China. The fact that most of them, with the notable exception of Hungary, failed to attract any significant amount of foreign investment despite these conditions, suggests that there was something deeply unattractive about the investment environment in these countries.[9]

Collapse of COMECON

Eastern European economies suffered a massive external shock due to the collapse of COMECON. If an advanced economy like Finland had to go through a massive adjustment programme due to the sudden collapse in its Soviet trade (which accounted for about one third of its trade), it may be argued, it is more than natural that poorer and less flexible economies in Eastern Europe suffered massively from such a dramatic shift in trade arrangements. In contrast, China was not a part of the COMECON trading bloc, and consequently did not have to suffer from such a shock during its reform process.

The collapse of COMECON certainly was an important factor in the downturn in Eastern Europe. However, a large part of the reason for the collapse of COMECON was precisely the attempts by its own members at an immediate and unconditional integration with the West through 'big bang' reforms. Especially for Russia, which held the key to the continued existence or otherwise of COMECON, the collapse of COMECON was not an external shock but more of an internal one. Moreover, it was long argued by Western commentators that COMECON constituted a large burden for the USSR, as it exported oil and natural gas to Eastern Europe at below world market prices in return for second rate manufactured goods. If this was the case, the collapse of COMECON should have benefited at least the former USSR. Eastern Europe's long-term future interest lay with the break up of COMECON and an eventual integration with the rest of the world economy. However, it is questionable whether such integration should have been attempted without a (potentially lengthy) prior restructuring of their economies. Moreover, the argument that deep integration into the COMECON system was sufficient to cause large post-Stalinist adjustment problems is belied by the case of Vietnam, which, despite its earlier almost total dependence on the COMECON trade, managed to redirect its trade and generate a rapid growth of exports.[10]

Legacy of repressed inflation

It has been argued that the legacy of repressed inflation in Eastern Europe and the former USSR necessitated a much greater priority in these countries for stabilization over output growth and employment. Much of the downturn in the early 1990s is argued as being caused by the need to control inflation inherited from the communist period.

This factor, however, cannot be taken seriously as an important element in the contrast in post-Stalinist economic performance. First, China itself, in common with other communist economies, inherited large problems of repressed inflation from the Stalinist period. Second, a large part of the inflationary difficulties faced by Eastern Europe emerged after the fall of the communist party, and in Russia began to emerge under Gorbachev's reforms. Third, in a country of China's size, in the absence of a comprehensive reform of the financial system, there was, in a 'prisoner's dilemma' fashion, little incentive for local authorities or banks to control the supply of money in the interests of control over the national rate of inflation. Fourth, it is quite possible for an economy undergoing a stabilization programme which sharply reduces inflation to grow rapidly, provided the correct policy choices are made to release the country's supply-side potential. Vietnam, for example, achieved a remarkable reduction in inflation through tight monetary policy, with reported inflation falling from 70 per cent in 1990 to below 10 per cent in 1992 (*Financial Times* 30 November 1993) yet simultaneously achieved greatly accelerated growth of national product.

Economic policy

China

The most striking characteristic of the Chinese reform was its cautious and gradual nature. Price reform was only finally completed in the early

1990s, 17 years after the post-Mao reforms cautiously began following the death of Mao. Even as of the early 1990s, the vast bulk of industrial output still was produced in state or local community owned enterprises (although their behaviour changed a lot), with the purely private sector playing only a small role. Not a single state enterprise of any size went bankrupt during the reform period. A massive decollectivization of farmland took place, but farmland remained in local community ownership. The economy remained largely shielded from international competition.

In almost all key aspects of institutional arrangements and policy, China's post-reform economy in the 1980s appears as the kind of interventionist half-way house that most mainstream economists would predict to perform very badly. Throughout the decade, private property rights existed in only a minor part of the economy; the government continued to intervene heavily in price setting; the economy remained substantially isolated from the impact of world prices; the communist party continued to rule in a sometimes brutal and always authoritarian fashion, and intervened at all levels of the economic process. Indeed, some observers believed that 'market socialism' was too charitable a description of this system and that 'market Stalinism' was more appropriate.

Non-Chinese Asian communist countries

Both Burma and Vietnam shifted in the late 1980s and early 1990s to a strategy that explicitly followed the Chinese path, with incremental economic reform occurring under communist rule. In Vietnam, for example, the industrial reform path was not one of a commitment to privatization, but rather to allow competition from the private sector alongside a slow transformation of state enterprises which focused on improving performance through better selection of managers, the effects of competition from the small scale private sector, delegating more powers to enterprise managers, allowing state enterprises to set up new semiautonomous companies and through encouraging foreign investment. As in China, genuinely private companies remain almost exclusively small scale, and property rights in the former state owned sector are still ambiguous and ill defined: 'What appears to be happening is a slow metamorphosis of state owned companies into private sector businesses, except that the legal ownership structure remains unclear' (*Financial Times* 30 November 1993).

USSR

Under Gorbachev, economic reform followed a remarkably similar path to that in China. It also began experimentally with similar hesitations and anxieties among the different factions in the leadership (see especially the careful account in Aslund 1991).[11] In the 'reform wave' of 1987–1988, a number of Chinese style reforms were introduced. In state industry, reforms were introduced to allow profit retention and an explicit commitment was made to undertake incremental reform of the pricing and material supply system. In agriculture, a beginning was made to a contract system for individual farm households. Individual business activity was legalized in many spheres. Co-operatives were given the green light and rapidly grew in number, entering one activity after another, often in competition with the state sector. In foreign trade, important devolution of control occurred, though, as in China, the economy still remained largely insulated from foreign competition. This 'reform wave' took place only three years after Gorbachev came to power.[12]

However, as the political events took over, the USSR collapsed and these reform measures never had the time to prove themselves, since, following the collapse of the USSR, the decision was taken to push ahead with comprehensive and rapid moves towards a privatized market economy. The programme began with the 'big bang' in the sphere of prices, with liberalization at a stroke in January 1992. The rouble was allowed to float freely. Foreign trade controls were largely removed, and a commitment was made to rapid privatization of state assets. The Soviet programme of economic reform now looked radically different from that pursued in China.

Eastern Europe

It is impossible to capture in a short space the complexity and heterogeneity of approach towards economic reform in the diverse countries of Eastern Europe since the political revolutions of 1989. However, not one country in the region followed what we call the East Asian path of state guided, experimental transition away from the planned economy. In the wake of the 1989 revolutions, confidence in the state as an effective instrument to play a large role in the economy disappeared. A form of commitment to a free market economy quickly gained the dominant position ideologically. All the countries in the region, with more or less rapidity, established freely convertible currencies, greatly reduced levels of protection, committed themselves to widespread privatization of state assets (though in practice the pace and methods adopted differed greatly), and quickly dismantled the state administrative planning system.

The political setting

The most important contrast between the Asian and the European paths to reforming the formerly centrally planned economies is the simplest: there is a sharp difference between the political paths followed in the two sets of countries. At the heart of the contrast lay the different outlook of the leadership. Let us take the cases of the two largest socialist countries, China and the USSR, and see how the different outlooks held by their respective leaders led to two distinctively different series of events.

USSR

The Soviet leadership had experienced a lifetime of political stability. They could not imagine that their country could be plunged into political turmoil by over-rapid political reform. Writing at the beginning of the Soviet reform process, Gorbachev expressed his hopes as follows:

> The main idea of the January [1986] Plenary Meeting – as regards ways of accomplishing the tasks of *perestroika* and protecting society from a repetition of errors of the past – was the development of democracy. It is the principal guarantee of the irreversibility of *perestroika*. The more socialist democracy there is, the more socialism we will have. This is our firm conviction, and we will not abandon it. We will promote democracy in the economy, in politics and within the Party itself. The creativity of the masses is the decisive force in *perestroika*. There is no other more powerful force.
>
> (Gorbachev 1987)

From as early as July 1986 Gorbachev had determined that a successful economic reform needed to proceed much more rapidly than the pace at which Soviet reforms were proceeding. He decided that this required a prior radical political reform. There was a chorus of praise from the West for Gorbachev's far-sighted vision and daring in moving the USSR rapidly towards multi-party democracy (the CPSU's monopoly of political power was formally ended just four years after Gorbachev began the programme of political *perestroika*) (for example, see Aslund 1991). Only in hindsight did some of the writers begin to acknowledge the dangers of the path that had been followed, and even then in the most equivocal terms.

The tentative, experimental economic reforms of the late 1980s were completely swamped by the effects of political *perestroika*. The communist party collapsed. The nation state disintegrated and a feeble, populist government was brought into being. The budgetary situation quickly became hopeless. The money supply ran wildly out of control. A disastrous spiral of withdrawal from the market was set in motion at every level from the republics down to the enterprise, and the system relapsed into a virtual barter economy. From having a relatively low level of indebtedness, the USSR rapidly moved towards becoming one of the world's most indebted countries, as the foreign trade situation careered out of control.

China

The aged Chinese leadership had personally experienced the anarchy of political life for much of the 'republican' period. Under the republic, the hopes of more Western-oriented Chinese intellectuals for the establishment of a stable democratic system in China after the 1911 revolution were dashed as China entered the prolonged turmoil of the warlord period. In addition, the same leaders had more recently been through the searing experience of the Cultural Revolution. They had seen the damage to economic life, the threat to ordinary citizens' safety and sense of security, brought about by the destruction of the party during the high years of the Cultural Revolution. Self-interest in clinging to power was, of course, extremely important in determining their approach towards political reform. However, an important, though indeterminable, part of their approach was also based on an extremely hard-headed appraisal of the options facing China. Writing early in China's reform process Deng (1979) presented the Chinese leadership's view of the relationship between different aspects of the reform process as follows:

> At present, when we are confronted with manifold difficulties in our economic life which can be overcome only by series of readjustments and by consolidation and reorganization, it is particularly necessary to stress publicly the importance of subordinating personal interests to collective ones, interests of the part to those of the whole, and immediate to long-term interests. ... [T]alk about democracy in the abstract will inevitably lead to the unchecked spread of ultra-democracy and anarchism, to the complete disruption of political stability and unity, and to the total failure of our modernization programme. If this happens then the decade of struggle against Lin Biao and the Gang of Four will have been in vain, China will once again be plunged into chaos, division, retrogression and darkness, and the Chinese people will be deprived of all hope.
>
> (Deng 1979: 55)

The Chinese leadership was determined not to allow any semblance of national disintegration. While the regime moved away from the depths of totalitarian intervention in social life, it remained an authoritarian one party state. Serious political opposition was dealt with brutally, most notably in the case of the Tiananmen massacre of 1989. The government believed that political democratization was a diversion from the most important task, namely that of improving the performance of the economic system in order to raise living standards and make China a more powerful and respected country.

A chorus of trenchant criticisms was made of the Chinese communist party in the 1980s. Western human rights groups spoke out against the undoubted harshness of the Chinese government. Many critics argued that the introduction of a market economy was impossible under communist rule: 'To survive and successfully evolve as a living social organism, the system of free markets, private property, and contractual buyer–seller transactions must operate within a legal order and in a politically democratic environment' (Prybyla 1990: 188).[13] It was argued that the CCP had the double burden of highly centralized traditions of Leninism plus millennia of centralized rule in China. The conventional wisdom, espoused in article after article and conference after conference, was that the CCP had to be removed from its monopoly of political power if the move to a market economy was to be put into effect. The Tiananmen massacre in 1989 confirmed the worst fears of the pessimistic view of the Chinese leadership, and few Western analysts thought the Chinese communist party could last for many more months let alone years. In fact, the same party led by largely the same old men led further sustained and controlled moves towards a market economy with remarkable results for the performance of the Chinese economy.

CONCLUSION

The reform experience of China and other Asian reforming communist countries demonstrates that for the Stalinist economic system to achieve a radical improvement in performance it was not necessary for there first to be a destructive systemic reform. It was not necessary that there be a programme of economic shock therapy based on the philosophy of 'more pain for more gain', or that drastic surgical operations were necessary to improve the health of the patient by cutting out the cancers, with long periods of convalescence being necessary after the operation.

The fact that the Chinese system of political economy in the 1980s and early 1990s (and the Vietnamese also after 1986) was 'market socialist' and yet was one of the most dynamic in terms both of output and income growth that the modern world has seen, presents the mainstream economists with a puzzle: why did it perform so well in the first decade and a half of reform, despite the fact that both economic and political institutions and policies were gravely inadequate in relation to mainstream Western theory and policy advice? There are a number of possibilities, of different orders of difficulty for mainstream Western political economy to digest.

The easy answer for economists reflecting on the shambles of post-Stalinism in Eastern Europe and the former USSR is that China entered its reform programme with important advantages compared to Eastern Europe and Russia. We have demonstrated that they are at best of secondary importance and at worst irrelevant. Indeed, it is questionable if on balance China (or Vietnam) did indeed enter its reform programme with any net advantages over the USSR or Eastern Europe in terms of its capacity to respond to the challenge of 'de-Stalinization', other than in the very deep sense discussed above of the historical and ideological factors that shaped the leadership perspective and the determination of policy.

A more worrying possibility is that China's incrementalist approach to economic reform may have been correct and the attempt in most of Eastern Europe and in the former USSR to move rapidly towards a market economy may have been a serious mistake. The enthusiasm of post-communist 'capitalist triumphalism' among advisers to Eastern Europe and the former USSR may have caused a major mistake in assessing not only the required speed of the transition but also the desirable economic functions of the state over an extended transition period (see essays in Chang and Nolan (eds) 1995).

An even more worrying possibility for mainstream economics is that a key part of the reason for the contrast may lie in the realm of politics. A successful formation of reform strategy may require a comprehensive perspective of political economy, which the mainstream economics lacks. A more successful transition away from a communist economy may be easier to achieve with a strong state which is able to place the overall national interest above that of powerful vested interest groups. A self-reforming communist party may be the least bad vehicle available to accomplish this. The causes for China's (and Vietnam's) success may lie above all in the set of historical factors which allowed the communist party to survive (whereas it was overthrown in Eastern Europe and Russia) and to preside over the introduction of an increasingly competitive economy.

The conclusion that the differences in economic performance of China and Eastern Europe largely originate from policy differences, and more importantly the different strategies of political change, becomes even more disturbing when we consider the possibility that all Stalinist economies possessed a huge inherent catch-up and overtaking possibility on account of the vast under-performance in relation to their huge physical and human capital inheritance. The tremendous success of the Chinese economy during the 1980s and into the early 1990s suggests that such potential was indeed large. The reform of the Stalinist economies may be seen by history to have been a knife edge situation in which correct choices in political economy could produce explosive growth and incorrect ones could send the system spinning backwards at high speed for an extended period.

NOTES

1 In the late 1980s, the UN began ranking countries by their 'Human Development Index' (HDI), two of the three main components of which were life expectancy and adult literacy. Almost without exception the communist countries' HDI ranking stood substantially above their ranking by per capita income (UNDP 1990: 128–129). In terms of the mass of citizens' capacity to be 'positively free' through education and a long life, it is paradoxical that even

the most brutal of communist dictatorships, such as Burma and Cambodia, performed exceptionally well.

2 For example, estimates for the USSR in the 1970s suggest that 30–40 per cent of personal income came from the private sector.

3 It may be argued that Chinese style agricultural reform cannot be applied to Eastern Europe or the former Soviet Union, because in the latter there is a greater need for 'lumpy' farm inputs. The more advanced European and Soviet agricultural systems at first sight appear to have been characterized generally by far greater 'lumpiness' than Chinese agriculture with large numbers of huge pieces of farm equipment. However, Chinese agriculture also had an important area of lumpiness which did not apply in Soviet agriculture, namely the high degree of dependence of farm production on irrigation and drainage facilities. Even quite small scale water conservation facilities could be well beyond the reach of individual households. The solution of the post-reform organization of these inputs is not in principle very complicated. In advanced capitalist countries a large part of lumpy inputs, from processing facilities through to combine harvesters and crop spraying aeroplanes, are owned either by non-farmers and hired out by specialist suppliers to individual farmers, or are co-operatively owned alongside individual farm operation. In principle, the land contract process could be combined with the maintenance of a large part of lumpy inputs in the hands of profit oriented co-operatives or state machinery and irrigation companies.

4 Eastern Europe and the former Soviet Union.

5 By the end of 1992 only around $3 billion in foreign investment had been attracted to the whole of Eastern Europe (*Transition* 4, 1 and 5) compared with a figure of $44 billion for China, where in the first six months of 1993 alone $9.4 billion in foreign investment occurred, with a further $170 billion projected (*Financial Times* 15 September 1993). By June 1993 Vietnam alone had implemented projects involving US$1.4 billion (and projects totalling US$6.2 billion had been approved) (*Financial Times* 30 November 1993).

6 The total value of imports for the seven largest Western European economies in 1991 was $1,155 billion, compared to $506 billion for the USA and $234 billion for Japan. The total value of exports from the Four Little Tigers in the same year was US$314 billion (World Bank 1993: 264–265).

7 Enterprises with foreign participation still account for only about 6 per cent of total industrial output. (*Financial Times* 15 September 1993).

8 India has a diaspora, which is perhaps as important as the Chinese one, but this did not (as yet) result in much capital inflow. The rapid growth of foreign investment in Vietnam in the early 1990s came almost entirely from non-Vietnamese sources.

9 According to an estimate of credit risk by the Economist Intelligence Unit, based on 11 factors, including indebtedness, current account position and political stability, Russia was the second riskiest country in the world in the second quarter of 1993, next to Iraq. China, despite having been downgraded recently on the basis of its overheating economy, ranked between Malaysia and Thailand (*The Economist* 21 August 1993: 88).

10 Exports have grown at a reported rate of 30 per cent per annum since the policy of *doi moi* began (*Financial Times* 23 November 1993).

11 While we disagree strongly with Aslund's overall view of the desirable path of Soviet reform, we find his account of the chronology of reform and the debates involved extremely useful.

12 A comparable stage in China's post-Stalinist reforms would be the late 1970s. At this point China had made less rapid progress in its reforms than the USSR had done by the late 1980s. The key decision to move ahead with fundamental

system reform in China was not made until December 1978, and even then the early reform measures following this were extremely cautious. As late as the spring of 1979 a major campaign was fought against the policy of agricultural contracting to a group, which had begun, cautiously, the previous year. In hindsight one frequently forgets the slow pace and great care with which the reforms were introduced in China.

13 The fact that this proposition was contradicted by the experience of almost all the industrializing countries in the nineteenth century doesn't seem to bother Prybyla nor most other economists who entered the fray of the political debate over economic reform in the former communist countries (for evidence, see Therborn 1977).

REFERENCES

Abramovitz, M. (1986) 'Catching up, forging ahead and falling behind', *Journal of Economic History* 2.

Acs, Z. and Audretsch, D. B. (1993) 'Has the role of small firms changed in the US?', in Z. Acs and D. B. Audretsch *Small Firms and Entrepreneurship*, Cambridge: Cambridge University Press.

—— (eds) (1993) *Small Firms and Entrepreneurship*, Cambridge: Cambridge University Press.

Amsden, A. (1989) *Asia's Next Giant*, Oxford: Oxford University Press.

Aslund, A. (1990) 'Gorbachev, perestroika, and economic crisis', *Problems of Communism* January–April: 13–41.

—— (1991) *Gorbachev's Struggle for Economic Reform*, London: Pinter.

Bergere, A. (1981) 'The "Other China": Shanghai from 1919–1949', in Howe, C. (ed.) *Shanghai*, Cambridge: Cambridge University Press.

Chandler, A. D. (1990) *Scale and Scope: The Dynamics of Industrial capitalism*, Cambridge, Mass.: Harvard University Press.

Chang, H.-J. (1993) 'The political economy of industrial policy in Korea', *Cambridge Journal of Economics* 16(2).

Chang, H.-J. and Nolan, P. (eds) (1995) *Transformation of the Communist Economies – Against the Mainstream*, London: Macmillan.

Deng, X. P. (1984) *Selected Works of Deng Xiaoping, (1975–1982)*, Beijing: Foreign Languages Press.

Ellman, M. (1994) 'The increase in death and disease rates under *katastroika*', *Cambridge Journal of Economics*.

Erlich, E. (1985) 'The size structure of manufacturing establishments and enterprises: an international comparison', *Journal of Comparative Economics* 9: 267–295.

Gattrell, P. (1986) *The Tsarist Economy, 1850–1917*, London: Batsford.

Gerschenkron, A. (1960) *Economic Backwardness in Historical Perspective*, New York: Praeger.

Gorbachev, M. (1987) *Perestroika*, London: Collins.

Guroff, G. and Carstenson, F. V. (eds) (1983) *Entrepreneurship in Imperial Russia and the Soviet Union*, Princeton, NJ: Princeton University Press.

Hicks, G. (ed) (1990) *The Broken Mirror*, Harlow, Essex: Longman.

Hobsbawm, E. and Ranger, T. (eds) (1983) *The Invention of Tradition*, Cambridge: Cambridge University Press.

Kornai, J. (1990) *The Road to a Free Economy*, London: Norton.

Lardy, N. (1983) *Agriculture in Modern China's Economic Development*, Cambridge: Cambridge University Press.

Levy, M. J. (1949) *The Rise of the Modern Chinese Business Class*, New York: Institute of Pacific Relations.

Little, I. M. D. (1979) 'An economic reconnaissance', in W. Galenson (ed.) *Economic Growth and Structural Change in Taiwan*, London: Cornell University Press.

Morishima, M. (1982) *Why Has Japan Succeeded?*, Cambridge: Cambridge University Press.

Nolan, P. (1988) *The Political Economy of Collective Farms*, Cambridge: Polity Press.

Prybyla, J. (1990) 'A broken system', in G. Hicks (ed.) *The Broken Mirror*, Harlow, Essex: Longman.

—— (1991) 'The road from socialism: why, where, what and how', *Problems of Communism* 40, January–April.

Sachs, J. and Woo, W. T. (1994) 'Structural factors in the economic reform of China, Eastern Europe and the former Soviet Union', *Economic Policy* 9(18).

Scherer, F. M., and Ross, D. (1990) *Industrial Market Structure and Performance*, Boston, Mass.: Houghton Mifflin (third edition).

State Statistical Bureau, various years *Chinese Statistical Outline* (*Zhongguo tongji zhaiyao*) (ZGTJZY), Beijing: Zhongguo tongji chubanshe.

State Statistical Bureau (SSB), various years *Chinese Statistical Yearboook* (*Zhongguo tongji nianjian*) (ZGTJNJ), Beijing: Zhongguo tongji chubanshe.

Steinherr, A. (1991) 'Essential ingredients for reforms in Eastern Europe', *MOCT* 3.

Sung, Y. (1991) 'The reintegration of southeast China', unpublished ms.

Therborn, G. (1977) 'The rule of capital and the rise rise of democracy', *New Left Review* 3, May–June.

Tian,Y. (1990) 'Prices', in Nolan, P. and Dong Fureng (eds) *Chinese Economy and its Future: Achievement and Problems of Post Mao Reform*, Oxford: Polity Press.

UNDP (1990) *Human Development Report*, New York: Oxford University Press.

United Nations, Economic Commission for Europe (1993) *Economic Survey of Europe, 1992/3*, New York: United Nations.

United States Congress, Joint Economic Committee (USCJEC) (1979) *Soviet Economy in a Time of Change* (2 vols), Washington, DC: US Government Printing Office.

Vogel, E. (1989) *One Step Ahead in China*, London: Harvard University Press.

Wade, R. (1990) *Governing the Market*, Princeton, NJ: Princeton University Press.

World Bank, various years, *World Development Report*, Washington, DC: Oxford University Press.

—— (1981) *China: Socialist Development*, annex D, *Challenges and Achievements in Industry*, Washington, DC: Oxford University Press.

Wu, Chengming and Xu Dixin (eds) forthcoming *China's Capitalist Sprouts*, (3 vols), Basingstoke: Macmillan.

2 The institutional nature of China's emerging economic order

Max Boisot and John Child

ABSTRACT

China's integration into the world economy and the dismantling of her state administered industrial infrastructure does not necessarily imply that she will in future conform to Western capitalist market models. In this paper the writers examine the nature of the newly emerging economic order in China in terms of the ways in which transactions are organized, the property rights and the criteria for ownership, and the role of government in making the system work. The application of research findings to an analytical framework enunciated at the beginning of the paper helps to draw out the comparisons and contrasts with Western practice. The authors conclude that conventional Western economic analysis of the development process may need to be re-appraised. While it may be possible to derive a conceptual language from Western theory to apply to the Chinese case, the relationships between the concepts will be different.

INTRODUCTION

Since initiating its reforms in 1979 – first in agriculture and then later in industry – China has sustained a rapid rate of economic growth and development, with only short-lived interruptions. Its success in this enterprise contrasts favourably with most other developing countries (*The Economist* 1993b), and invites a closer examination of the kind of economic organization that is facilitating such an impressive performance. China's growth has been stimulated by two main policy measures which appear *prima facie* to be moving its economic system towards the Western model: the dismantling of its state administered industrial structure and its integration with the world economy. However, contact with the country suggests that the emerging economic order may not conform to familiar Western capitalist market-system models in regard to property rights and the organization of transactions, and that the role played by government may also be of a different order.

In this chapter we discuss a number of specific issues that can be subsumed under these broad questions. The first concerns the type of business system now operating in China. If, as Nee (1992) suggests, there is a newer system of marketized transactions in addition to state dominated 'non-market firms', does this merit special attention as the Chinese economic system of the future (cf. Qian and Xu 1993)? Second, do the arrangements through which the marketized sector operates conform to the conventional Western model? Are Chinese market arrangements weak in Western terms, because they do not rely primarily on formal, legally enforceable contracts, but strong in their reliance on trust and social ties which are firmly embedded in traditional social norms (cf. Granovetter 1985)? Third, does the economic order that is emerging in China from the dismantling of the socialist system incorporate a new form of capitalism (as judged by the criteria of ownership and property rights) or does it require its own specific designation? Fourth, if a distinctive economic system is emerging in China, what part does government play in its operation and what amendments does this require to our conventional theories about the role of the state in economic life?

Even if only tentatively formulated, answers to these questions would be of considerable moment for Western academics and business people. A good understanding of Chinese economic organization would have a bearing upon Western discussions of modernization, many of which assume that this requires the building of markets, property rights and other institutional systems of essentially the same kind that supported earlier instances of industrialization. Such answers would also carry useful implications for foreign investors and business people. Better knowledge of the Chinese business system would help to indicate how foreign business people can enter the system and point to where power and decision making is located within it.

The paper begins with an analytical framework which helps to differentiate China's system of economic governance in relation to ideal types familiar to Western institutional economists. Application of the framework suggests *a priori* that China is treading a distinctive path towards modernization. Distinctive characteristics of China's emerging economic order are then tentatively identified by reference to the four issues just mentioned. A concluding comment is finally offered on the potential significance of the subject. The chapter as a whole should be read as a prolegomenon to the research that its subject richly deserves, its purpose being to elaborate relevant questions rather than to offer adequate answers at this stage.

AN INSTITUTIONAL PERSPECTIVE ON THE CHINESE ECONOMIC SYSTEM

The Chinese have explained the economic reforms they have undertaken since 1978 as a move from bureaucracies to markets. The shift away from bureaucracy has taken two forms:

1 A decentralization of administrative power from the central government to provincial and city governments. For example, responsibility
for large state owned enterprises was transferred from central to provincial governments, while for medium sized state owned enterprises it
was transferred from provincial to city or county governments. Powers
to enter into foreign trade relations and to approve the establishment
of smaller joint ventures have also been decentralized.
2 A decentralization of economic power from the state to economic
agents – state owned firms, collective enterprises, and family businesses.
These have now been given a measure of managerial discretion
over what they produce, over marketing their output, and personnel
policies (Child and Lu 1990; Lu and Child 1994).

Economic reform measures were enacted at an ever accelerating pace
throughout the 1980s and the early 1990s. Yet as Boisot and Child (1988)
have shown, delegation and decentralization measures have encountered
problems on the ground. The state has lacked both the appropriate
economic and institutional concepts as well as the 'low context' (Hall 1976)
institutional culture that would allow such measures to usher in a work-
able market order.

In developing their argument, Boisot and Child drew upon a two-dimen-
sional framework that relates the transactional options available to a given
group or population to the way that information is processed within it.
This framework takes the diffusibility of transactionally relevant knowledge to be related to its degree of codification (Figure 2.1). Thus price
information, being well codified, can diffuse rapidly and anonymously
within a group, whereas the uncodified knowledge that a Zen master holds
in his head can only be shared face-to-face with a few disciples, and this
only over extended periods of time.

The codification and diffusion of information create an information
environment which conditions the transactional characteristics to be found

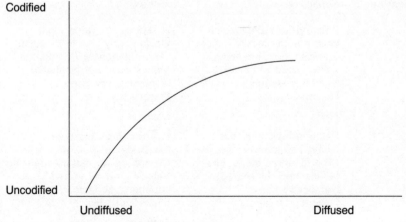

Figure 2.1 Codification and diffusion of information

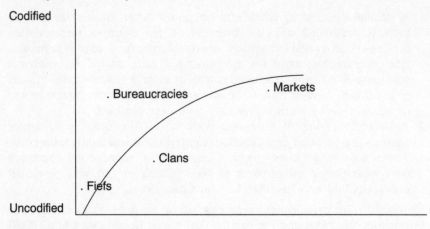

Figure 2.2 Transactional systems

in different regions of the framework (Figure 2.2) and endows each of them with some quite specific features. These are listed in Table 2.1.

Using the framework as an analytical tool, Boisot and Child then argued that China could not be decentralizing from bureaucracies to markets because it had not actually built up a stable codified bureaucratic order from which to decentralize. A preference for interpersonal accommodation was always undermining the country's attempt to develop into bureaucracies and pulling China towards fiefdoms, its traditional mode of social organization (Figure 2.3). Boisot and Child labelled this tendency 'the iron law of fiefs'.

The situation has not appreciably changed in the 1990s. The institutions

Table 2.1 Transactional characteristics

Codified	Bureaucracies	Markets
	Relationships: impersonal	Relationships: impersonal
	Goals: hierarchically imposed	Goals: freely chosen by agent
	Co-ordination: hierarchical	Co-ordination: self-regulation
	Values: need to be shared	Values: need not be shared
	Numbers: medium	Numbers: very large
	Uncertainty: low	Uncertainty: low
	Fiefs	*Clans*
	Relationships: personal	Relationships: personal
	Goals: hierarchically imposed	Goals: by negotiation
	Co-ordination: hierarchical	Co-ordination: mutual adjustment
	Values: must be shared	Values: must be shared
	Numbers: small	Numbers: medium
	Uncertainty: high	Uncertainty: high
Uncodified	*Undiffused*	*Diffused*

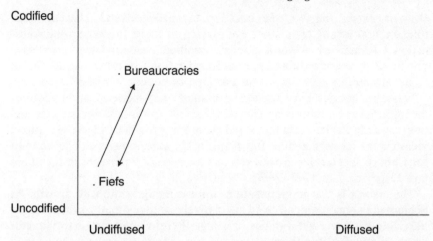

Figure 2.3 The iron law of fiefs

that characterize a rational–legal system – an effective central bank, macroeconomic levers, enforceable and consistent laws – remain absent, all official rhetoric to the contrary notwithstanding. The freeing up of the financial system, for example, has led to the emergence of a sizeable secondary credit sector in which lending takes place through direct relationships between firms and other bodies at very high interest rates; this sector is beyond the control of the monetary and regulatory authorities. As happened in 1987–1988, China's economy is once more overheating and the only tools available to policy makers for bringing the economy under control remain the microeconomic ones designed for a command economy. Yet since these are of proven ineffectiveness, to function at all they require direct interpersonal encounters between state actors and a myriad of economic agents in highly particularistic circumstances.

China once more confronts its age-old problem: centralize and face stagnation or decentralize and face chaos. How much chaos is evidenced by the centre's rapid loss of control over the provinces. According to the World Bank, for example, the share of tax revenue accruing to the central government at the beginning of the reform process 14 years ago amounted to 34 per cent of China's GDP. With the decentralization of economic power, this has now shrunk to 19 per cent (*The Economist* 1993c). Many of the central government's measures to cool down the economy are at the same time attempts to wrest control of tax revenues away from the regions.

Yet, since the PRC has now had more than 10 years in which to observe how other countries build their rational–legal bureaucracies and markets and then to emulate them, we are tempted to ask what the blockages are. Why is mimetic isomorphism proving so difficult in China whereas in Eastern Europe it is proceeding much faster? (cf. Powell and DiMaggio 1991). There is, however, another possibility: *could it be that, put in this*

Western-centred manner, the question is misconceived? That at some fundamental level China is not even trying to move further up the transactional framework towards a more codified rational–legal order as a precursor to a less troublesome decentralization? In other words, that it is not attempting to build a Western type of economic order?

Western theories have tended to assume that modernization requires institutional choices moving transactions first towards bureaucracies and then towards markets and that rapid economic growth can serve as a proxy measure for modernization. But if this is the case, how does one account for China's spectacular growth rate, an average of 9 per cent in the 1980s and 13 per cent in 1992–1993?

The answer is that modernization is not commensurate with growth. As Schumpeter once quipped 'Add successively as many mail coaches as you like, you will never get a railway carriage thereby'. Yet just as total factor productivity identifies those elements of growth that cannot be attributed to any single factor but are rather the product of how the factors are organized,[1] so we might consider that modernization speaks about how growth is organized, about its quality, and about the institutional choices which drive the process. This means the question can now be reformulated: if modernization requires institutional choices that move transactions first towards bureaucracies and then towards markets, and if rapid economic growth can serve as a proxy measure for modernization, then how can China be achieving such rapid rates of growth while retaining an institutional order so heavily invested in the lower (uncodified) regions of Table 2.1?

Two explanations suggest themselves. The first is that with a per capita income of $300 or so in 1980 (in 1980 dollars), the country started its reforms from a very low base (World Bank 1985). Most of its growth results from a more efficient use of productive factors rather than from some elusive residual associated with how these are institutionalized. According to this explanation, the latter has a part to play but it hardly drives the process.

Many countries that undergo economic take-off indeed start from a low base and in the case of China this must certainly count as part of the explanation for its spectacular growth rate in the 1980s. For the 1990s, however, the explanation begins to lose some of its force. The World Bank's *World Development Report* has recently taken to estimating GDP per head for various countries on a purchasing power parity basis in order to take into account international differences in prices (*The Economist* 1993a). Using such calculations, China's GDP per head was US$1,680 in 1991, a figure which not only places it among middle income countries but, when multiplied by its vast population, converts it into the world's third largest economy after the United States and Japan. From such a perspective the 'low base' vanishes, as do the arguments that it was used to support. At this income level, many economies have already acquired the rudiments of a rational–legal bureaucracy as well as those of efficient market institutions – hence their claim to be modernizing.

The second explanation is that the iron law of fiefs only applies to the state sector, victim of the continuing irrationalities of the planned economy. It is argued that the non-state sector is becoming codified, as it should (Fischer 1993). The significance of the non-state sector in China today is undeniable; it now accounts for around 50 per cent of industrial output (Qian and Xu 1993). Indeed, the state sector is 'hollowing' itself out through sub-contracting to non-state firms and/or through forming joint ventures both with non-state firms and foreign partners. Yet the non-state sector is, by and large, made up of small, undercapitalized collective or family businesses. They operate discreetly, sometimes clandestinely and, where they do so most successfully, it is because they are beyond the reach of the state central bureaucracy. They do not, however, escape the exactions of local bureaucracies with which they must reach some accommodation if they are to survive (Nee 1992). Here the relationship remains essentially feudal, with the local bureaucracy offering protection in return for loyalty from the private and collective enterprises that come under their jurisdiction. The infrastructure available at the local level does not, however, necessarily energize such enterprises; it can also impede them. The considerable growth of official corruption in recent years bears eloquent testimony to this problem. The non-state sector in China is not pushing towards the codified areas of our framework. Rather, it is having once more to fend off, or at least 'manage', the impositions of ostensibly formal governmental organization as it had to in late-imperial times (Mann 1987).

We are thus left with a country representing over a fifth of the world's population that is achieving an unprecedented level of economic performance through a relatively uncodified system of ownership and transacting. In effect, China's rapid growth and development over the last fifteen years challenges our concepts of modernization initially as an institutionalization towards greater codification (cf. Durkheim 1933; Tonnies 1955; Habermas 1970), followed by a decentralization towards a market order. We either have to imagine a country as being capable of growing at 13 per cent per annum without modernizing – theoretically conceivable at least – or we have to re-conceptualize the process of modernization itself.

Casual empiricism refutes the first option – a visit to any of China's cities or to the villages of its coastal regions overwhelmingly confirms that something we can call modernization is taking place. As in the case of the proverbial elephant, we may not be able to define its constituent elements, but we surely recognize it when we see it. We are then left with the need to rethink the concept of modernization itself. A deeper understanding of China's system of economic organization and its institutional supports would make an invaluable contribution to that larger end.

IS CHINA FOLLOWING A DISTINCTIVE PATH TOWARDS MODERNIZATION?

Modernization reflects the working of the law of codification and diffusion (Boisot 1986). The more you codify or formalize a transaction, the easier it is to decentralize it within a transactional population. The more you fail to do so, conversely, the more local the transaction must remain. Codification sacrifices contextual data. Transactional coverage is achieved at the expense of transactional nuance and richness. The depersonalization associated with codified transactions merely reflects the difficulty of maintaining a dense network of interpersonal obligations as small numbers transacting gives way to large numbers transacting. What Williamson (1975) terms 'atmosphere' vanishes as exchange loses its 'embeddedness' (Granovetter 1985). The move towards greater codification thus corresponds to what Hall (1976) terms a shift from high context to low context or to what Habermas (1970) calls a shift from 'lifeworld' to 'system'. It stimulates and facilitates but does not guarantee decentralization.

Prior to developing a market order, for example, Europe went through an absolutist phase in which emergent nation states created strong centralizing bureaucracies. Only with the advent of a liberal ideology in the eighteenth and nineteenth centuries did a decentralization to a market order gradually take place. A bureaucratic order, however, could only stabilize on the basis of a rational–legal approach to the problems of statecraft and institution building. In many countries of Eastern Europe rational–legal state bureaucracies predated the advent of Marxism-Leninism. When Eastern Europe came under Soviet domination in the post-war years, therefore, the institutional infrastructure that already existed allowed Marxism–Leninism to operate at a higher level of codification than it could in China, and this in spite of the 'iron law of fiefs' – the tendency of agents to seek mutual accommodation based on the informal exercise of personal power to compensate for the system's lack of rationality. Thus, while Marxism–Leninism may have been erosive of legality and economic rationality, in Eastern Europe it still had to contend with the countervailing effects of what was already in place.

This was not so in China. The bureaucracy that the communists inherited in 1949 was 'patrimonial' (Weber 1964) and feudal in its operations. For the modernizing Chinese, Marxism–Leninism was assumed to show the way to the attainment of a codified rational–legal order. Stalin's forced collectivization of the Soviet Union in the 1930s and the latter's subsequent ability to confront an armed Germany's industrial might in the second world war had suggested that, with the right policies, socialism in one country was indeed a live option. However, Marxism–Leninism in the event led in the opposite direction, towards fiefs, a move that was reinforced in China by a cultural and cognitive bias against abstraction (Bond and Hwang 1986).

Abstraction is a prerequisite for the creation of robust codifications and the construction of a rational-legal order. It involves a move away from treating each specific exchange *sui generis* and towards the employment of general principles which apply predictably and systematically to every case. The central role of law in modern societies illustrates the importance of abstraction to the notion of modernization. The modernization hypothesis assumes that there is a shift from particularism to universalism and from substantive to procedural rationality. Thus the ability to move towards higher levels of codification and to stay there, requires a greater disposition for abstract thought than Chinese culture has shown up until now. Absent abstraction from efforts at codification and you obtain little more than ritual and mock bureaucracies (Gouldner 1954).

What appears to be happening in China in the economic sphere is that the system continues to reproduce a model of organization specific to the relations between governmental authorities and enterprises which are themselves particular to given industries and/or localities. Interorganizational relations between state bodies and enterprises, relations that in other industrial economies would be conducted at arm's length through markets, are managed hierarchically (though often executed through horizontal relationships) as if they were intraorganizational in nature. The impersonal abstract order associated with a decentralization to markets has yet to replace the much more concrete personalized order that delegation within a patrimonial system can allow. The model currently in use thus fails the test of abstraction implicitly posed by the modernization thesis. Instead, people 'make out' through interpersonal accommodation and negotiation, and they continue to sustain the iron law of fiefs. Indeed, the rapid spread in China today of modern technology for personal communications (such as pagers and mobile phones) is beginning to facilitate the extension of these fiefs into clan-type networks which achieve a measure of market coverage through relatively uncodified, personal means.

If, then, rapid development in China is being pursued through its own model of economic and social organization, can more be said about the distinctive features of this model? These questions are now addressed by reference to the four issues identified in the introduction.

SOME FEATURES OF CHINA'S EMERGING ECONOMIC ORDER

What kind of business system?

Whitley (1991, 1992, 1994) argues that business systems vary internationally in terms of three main sets of characteristics: the nature of firms as economic actors, especially their autonomy; the way relations between firms are structured to form markets; and the logic which governs managerial systems of co-ordination and control within firms. His analysis of these three constituents is applied to 'market economies' in which 'control over economic resources is decentralized to private owners' (1994: 155). This definition would still exclude the bulk of China's economic activity. Nevertheless, Whitley employs his framework to compare the business systems of post-war Japan, South Korea, Taiwan and Hong Kong and it should be instructive to add China to this comparison, both because it has a broad cultural affinity with these countries and because the exercise can help to clarify whether, and how far, China has moved towards establishing a business system based on non-state control of economic resources.

China has always had a significant amount of small scale commercial and industrial activity outside the centrally planned command economy, but since 1979 the industrial system has become considerably more diversified (Hussain 1990, 1992). Indeed, an outstanding feature of China's economic reform has been the steady and substantial growth in the share of the non-state sector in the national total (Qian and Xu 1993). Today, there is a free market for most consumer goods, while the market remains supplementary to planning in the production and supply of some industrial goods and materials, especially those considered to be of strategic significance. Moreover, several different forms of industrial property rights have now emerged alongside a diversification in the forms of enterprise ownership and of relationships with the organs of government, including different types of contract for the management of state owned enterprises.

It is necessary therefore to employ a framework for analysis within which the spread of markets and changing structure of property rights in China can be taken into account. Nee (1992) has made a useful contribution to this end by identifying three categories of Chinese enterprise according to the predominant mode through which their transactions are co-ordinated and the rights over industrial property they embody. He calls the three types the 'non-marketised firm', the 'marketised firm' and the 'private firm'.

Non-marketized firms form part of a centralized structure of economic transactions in which state agencies control the circulation of goods and services through their redistributive mechanisms; indeed to a large extent they also redistribute income between the firms. Those goods for which the state still sets fixed plan prices come within this category.

The marketized firm, according to Nee, falls outside the bounds of central planning, though it often relies to some extent on local government to secure access to resources allocated through the plan. He regards the collectively owned enterprise as the stereotypical marketized firm, though it is clear that some state enterprises also fall within the category (see Child 1994: Chapter 7). The economic contribution of collective enterprises has grown considerably under the reform.

Many collective enterprises, especially the generally smaller ones located in townships and villages (the so-called township–village enterprises or TVEs), today operate entirely in the market and with greater freedom from government control. Together with purely privately owned firms, which also deal wholly through market channels, they constitute Nee's third 'private firm' category. Foreign funded firms also enjoy a private status, albeit usually with state owned partners, and operate through markets. These are not 'efficient' neo-classical markets, however, since they remain for the most part small, local and hierarchically ordered.

The distinctions which Nee draws have to be borne in mind when assessing how far a business system has now developed in China. Not only is the situation a mixed one, but it is changing quite rapidly. The general direction of the change is indicated by the fact that marketized non-state firms constitute the most rapidly growing part of the Chinese economy, and that this growth suffered only a short-term set-back because of political reaction after the Tiananmen incident. A potentially significant factor behind the shift towards the marketized and non-state sectors is the 'hollowing out' of state owned enterprises through the growth in their sub-contracting to non-state (primarily collective) firms.

Whitley (1994) identifies five types of business system that have become established in East Asia, Europe and North America. His three sets of criterial characteristics – nature of economic agents, organization of economic relations between them, internal co-ordination and control – point up the distinctions between the private, marketized and non-marketized sectors in China. They indicate that the country at present contains two business systems and one non-business system.

In several respects, the characteristics of the Chinese private sector bear similarities to those of Whitley's 'centrifugal' business system. Indeed, he cites the non-PRC Chinese family business as an example of this type. Within this system, economic power is decentralized to firms only to a limited extent, partly because there is a lack of stable institutional procedures (especially laws) governing economic relations. A salient example of the arbitrary regulation to which private business in China remains subject was illustrated by the political disfavour into which private business fell for a time after 1989. Whitley suggests that this insecurity encourages dependence in this system on personal relationships and a strong preference for skills, products and processes which restrict commitments to particular markets and technologies: 'Thus, strong owner control, a reluctance to invest in capital intensive industries and highly personal connections with employees, customers and suppliers are likely to be distinctive characteristics of business systems in this context . . .' (Whitley 1994: 171).

Firms in the private sector cannot expect much support from intermediaries like banks.[2] They operate under hard budget constraints and have to be self-reliant; as a result they remain small and undercapitalized. Many private firms attempt to compensate for these disadvantages by seeking close ties with local government, but they cannot take support from that quarter for granted. Thus they often have to pay a 'management fee' to the local authority for assistance in securing access to resources and political protection, or they have to register as collective enterprises (Nee 1992: 9–10). This mode of compensation parallels a characteristic of the centrifugal business system posited by Whitley, namely that in the absence of well-developed private intermediaries the managers of firms have to seek and utilize personal connections. A difference is that the key personal connections in China lie with local government officials rather than with other firms.

While there are some similarities between the PRC private sector and Whitley's centrifugal type of business system, they nevertheless diverge in two main respects. The first is that private firms in China remain, for the most part, small-scale organizations. Thus the diversity of their operations is limited (which Whitley suggests is not the case when centrifugal systems contain large firms), and they achieve a relatively high level of internal integration under the close personal control of their owners. The second difference stems from the fact that in China the ownership of property does not furnish legal property rights as it normally does in Western business systems – these rights continue to depend importantly on the sanction of government and its officials.

The marketized non-private sector of the Chinese economy, comprising many collective firms and most state enterprises responsible to local authorities, fits much of the profile of Whitley's 'state-dependent' type of business system. Firms in this sector do not enjoy the same degree of formal autonomy as do private firms, although their effective freedom of economic action is usually greater because of the support they receive from local institutional intermediaries. The growth and profitability of marketized firms have a larger and more direct impact on the income of local government than those of either private or non-marketized firms (Nee 1992:11). This encourages local authorities to assist such firms by providing them with valuable networks and assistance in access to capital, raw materials and labour. Thus local agencies of the state fill many of the roles which in other business systems are played by private intermediary institutions. The localized nature of 'state-dependency' for firms in this sector supports the development of their personal interorganizational connections, which are of greater importance than appears to be the norm for this type of business system, as described by Whitley. These connections are often arranged by local officials and they may be a continuation of arrangements previously made under the planning system, as Solinger (1989) has illustrated through her study of 'relational contracting' in Wuhan.

It is not so clear how far the internal management of non-private marketized firms in China fits Whitley's state-dependent type. Much depends on specific factors such as the size of the firm, the standing and experience of the director and the relations he and his immediate colleagues enjoy with the supervisory bureau, the local party organization and the trade union. The managers, at least of the larger firms falling within this category, find themselves within the web of interests which Walder (1989) has identified. The way this web is handled can have a significant effect, not only on external resourcing of the enterprise but also on the quality of its internal operation.

The non-private marketized sector in China can be said to be a business system in Whitley's terms because it constitutes a mode of organizing market transactions even though this organization relies a great deal upon local government intervention. However, the third major sector comprising state owned non-marketized firms remains as much an administrative as a business system. Despite the formal decentralization of decision making to their managements under the responsibility system, state enterprises in this category continue to depend on vertical ties to higher level agencies which transfer to them resources of materials and capital according to central plans. They can only produce for the market once they have satisfied the requirements of the plan, and in many cases the prices of both inputs and outputs under the plan are fixed administratively. Their performance is judged more in the light of plan fulfilment than of hard budget criteria. One may recall that one-third of state enterprises are overtly loss-making while another third have so-called 'hidden' (unpaid) debts; these firms rely on subsidies to keep them afloat. This undermines the decentralization of responsibility to enterprises as economic actors since it is not clear under a non-market system who should bear the responsibility for losses; under soft budget constraints it is effectively government that does so.

The present declared policy of the Chinese government is to convert the non-marketized sector into a business system through a number of measures, including the abolition of administered prices over the next five years in favour of market regulation for industrial materials; the granting of autonomy to state enterprises to determine their own production, imports and exports, investment and employment through engaging in market transactions for these; making these enterprises accountable for their own performance and eliminating subsidies to them even at the cost of bankruptcies; and decentralizing ownership through experiments in stockholding. If these measures are implemented across the non-marketized sector, and most commentators regard them as ultimately inevitable, China's economy will have transformed itself into what would appear to be a market-based business system. How transactions will be governed within this system, and whether it will become capitalist in nature, remain open questions which are now discussed in turn.

The nature of market arrangements

Whatever economic decentralization has taken place in China, it has not occurred within the formalized, legal–rational, institutional systems that characterize Western countries, such as consistent and enforceable laws and effective fiscal and monetary systems. Rather, China would appear to be managing its economic development on another basis, which relies less on formalized contractual relations than on personal trust-based relationships of an essentially localized nature, characteristic of fiefs when centralized and of clans when decentralized (Boisot and Child 1988). Within this system, much seems to be settled through negotiation and the identification of reciprocal obligations, with local government being a major player as resource provider, facilitator and tax collector. These transactional arrangements, weak in Western terms (Granovetter 1985), appear to have considerable latent strengths. Thus, the institutionalized use of negotiation between enterprises and local authorities appears to introduce flexibility into regional property rights and to allow for the reconstitution of transactions to meet new opportunities and changing circumstances.

Solinger (1989) has indicated how, in Wuhan, the withdrawal of the planning system based on quotas and local government-directed input and output transactions gave rise to relational contracting in which many of the former business relationships were maintained. She points to the advantages these long-established relationships could provide in an economic environment where uncertainties persisted in regard to the honouring of trading agreements, the assurance of quality in goods exchanged, the provision of working capital, and so forth. These transactions were founded upon long-standing economic relationships between key individuals within the organizations concerned. The assurances that underpinned the transactions derived from mutual trust.

The description offered by Solinger appears to be broadly consistent with Nee's analysis (1992) of local quasi-market networks in which local government agencies play a facilitating role (and benefit from the tax revenues that derive from the stimulation that dynamic networks provide for local economic growth). The development of both internal and external sub-contracting, particularly by larger enterprises, also serves to extend such networks. External sub-contracting encourages the growth of close personal relations between managers and technical staff of the collaborating firms, particularly when technical quality specifications and delivery schedules need to be tightly controlled (Child 1994: Chapter 7).

As Su (1994) indicates, it has also become quite common for Chinese enterprises to form alliances (including mergers) to provide horizontal and vertical integration. These alliances contribute to the development of the quasi-market within China and appear to constitute a growing trend. In cases known first-hand to the writers, the initial moves in establishing these alliances each consisted of an approach by the enterprise director to persons in other units from his home town and acquainted with him personally. Later on, endorsement from the relevant government ministry became necessary in order to ensure the support of local government departments and to encourage co-ordination between them. Once in operation, integration between the constituent units of these alliances appears to depend heavily upon close personal relations among senior managers and to some extent the interlocking of roles between the units.

At quite an early stage, Richardson (1972) came close to recognizing the phenomenon of relational contracting in his discussion of co-operative interfirm relationships. Williamson (1985) also brought relational contracting into his perspective, but regarded it as falling within the domain of codified transactions at an intermediate point between hierarchy and market. The Chinese system of networked transactions, however, appears to be relatively uncodified and to be based on trust and long-standing connections. It does not therefore conform to this analysis, and indicates the need to re-evaluate, or at least qualify, the conventional Western economic model.

It is not clear to what extent the new market arrangements in China derive their distinct character from the influence of pre-1949 modes of economic transacting and the institutional supports for these. Do those who have helped to build up the Chinese market system take pre-1949, or overseas Chinese, communities as their exemplars? For example, do the entrepreneurs of contemporary regional networks borrow from the role formerly played by merchants? Are the values and expectations of Chinese businessmen still informed by the lineage system, which from the late Ming dynasty became the *de facto* social unit that interceded between state and community, at least in southern China? An important issue here is whether we are now seeing in Chinese economic organization the re-emergence of traditional social structures and behaviour patterns or, rather, the establishment of new forms (cf. Sui 1989).

There is some reason to expect a degree of continuity with pre-communist society, because it is recognized that social institutions and traditions are deeply embedded and extremely persistent (Granovetter 1985; Powell and DiMaggio 1991). Cohen (1993: 156) remarks that 'China was notable for the cultural, social, political, and economic interpenetration of city and countryside' during the later imperial era. Wong and Perdue (1992) comment on the 'mounting evidence of active, integrated markets' in Qing China (pp. 143–144), while Rawski and Li (1992) note the active intervention of the Qing government in the grain market to stabilize prices and avert catastrophes. Skinner (1964, 1965) has analysed the hierarchical ordering of market structures in pre-communist China and the extent to which this subsumed a conjunction of administrative and market units especially at prefectural level and above. The previous politico–economic system therefore appears *prima facie* to provide precedents for the administratively-supported system of locally networked transacting which has developed in China's non-state sector, and which points to the emergence, if not of a full-blooded market order, at least of a market orientation. Institutional continuities link the future of China's economic order to its past.

Further investigation of these issues is required through the medium of concentrated enquiry within selected local districts. This should benefit both from access to records relevant to a re-construction of the pre-1949 economic system and from the questioning of those influential in establishing the new system as to the origins of their design and normative framework. A local focus is further justified by the emergence of the non-state sector, to which many state enterprises are becoming increasingly tied through sub-contracting and alliances (Su 1994). It is the sector from which much of the 'bottom-up' momentum of the reform has derived and within which new business networks are emerging with local government support. Questions of ownership, financing, trading and regulation need to be investigated as components of a wider regional commercial system, and with regard to its historical antecedents, and this comprehensive perspective can only be accomplished practically on a local basis.

A new form of capitalism?[3]

There is a major debate in economics about the relevance of property rights to economic performance. Economic reform in different socialist countries since the 1970s has intensified this debate, on which the Chinese case should offer an important comment. Arguably the seminal text in the modern debate is North and Thomas (1973). It maintains that the key factor explaining the 'rise of the Western world' was the evolution of 'a set of property rights that provided the incentives necessary for sustained growth'. It attributes economic failure, including that of 'much of Latin America, Asia and Africa in our times', to 'inefficient property rights' (North and Thomas 1973: 157). A large literature has emerged arguing on both theoretical and practical grounds that, with certain exceptions, state ownership of industrial assets is incompatible with efficient operation. This argument has shaped the policy advice received by developing countries, often as a condition of further aid from the Bretton Woods organizations (Cook and Kirkpatrick 1988). Most recently, it has informed the advice given to the reforming communist countries: 'The hallmark of market capitalism is that private capital has wide autonomy to enter or leave industries by creating or closing enterprises and it has substantial control over the management of the enterprises it owns' (EBRD 1993: 113).

China's rapid growth, and indeed that of a wide spectrum of East Asian countries, calls these broad judgments into question. The highly complex forms of property rights in China have prompted the realization that 'property rights' do not constitute a simple binary set of possibilities – state versus private. Instead, they may incorporate a bundle of rights, relating to such diverse matters as the appointment of managers, determination of output mix, terms of employment and allocation of profits. They also tolerate a great variety of institutional structures, which in different activities in different cultures and at different stages in their evolution may be more or less capable of generating economic growth.

While the Chinese have explained the post-1978 economic reforms as a move from a bureaucratic to a market-led system of industrial governance, they have been at pains not to present this as a move towards capitalism and private property rights. Chinese economists and political theorists have repeatedly claimed that a market economy does not equate with a capitalist one, just as a planned economy does not necessarily amount to a socialist one (Jiang 1993; Gong 1992; Wang 1993). Markets and hierarchies, in this perspective, are just tools – mechanisms for co-ordinating transactions – that with suitable adjustments can be placed equally effectively at the service of a socialist or a capitalist order.

Whether these claims are true or not, their disassociation of marketization from private ownership reflects a distinctive feature of China's economic development which merits close attention. Before 1949, industrial property rights in China were granted more or less under licence from the state with the continued approval of local officials being required (Jiang 1992). Similarly, the property rights enjoyed by state owned enterprises are today negotiated with higher authorities under the contract responsibility system (CRS) (Chen 1993). In the rapidly growing non-state sector, the ownership of collectives has not been clearly defined and local government retains an important supportive and supervisory role in their operation (Nee 1992).

State enterprises in China are officially owned by 'the whole people', government being the *de facto* representative of their owners. However, the intention of the economic reformers has been to separate public administration from business management by decentralizing powers of enterprise decision making to the latter through the CRS (Byrd 1991). As Chen (1993) has shown, the property rights enjoyed by the managers of state enterprises under the CRS are established through negotiation with administering authorities rather than on the basis of codification, with the result that the rights of their official owners are becoming increasingly attenuated. The lively current discussion on the possibility of introducing stock-holding systems to state enterprises points to a further impending re-definition of their ownership. The nature of such re-definition is uncertain since it will depend on the determination of which groups are entitled to own stock and the percentage of enterprise assets allocated to stockholders. It is therefore quite difficult at this moment to comment on whether the state sector will be privatized and whether, in this respect, there will be a move towards a capitalist regime. If there is, it is quite likely that the institutional basis on which ownership rights are defined will not accord to the highly formal and legalized Western pattern.

Whereas the reform of state enterprises has been top-down in nature, the township–village enterprises (TVEs) have emerged and proliferated from the bottom up. The consequence is that their ownership status is very ill-defined. Weitzman and Xu (1993) argue that TVEs do not have any owners in the spirit of Western property rights theory. Nominally, TVEs are collectively owned enterprises, with all the community members being owners. These 'collective owners' do not, however, have shares in a formal sense and are only permitted to participate in the TVE on the basis of their residency, a right that is mandated by the community government. The community government is the *de facto* executive owner of the TVEs and would appear normally to exercise ultimate control over them. The TVE therefore is not a private capitalist firm in disguise, and there are indeed legal restrictions to prevent it from converting into one. So, while TVEs are highly successful non-state enterprises, with a growth rate of total factor productivity about ten times that of state enterprises, and accounting by 1991 for about 38 per cent of China's industrial output, they do not represent a shift towards capitalism of the Western variety. In other words TVEs – and indeed other Chinese enterprises – may today behave like capitalist firms, but this does not necessarily mean that they are capitalistic in their constitution.

This failure to match the Western model generates ambiguity in the minds of some Western writers. Bolton (1993), for example, questions whether 'TVEs can be seen as a stable institutional arrangement which could form a long term alternative to private ownership of firms' (p. 12). An alternative reaction would be to suggest that if TVEs have emerged from, and retain their roots within, a traditional system of community co-operation and transacting based on collective property rights, then they are founded on a sound institutional bedrock. Further investigation into this question will require close attention to the property rights and trans-actional arrangements pertaining to TVEs and other collectives in particular communities. It is not clear, for instance, how much variance there is in such arrangements between different local areas. Overall, it seems appropriate to break away from the legally-based Western notion of property rights which emanates from ownership and instead to adopt a concept more appropriate to China which allows for the possibility that such rights may be granted upon administrative sufferance and that their terms can be subject to a continuing process of re-negotiation. In that case, the significant research question is not so much who owns Chinese business assets as who controls and regulates them and through what social process.

Another feature of growing importance in the Chinese economy, in which government agencies are often active partners, is the development of various forms of hybrid firm (Su 1994 and cf. Borys and Jemison 1989). These organize business activities across ownership forms and systems and include Sino–foreign joint ventures, Sino–Sino joint ventures and part-nerships between state, collective and private ownership forms. Su concludes from his research in Xiamen that hybrid firms have provided an extremely important dynamic for economic growth and development at the micro level. They also contribute importantly to the formation of business networks which inter alia stimulate innovation through information exchange and innovation.

Overall, the combination in China of decentralization from central authorities with the bottom-up dynamic provided by township and village enterprises generates the need for a new perspective on the role that government can play in facilitating business networks at the local level. As Tu Wei-ming notes in his introduction to the spring 1993 issue of *Daedalus* on 'China in Transformation':

> The immediate cause of economic dynamism may be due to individual and collective entrepreneurial initiatives. The peculiar economic strength lies in the intricate relationship between state and economy, involving the continuous negotiation and collusion of central, provincial and local governments. The interdependence of economy and polity is such that the state plays a vitally important role at all levels in removing 'structural impediments' to development and building necessary infrastructures for manufacturing industry, commerce, and trade. The mixed pattern is certainly not a socialist planned economy, nor is it a Western capitalist system. The so-called township village enterprise is a new animal, a species in economic development that has yet to be properly defined.
>
> (Tu 1993: XI)

The role of government

Frequent reference has already been made to the part that government plays in the emerging non-state Chinese economic system. Rather than reiterate, we simply advance what may be a key analytical distinction for further research. This lies in the contrast between the concept of a 'nation state' and that of 'the nation and the state', even 'the nation or the state'. The former assumes that there is a positive valence between government and society, with the state being the codification of the nation through the constitutional and legal system. This approximates to the Western model. The latter concept envisages a sharp distinction between government and nation, where the state may be oppressive and fail to secure popular legitimacy. It may be conjectured that in the former Soviet Union and in China by 1976, the situation was one of 'the state or the nation', and that this contributed importantly to the failure of the planning system.

Should this have been the case, it would have applied in China much more to the central government than to local authorities, and this returns us to a focus on the local community. The question arises at this level as to whether or not local government enjoys the legitimacy to run local networks. If it does, is the system similar to Gellner's (1981) notion of 'segmented society' where there is a collection of local systems in competition with each other but co-ordinated by government at the next level up? (At this higher meso level the co-ordinated group may find itself in competition with other meso level groups, with government at the next level up resolving the competition.) The notion of a segmented society posits a clear functional role for government with a networked economic system, and the parallel with Skinner's concept of hierarchically ordered markets in pre-communist times is also evident (Skinner 1964). We might label the resulting arrangement 'network capitalism'. It can be viewed not as a complete decentralization towards a market order in the codified region of Figure 2.2, but as a more limited decentralization towards clan-like forms of exchange in the uncodified region of the space – a region where networks thrive.

CONCLUSION: THEORETICAL AND PRACTICAL SIGNIFICANCE

It has already been argued that even a superficial examination of the emerging Chinese economic system calls for a re-appraisal of conventional Western economic analysis of the development process. That analysis has largely confined itself to the coded reaches of the framework presented earlier. Our expectation is that we can derive a conceptual language from much of Western economic and social analysis that is useful for elucidating the Chinese case, but that Western assumptions about the relationships between the variables identified by the concepts – in this case modernization and economic organization – will not apply. In other words, the nature of the Chinese system, in particular its underlying logic and its gestalt, will be different.

The reverse may also prove to be the case. Analysis of the Chinese economic order draws attention, among other things, to the processes that arise from the operation of personal relationships. The Chinese have their own concepts pertinent to such processes, such as *'guanxi'*, which are themselves being refined in China through an exploration of their range of meanings. It is quite evident that, to a degree at least, personal relationships play a role in the organization and governance of Western economic transactions. This role may well vary between countries, between small local firms and large ones, and so forth, but despite the assumptions of conventional economic theory, it is there. This suggests analysis of the Chinese case may in turn be able to contribute to our conceptual language for the understanding of economic and organizational phenomena, even though the role of, and the relationships between, the variables identified by the concepts may not apply as they do in China.

Several practical insights would arise from further successful investigation of the issues addressed in this chapter. Light should be thrown on entry points into Chinese economic networks, and this would have direct implications for European companies' market entry and marketing policies in respect of China. The possibility arises here of comparing foreign companies which have achieved contrasting levels of success in their China market policies. One might, for example, expect to find differences between overseas Chinese and Western companies. Westerners may well believe that their best policy is to enact their Chinese business environment via formal dealings with the state, whereas the Chinese investor may well enact his environment via the invisible, weak network. Research on local economic systems would also hope to throw light on the question of where the key decision makers are located within what appear to be quite fluid and dynamic systems. This is of obvious potential importance to foreign firms seeking to secure a commitment to actions that are positive for their business operations.

Rather more far-reaching in nature, but nonetheless consequential, is the distinct possibility that from a close study of successful Chinese economic organization, some guidelines might emerge for foreign policy makers seeking to inject greater dynamism into their mature economies via the encouragement of regional networks. This is not to ignore the point which has been stressed throughout the discussion, namely that Chinese practices are likely to be strongly embedded in particular inherited traditions, but it is to assert that a degree of cross-cultural learning can take place. This is, after all, how the Chinese aspire to acquire knowledge from the West and, through its adaptation, to endow such knowledge with Chinese characteristics. The conceptual cross-fertilization suggested earlier would assist this mutual learning.

ACKNOWLEDGEMENTS

The authors wish to thank the British Council, the Economic and Social Research Council (ESRC) and the European Commission for their financial support of research work which has informed this chapter

NOTES

1 In many industrialized countries today, the quality of economic organization at both macro and micro levels identifies the larger part of growth (cf. Porter 1990).
2 Chinese banks have hitherto remained government agencies which offer loans as much on the basis of political as economic criteria, so favouring state and larger collectively-owned firms. Similar considerations tend to govern the allocation of materials in short supply. The situation will probably change as, for example, foreign banks are permitted to play a more active role in the Chinese economy.
3 This section has been informed by comments from our colleague Peter Nolan.

REFERENCES

Boisot, M. H. (1986) 'Markets and hierarchies in a cultural perspective', *Organisation Studies* 7: 135–158.

Boisot, M. H. and Child, J. (1988) 'The iron law of fiefs: bureaucratic failure and the problem of governance in the Chinese economic reforms', *Administrative Science Quarterly* 33: 507–527.

Bolton, P. (1993) 'Privatisation in the presence of ownership and control,' paper given to the Chinese Economic Association (UK), Fifth Annual Conference, December, London.

Bond, M. H. and Hwang K.-K. (1986) 'The social psychology of Chinese people', in M. H. Bond (ed.) *The Psychology of the Chinese People*, Hong Kong: Oxford University Press, Chapter 6.

Borys, B. and Jemison, D. (1989) 'Hybrid arrangements as strategic alliances', *Academy of Management Review* 14.

Byrd, W. A. (1991) 'Contractual responsibility systems in Chinese state-owned industry: a preliminary assessment', in N. Campbell, S. R. F. Plasschaert and D. H. Brown (eds) *The Changing Nature of Management in China*, Advances in Chinese Industrial Studies 2, Greenwich, Conn.: JAI Press.

Chen Derong (1993) 'The contract management responsibility system in China: an institutional interpretation', unpublished PhD thesis, Birmingham. Aston University.

Child J. (1994) *Management in China During the Age of Reform*, Cambridge: Cambridge University Press.

Child, J. and Lu, Y. (1990) 'Industrial decision making under China's reform 1985–8', *Organisation Studies* 11: 321–351.

Cohen, M. L. (1993) 'Cultural and political inventions in modern China: the case of the Chinese "peasant" ', *Daedalus* 122: 151–170.

Cook, P. and Kirkpatrick, C. (eds) (1988) *Privatisation in Less Developed Countries*, New York: Harvester.

Durkheim, W. (1933) *The Division of Labour in Society*, New York: Free Press.

Economist, The (1993a), 'Economic giants' 10 July: 89.

Economist, The (1993b) 'Developing countries' growth' 18 September: 143.

Economist, The (1993c) 'Can the centre hold?' 6 November: 90.

European Bank for Reconstruction and Development (EBRD) (1993) *Annual Economic Outlook*, London: EBRD.

Fischer, S. (1993) 'Socialist economy reform: lessons of the first three years', *American Economic Association*, Papers and Proceedings, May.

Gellner, E. (1981) *Muslim Society*, Cambridge: Cambridge University Press.

Gong Yuzhi (1992) 'Dialogue on the socialist market economy', *Beijing Review* 26 October–1 November: 34–38.

Gouldner, A. W. (1954) *Patterns of Industrial Bureacracy*, Glencoe, Ill.: Free Press.

Granovetter, M. (1985) 'Economic action and social structure: the problem of embeddedness', *American Journal of Sociology* 91: 481–510.

Habermas, J. (1970) *Towards a Rational Society*, London: Heinemann.

Hall, E. T. (1976) *Beyond Culture*, Garden City, NY: Doubleday.

Hussain, A. (1990) *The Chinese Enterprise Reforms*, Development Economics Research Programme, London: London School of Economics CP 5, June.

Hussain, A. (1992) *The Chinese Economic Reforms in Retrospect and Prospect*, Development Economics Research Programme, London: London School of Economics CP 24, August.

Jiang Xiaoming (1992) 'The evolution of property rights in China: a long-run analysis with special reference to the Hefeng textile mill', unpublished PhD thesis, Cambridge: University of Cambridge.

Jiang Chunze (1993) 'China embarks on the road to a socialist market economy', *China Scholars Abroad* 1: 7–8.

Lu, Y. and Child, J. (1994) 'Decentralization of decision making in China's state enterprises', paper given to the Conference on 'Management Issues for China in the 1990s', Cambridge, March.

Mann, S. (1987) *Local Merchants and the Chinese Bureaucracy 1750–1950*, Stanford, Cal.: Stanford University Press.

Nee, V. (1992) 'Organisational dynamics of market transition: hybrid forms, property rights, and mixed economy in China', *Administrative Science Quarterly* 37: 1–27.

North, D. C. and Thomas, R. P. (1973) *The Rise of the Western World*, Cambridge: Cambridge University Press.

Porter, M. E. (1990) *The Competitive Advantages of Nations*, New York: Free Press.

Powell, W. W. and DiMaggio, P. J. (1991) *The New Institutionalism in Organisational Analysis*, Chicago: University of Chicago Press.

Qian Yingyi and Xu Chenggang (1993) *Why China's Economic Reforms Differ*, Development Economics Research Programme, London: London School of Economics CP 25, July.

Rawski, T. G. and Li, L. M. (eds) (1992) *Chinese History in Economic Perspective*, Berkeley, Cal.: University of California Press.

Richardson, G. B. (1972) 'The organisation of industry', *Economic Journal* 82: 883–896.

Skinner, C. W. (1964) (1965) 'Marketing and social structure in rural China, Parts I, II and III', *Journal of Asian Studies* 14: 3–43, 195–228, 363–399.

Solinger, D. J. (1989) 'Urban reform and relational contracting in Post-Mao China. An interpretation of the transition from plan to market', *Studies in Comparative Communism* 23: 171–185.

Su Sijin (1994) 'The dynamics of market-oriented growth of Chinese firms in post-Maoist China: an institutional approach', unpublished PhD thesis, Cornell University.

Sui, H. F. (1989) *Agents and Victims in South China*, New Haven, Conn.: Yale University Press.

Tonnies, F. (1955) *Community and Society, Gemeinschaft und Gesellschaft*, London: Routledge.

Tu Wei-ming (1993). Introduction: special issue on 'China in transformation', *Daedalus* 122: VII–XXIII.

Walder, A. G. (1989) 'Factory and manager in an era of reform', *The China Quarterly* 118: 242–264.

Wang Shiyuan (1993) 'Basic framework and advanced pattern of the economic systems of the socialist market economy', *China's Economic Structure Reform* 1: 16–18.

Weber, M. (1964) *The Theory of Social and Economic Organisation* (trans. A. M. Henderson and T. Parsons), New York: Free Press.

Weitzman, M. L. and Xu Chenggang (1993) *Chinese Township Village Enterprises as Vaguely Defined Co-operatives*, Development Economics Research Programme, London: London School of Economics CP 26, September.

Whitley, R. D. (1991) 'The social construction of business systems in East Asia', *Organisation Studies* 12: 1–28.

—— (1992) *Business Systems in East Asia: Firms, Markets and Societies*, London: Sage.

—— (1994) 'Dominant forms of economic organization in market economies', *Organisation Studies* 15: 153–182.

Williamson, O. E. (1975) *Markets and Hierarchies*, New York: Free Press.

—— (1985) *The Economic Institutions of Capitalism: Firms, Markets, Relational Contracting*, New York: Free Press.
Wong, R. B. and Perdue, P. C. (1992) 'Grain markets and food supplies in eighteenth-century Hunan', in T. G. Rawski and L. M. Li (eds) *Chinese History in Economic Perspective*, Berkeley, Cal.: University of California Press, Chapter 4.
World Bank (1985) *China: Long-Term Issues and Options*, Baltimore, Md: Johns Hopkins University Press.

Part II
Decision making

Part II

Decision making

3 Decentralization of decision making in China's state enterprises

Yuan Lu and John Child

ABSTRACT

A central objective of China's reform of state enterprises, begun cautiously in the early 1980s, has been to decentralize decision making from the planning authorities to enterprise management. This chapter presents the result of a study of decision levels for six state enterprises in Beijing during 1985, 1988 and 1993. Results show that

1 the enterprises now enjoy autonomy of decision making for most issues and bureaux are kept separate from enterprise operations;
2 a new governance structure has emerged within large industrial firms, where strategic decisions are now taken by the headquarters or the board, which has replaced the bureau as the managerial authority;
3 within enterprise management the trend is to delegate less, as the directors and senior executives exert more control over activities.

The progress of the decentralization programme has been accomplished by separating the government from management, and a hybrid economy has appeared in which the state more frequently applies regulatory measures and exerts its control over infrastructure to administer both the enterprises and economic relations governing transactions. As the enterprises are now more exposed to market transactions, decision making has become concentrated at the director and executive levels. These findings highlight the growth of strategic business decision making and the development of a professional management class in China.

INTRODUCTION

The aim of China's economic reform has been to shift the governance of economic relations from the state bureaucracy to the market. A central objective was to widen decision making to include enterprise management and to establish a professional managerial elite as key players in this decision making. In 1984, the State Council published a policy document 'On the Further Expansion of Autonomy in Large and Medium-sized State

Enterprises', granting enterprise management decision making powers in areas of production planning, sales, purchasing, labour and personal management, organizational change, financial investment and the formation of an alliance with other firms. Since then, the so-called decentralization programme has been adopted as the essential strategy for reforming state enterprises through delegating decision making from industrial ministries and bureaux to enterprise management. At the same time, two institutional changes were introduced.

The first involved the creation of markets through, inter alia, the reduction of state mandatory plans and the abolition of price controls. From 1978–1993, the proportion of overall industrial outputs subject to state planning was reduced from more than 90 per cent to 6.3 per cent (*People's Daily*, 9 December 1993: 1). The percentage of industrial products subject to state price control was reduced from 100 per cent in 1978 to 18.7 per cent in 1993 (Ma Hong and Sun Shangqing 1994: 127). Factor markets, such as labour, technology, estate property and capital, were gradually created (*China's Reform and Development Report* 1993; Ma Hong and Sun Shangqing 1994). Following the transition from a centrally planned economy to a market one, the management objectives of state enterprises changed from the fulfilment of production plans set by the state to profitability. This required the separation of government from the management of state enterprises. In order to transform state enterprises into independent business units, various economic measures were introduced. During the early 1980s, the profit retention system (PRS) was widely adopted for the purpose of motivating enterprises to pursue a profit target. From 1986 onwards, the contract responsibility system (CRS) was introduced nation-wide. Enterprises that were part of the CRS had full responsibility for attaining agreed profit targets and formulating appropriate business plans without government intervention.

The second change was to delegate within enterprise management specific decisions to a trained body of managers. The power of decision making shifted from the party secretary to the director, who became the dominant administrator exerting control over enterprise activities. From 1984–1986, the director responsibility system (DRS) was introduced in most state enterprises, giving the director full responsibility for operations and staffing without requiring permission from its communist party committee. In August 1988, the Enterprise Law took effect, which designated the director as the legal representative of a state enterprise, while the party and trade union were now to assist the director.

The essential premise of decentralization as a means of improving organization performance was based on the assumption that managers would make better decisions than the authority at the top, because they had more information about markets and a better understanding of business. But China's decentralization programme, as a national reform policy, had a mixed result. The contribution of state enterprises to total industrial output value declined from almost 78 per cent in 1978, when the economic reforms were launched, to about 52 per cent in 1993 (*China Industrial Statistical Yearbook* 1993; Ma Hong and Sun Shangqing 1994). Over the last 15 years, the growth rate of state enterprises only reached an average of 8 per cent a year, behind those of township and private enterprises, which achieved about 35 and 60 per cent respectively (Ma Hong and Sun Shangqing 1994). In 1991 it was reported that of those enterprises adopting the CRS, only 30 per cent were able to fulfil their contracts, whilst the majority of the enterprises failed to meet their contract targets (Wu Zhenkun 1993: 131). By the end of 1992, about 45 per cent of state enterprises ran into loss (Liu Zishen and Sun Yong 1993). In fact, the situation could be worse than that presented by official statistics. It was estimated that in 1990 about 70–80 per cent of state enterprises had a hidden loss, i.e. the loss, such as bad debts and considerable waste of materials and human resources, was not presented in the official records (*China's Reform and Development Report* 1993). The inefficiency and poor performance of state enterprises have become serious problems.

The main difficulties of the decentralization programme were embedded in the high degree of market imperfection, together with constraints set by remaining planning institutions. As Child and Lu (1990) noted, industrial decision making is located within a network of interlocking relationships comprising industrial bureaux as planning administrative authorities, regulatory bureaux as functional authorities and local government holding statutory authority as the representative of the state, in addition to central ministries and government issuing instructions, policies and regulations. This complex of institutional settings, as Granick (1990) noted, leads to the phenomenon of multilevel supervision over state enterprises. Regarding property rights, Granick argued that local authorities, i.e. all regional government, intervened in state enterprises both traditionally and/or through government sponsored investment. Thus, local authorities could load social, political and communal obligations on to enterprises, imposing multi-performance criteria (Walder 1989; Lu 1991; Lu and Heard 1995).

Nee (1992) noted that state enterprises were still dependent on state institutions for resources and transactional arrangements. As a consequence, they did not have the required autonomy to obtain the maximum economic efficiency as do those firms with non-state ownership. This observation was consistent with what Wang and his colleagues found in their comparison of state and non-state enterprises in Shanghai and Shashou. They showed that state enterprises were forced to follow various directives and state guidance, and that they only partially reflected market forces. This was in contrast to township enterprises which operated in response to market forces. Managers of state enterprises complained about their lack of real decision making power concerning transaction activities, such as purchasing and distribution, as well as government constraints on employment issues (Wang *et al.* 1991).

Table 3.1 Profile of the six enterprises in 1985, 1988 and 1992

Product category	Date of foundation	Total employment			Sales turnover (Y million)			Net profit before tax (Y million)			Net profit after tax (Y million)			Official size category*			Quota(Q) or profit(P) target		
		1985	1988	1992	1985	1988	1992	1985	1988	1992	1985	1988	1992	1985	1988	1992	1985	1988	1992
A Automotive	1966	3883	5100	6000	205	467	1300	53.0	86.0	150.0	6.6	21.1	28.6	M	L	L	Q	Q	P
B Audio-visual	1973	2200	3000	6800	183	418	1070	13.0	13.0	128.0	3.1	4.1	8.4	M	L	L	Q	Q	P
C Heavy electrical	1956	1869	1798	2700	23	44	86	4.8	8.6	4.8	0.9	1.7	0.2	M	M	L	Q	Q	P
D Pharmaceutical	1973	957	912	910	27	43	67	4.0	8.6	4.7	0.8	3.0	0.1	S	M	M	P	P	P
E Audio	1955	848	890	900	25	24	60	4.7	0.9	2.5	1.7	0.3	0.6	S	M	M	P	P	P
F Electrical switchgear	1955	718	695	630	6	8	16	1.5	2.1	1.3	0.2	0.4	0.2	S	M	M	P	P	P

Sources: Data for 1984, 1985, and 1988, Child and Lu (1990: 330); data for 1992: interviews and documents in the enterprises, August 1993

Notes: * L = large, M = medium, S = small. Chinese state owned enterprises are designated as large, medium or small depending on their output level, asset value and number employed

THE REFORMS IN BEIJING

Beijing was one of the first locations to pioneer the reform of state enterprises. As early as in 1979, three large firms in Beijing were selected by the State Economic Commission to test a profit-sharing scheme. In 1985 the PRS, in which an enterprise was assigned a profit target by the industrial bureau, was introduced to most state enterprises in Beijing. In 1986, the DRS, through which the decision making power was transferred from the party secretary to the director, was adopted by all state enterprises in Beijing. During 1987 and 1988, the municipal government decided to implement the CRS in more than 300 large and medium sized firms. Enterprises participating in the CRS were obliged to guarantee, during a contractual period of three or four years, the growth of asset value and the annual profit target, while the municipal government permitted them to increase their employee salaries and bonuses according to the rate of profit growth. Through the CRS, the government transferred its control over the enterprise management process, for instance drawing up a production plan and allocating raw materials, to control the enterprise's outcome, i.e. profitability. The director was the legitimate decision making authority, while the party and trade union supported the director.

In 1992, following the State Council's call for the transfer of business systems in state enterprises to a market economy, the Beijing Municipal government issued a policy delegating further decision making authority to managers. This covered a wide range of business activities, including sales, pricing, investment, rewards and incentives, labour and personnel management and organization design and change. These were intended to advance the decentralization programme. As a result, according to a survey of 898 state enterprises in six municipalities and regions, Beijing came second in the adoption of the decentralization process following Guangdong province. Managers in Beijing were satisfied with the autonomy they had gained – mostly in sales, rewards and production planning – but foreign trading was still highly centralized (Wu Zhenkun 1993: 160).

The six state enterprises in Beijing in which this research took place are those described by Child (1987, 1994), Child and Lu (1990, 1995), and Lu (1991). Table 3.1 identifies, for each year studied, the industrial sector, size, financial profile and official category of the six enterprises and whether or not they produced primarily to a quota or a profit target.

Between 1985 and 1993, three enterprises, automotive, audio-visual and heavy electrical, had expanded considerably in sales and employment, and their status had changed from medium to large categories. Automotive in mid-1988 changed its ownership and entered into a joint venture with a Hong Kong company. As a consequence, its governance structure shifted from administration by an industrial bureau to a board of directors, and the firm enjoyed prestige through foreign trade and favourable government policies. However, it was reported that this ownership change did not seem to affect its management in practice. This was partly because the Hong Kong partner was actually an overseas subsidiary of a Chinese investment corporation. Therefore, it did not bring foreign ownership into the joint venture, though it claimed to be 'international' and benefited from policies for foreign-invested firms. Furthermore, the Hong Kong company had no expatriate staff in the joint venture. Finally, despite its complete autonomy in sales and price setting, it still relied on the state distribution system controlled by the ministry and bureaux. Consequently, the management in automotive shared some of the characteristics of a state enterprise.

The other two large enterprises, audio-visual and heavy electrical started taking over other small factories after 1989 and became an industrial group. The group headquarters was established as the top layer of management. Three other enterprises, pharmaceutical, audio and electrical switchgear, remained in the medium sized category after 1988 with a similar level of employment, but maintained an increase in sales. The five state enterprises, apart from automotive as a joint venture, were in three industrial sectors, each headed by a municipal industrial bureau: audio-visual and audio were electronic industrial; heavy electrical and electrical switchgear were machine building industrial; and pharmaceutical was medical.

As in 1985 and 1988, data were gathered in 1993 about the extent of decentralization within the enterprises and about how 48 decisions had been delegated. These decisions related to the main areas of activity normally found in an enterprise, namely marketing, production and contingent functions, purchasing, finance and investment, organization, R&D, employment and personnel. Since by 1993 there were only a few products still subject to state planning quotas, the decision on the pricing of products in the plan will not be used for comparative purposes. This reduces the total to 47 decisions, a full list of which is given in the Appendix.

The method of assessment used is derived from the 'Aston Programme' of organizational studies. It particularly focuses on the extent to which decision making powers are passed down through a set of hierarchical levels, both within the enterprise and between the enterprise and a higher authority and/or a governing board on which enterprise managers do not constitute a majority. Questioning was directed to establishing the lowest hierarchical role in which the incumbent could authorize action to be taken without this requiring further ratification.

The research findings comparing decision levels in 1985 and 1988 have already been published (Child and Lu 1990). In 1993, the two authors jointly visited the six enterprises again. The replication was undertaken in a similar way to the investigations in 1985 and 1988. Interviews with directors (in some cases) and relevant managers were also conducted.

Questions about the 47 decisions, changes in organizational structure and development and the relationship between the party and management were asked. Where appropriate, access to documents and statistics was requested.

CHANGES IN ENTERPRISE AUTONOMY AND DECISION MAKING WITHIN MANAGEMENT

The emergence of new industrial governance and the progress of the decentralization programme

Table 3.2 shows decisions which were not decentralized to enterprise managers. The number of decisions taken above the directors' level was considerably reduced from a total of 45 activities in 1985 to 10 in 1988 and variation between the six enterprises was reduced (Child and Lu 1990). This suggests that the managers in all the enterprises had secured a substantial increase in autonomy. However, the survey in 1993 offers a more complex picture. The degree of autonomy held by the director over decision making varied among the six enterprises. In the three large firms, namely A (automotive), B (audio-visual) and C (heavy electrical), centralization had increased whereas there was a continuous trend towards decentralization in the remaining enterprises. As Table 3.2 shows, the number of decisions taken at the level above the director increased from three in 1988 to eight in 1993 in automotive, from nought to seven in audio-visual and from one to two in heavy electrical. But a difference from the earlier situation was that these decisions were now not taken by governmental bureaux, they were in the hands of a new regime. In automotive, this was a board of directors representing its owners, while in audio-visual and heavy electrical this was the industrial group headquarters. This form of corporate governance structure had not emerged in the three medium sized enterprises.

One explanation for these differences in decision making levels and governance structures stems from organization size and the relationship between the enterprises and government. The expansion of these large enterprises, which had enjoyed strong support from the municipal government under the planning system, proceeded rapidly and gave rise to a new industrial governance structure. Automotive established a joint venture supported by both the central and local governments. The firm benefited from the government policies favourable to foreign firms in areas of foreign trade and labour management. Furthermore, the joint venture was governed by a board of directors, which gave the general manager decision making powers over operational activities. There was no direct administrative relationship between the venture and the bureau.

The other two large firms, audio-visual and heavy electrical, diversified through mergers and acquisitions. Audio-visual acquired its local

Table 3.2 Limits to enterprise decentralization 1985, 1988 and 1993 (decisions for which authority was withheld from some or all enterprises, x = authority withheld 1985, y = authority withheld 1988, and z = authority withheld 1993)

Decisions	A			B			C			D			E			F	
	1985	1988	1993	1985	1988	1993	1985	1988	1993	1985	1988	1993	1985	1988	1993	1988	1993
Marketing																	
Price			z	x		z							x			x	y
New product		y														y	
Type of market served	x																
Market territories																	
Production																	
Production plan		y															
Schedule against plan							z										
Quality standards: inputs																	
Quality standards: outputs	x							y			y					y	
Purchasing procedures:																	
Investment and accounting																	
Level of investment	x		z			z	x		z	x		z	x				
Choice of capital equipment					x												
Scope of costing system	x		z	z	z		z			z			x	z			z
Unbudgeted capital items						z											
Unbudgeted revenue			z														
Personnel																	
Recruiting workers																	
Recruiting supervisor											x			x			
Recruiting managers	x			x							x		x			x	
Selecting methods													x				
Size of total establishment	x		z			z	x					z	x			x	

Table 3.2 Cont.

Decisions	Enterprises																	
	A			*B*			*C*			*D*			*E*			*F*		
	1985	1988	1993	1985	1988	1993	1985	1988	1993	1985	1988	1993	1985	1988	1993	1985	1988	1993
Workers' basic salaries	x				x			x			x						x	
Cadres' basic salaries		z		x			x			x			x					x
Dismissing workers				x			x			x			x					
Dismissing cadres				x			x			x			x					
Design of office systems			y															
Total of above decisions which authorities withheld from the enterprise	7	3	8[a]	7	0	7[b]	7	1	2[c]	5	3	1	12	0	0	6	3	1

Sources: Data for the comparison between 1985 and 1988: adopted from Child and Lu (1990: 333); data for the comparison between 1988 and 1993: interviews in the enterprises, August 1993

Notes: a = board of directors; b and c = industrial group headquarters

Key:

A = automotive D = pharmaceutical
B = audio-visual E = audio
C = heavy electrical F = electrical switchgear

competitor and merged with another two small factories. Its product range now extended beyond consumer electronic goods and included computer support systems, estate and property, services and foreign trading. The firm also invested in shares of other corporations as a way of controlling the distribution and retailing of its products. Heavy electrical took over three small factories after 1988. In 1992, it allowed one factory to enter into a joint venture with a Thai company. The enterprise also ran services and formed an alliance with a local factory in a suburb of Beijing, with help from the municipal government, to supply its main components. What was common to these large firms was that this governance structure, consisting of a board or the headquarters, acted as the managerial authority over its manufacturing sites. Strategic decisions with respect to areas of marketing, investment and personnel, were now taken at the board and headquarters level, as Table 3.2 shows.

The remaining three medium sized enterprises were in a different position. They lacked resources and did not receive significant government support. In 1993, they were still limited to a single manufacturing site and had not engaged in any appreciable growth. As a result, pharmaceutical and audio became more entrepreneurial. Their workshops were re-grouped into smaller manufacturing units, each of which entered into joint ventures with partners from Japan, the US, Korea, Taiwan and Hong Kong. These two enterprises also established a number of small companies which sub-contracted purchasing, packaging and services. Pharmaceutical invested its technology in a local firm outside Beijing, with support from the local government, to establish a bottling factory and sell its products in the regional market. Only electrical switchgear had shrunk in size, because the municipal government took over a piece of land from its site. This cut back the enterprise's production capacity, and the municipal government in return ordered a compensation scheme to reduce the enterprise's contract profit target for three years.

The bureaux' power over management decision making had clearly declined by 1993. One indicator of management autonomy from bureaux is the state-set operational target and the number of decisions approved at bureau level. The 1993 survey shows that none of the enterprises were obliged to follow state plans for their production and sales, as Table 3.1 exhibits. In the case of decision making, the bureaux still controlled four areas in 1988 – product pricing, production plans, the quality standards and the design of office systems. But by 1993, bureau permission was not required for most decisions. The enterprises were now heavily involved in market transactions, so they relied less on the bureau for raw materials, product prices, quality controls and production planning. The only area where the bureaux retained control concerned cost systems, in the cases of pharmaceutical and electrical switchgear. Managers in these two enterprises stated that this was caused by a directive to implement a new cost system in July 1993.

Regarding day-to-day operations, the bureaux had no direct administrative authority. But they still intervened over 'soft budget constraints',
the term used by Kornai (1980, 1986) to describe an enterprise's depen-
dency on the planning authority. The bureau's power was retained in
three areas. First, the bureau assessed the enterprises' performances and
determined their targets, for instance the profit contract. The negotiating
relationship between the bureau and enterprises which Montias (1988)
noted for the planning hierarchy, remained with the CRS. Intensive
bargaining and negotiation took place in 1992 when the enterprises
renewed their profit contracts. Audio-visual was allowed to adopt the
contractual system for large firms with a favourable scheme of lower
interest bank loans and financing autonomy. Heavy electrical and pharmaceutical were assigned policies with low taxation and freedom of foreign
trade. Electrical switchgear benefited from interest-free loans for its technological innovation. Although audio failed to meet its contracted profit
target, the bureau, instead of penalizing the enterprise, decided to lower
the profit threshold in the new contract.

Second, the bureau determined who would be the enterprise director
and party secretary. Although the workers' congress was in principle the
constitutional body holding such authority, in fact in the six enterprises,
none of the directors had been elected by the congress, they were all
appointed by the bureaux. Finally, and most importantly, the bureau had
control over the strategic activities of the enterprises, including acquisitions, the formation of joint ventures, exports and cross-regional investment. Both audio-visual and heavy electrical sought their bureaux' consent
when they intended to merge other factories to develop an industrial
group. In other words, the bureaux normally had the power to halt actions
by the enterprises.

Although the enterprises had more decision making autonomy,
supporting intermediate institutions providing resources and distribution
channels, such as banks, financial institutions and national distributors,
were still under the state monopoly. As a result, a state policy could affect
a large number of firms if they relied on the state-controlled networks.
For instance, during July and August 1993, the state imposed an austerity
policy to control investment funding – a corrective measure frequently
used by the government during the reform (Wu Jinglian 1991). This immediately led to a shortage of capital, as the banks reduced their credit to
enterprises. More seriously for enterprises such as heavy electrical and
electrical switchgear, whose products were sold to industrial customers,
they were unable to collect their money, as buyers had no cash, due to
the banks cutting down money supply under directives from the central
government. Automotive's situation was also difficult. In spite of its
complete transactional autonomy as a joint venture, both its national
distributors and a majority of its customers were controlled by the state.
Faced with a capital shortage, these distributors either cancelled customers'

orders or delayed payment. However, those enterprises producing consumer goods, such as audio-visual, pharmaceutical and audio, appeared to be in a better situation, because their products went directly to the market through many local distributors and private retailers.

In addition to these austerity measures, the government also intervened through other regulatory powers. Part of the reason most enterprises diversified their business and engaged in a wide range of activities, such as services, was because the enterprises were obliged to maintain their level of employees. Although official policies granted directors autonomy over labour management, they were not permitted to lay off redundant workers. The local labour arbitration committee reserved the right to review a dismissal decision and order a firm to take back the worker. Thus, the enterprises had to establish many small units to retain a large number of employees who were no longer required on the production lines.

CHANGES OF DECISION MAKING LEVELS WITHIN ENTERPRISES

In our earlier study, a comparison of results of responses to the 47 decisions between 1985 and 1988 regarding delegation within management showed a mixed result, apart from the growth of enterprise autonomy. During the period from 1985 to 1988, decisions concerned with routine matters tended to have been delegated down to lower levels within enterprises. These included labour and personnel issues, production and work allocation, purchasing and customer priority. But in some more strategic areas, decision making had become more centralized within enterprises. These included new products, finance and investment and design of office systems (Child and Lu 1990: 336). Data collected in the 1993 survey were consistent with the 1988 findings, namely that the overall tendency within management was centralization. Table 3.3 lists the kinds of decision of where change was evident between 1988 and 1993.

Delegation of decision making within management had increased in limited areas. The level at which prices were determined varied among the enterprises. An extreme case was found in heavy electrical, where individual salespersons had the power to determine prices, whereas in audio sales managers set prices. In the other enterprises, pricing was decided by the deputy director or director. Decisions concerning quality standards of inputs and outputs were similar. Directors, including the deputy directors, were now mostly in charge of these. In automotive, heavy electrical, pharmaceutical and electrical switchgear, quality decisions were delegated, but in audio-visual and audio, these quality decisions which had been taken by department managers were now taken at the deputy manager level. Overall, there was an increase in delegating the promotion of work group leaders or supervisors. This decision was now taken

Table 3.3 Main decisions and change in delegation within management, 1985–1993

Delegation	Decision
From 1985 to 1988	
Generally increased	Labour and personnel issues (but not organization)
	Production and work allocation
	Purchasing
	Customer priority
Generally decreased	Introduction of new products
	Finance and investment
	Design of office system
From 1988 to 1993	
Generally increased	Price
	Quality inspection
	The promotion of work group leaders
Generally decreased	Marketing (selection of markets and customers)
	Purchasing
	Finance and investment (unbudgeted expenses, cost systems, etc.)
	Staffing (size of employment and salaries)

Sources: Data for the comparison between 1985 and 1988: adopted from Child and Lu (1990: 336); data for the comparison between 1988 and 1993: interviews in the enterprises, August 1993

by the deputy directors, but previously had been at the director level – except for automotive where it was the province of the department manager.

Apart from the above limited amount of additional delegation, there were rather more decision areas where authority had been rescinded, such as marketing, financing and investment, personnel and labour management. For instance, the decision to set salaries used to be delegated to deputy directors and work group supervisors identified in the earlier studies. But in 1993, it was mostly controlled by the director. In large enterprises, the headquarters or the board, rather than the director, took decisions regarding the size of the employment establishment. Another area where control had become more centralized was unbudgeted expenses. Purchasing decisions in 1993 were retained by the deputy directors, but in 1988 these had in many cases been taken by department managers. Table 3.4 summarizes the distribution of decisions and indicates the pattern of decentralization and delegation in each enterprise.

Six standardized hierarchical levels are distinguished in Table 3.4. Level 5 is above the enterprise and indicates the joint venture board in the case of automotive, the group headquarters in audio-visual and heavy electrical and a municipal bureau for others. Level 4 is that of the enterprise

Table 3.4 Distribution of decisions by hierarchical level (number of decisions from a total of 47 delegated to each of five hierarchical levels in six Beijing enterprises, 1985, 1988 and 1992)

Hierarchical level	A (Automotive)			B (Audio-visual)			C (Heavy electrical)			D (Pharmaceutical)			E (Audio)			F (Switchgear)			Average for all six enterprises		
	1985	1988	1993	1985	1988	1993	1985	1988	1993	1985	1988	1993	1985	1988	1993	1985	1988	1993	1985	1988	1993
5 Above the enterprise directors (bureau, or for audio-visual and heavy-electrical in 1993 the group headquarters, or for automotive in 1988 and 1993 the joint venture board)	7	3	8	8	0	7	7	1	2	5	3	1	12	0	0	6	3	1	7.5	1.7	3.1
4 Enterprise director	15	8	18	7	19	22	4	17	20	20	20	19	12	19	22	15	21	20	12.2	17.3	20.2
3 Head of several departments (e.g. deputy director, chief engineer)	12	13	15	5	4	14	8	16	19	2	4	19	7	6	17	8	4	21	7.0	7.8	17.5
2 Head of department, workshop or single function	10	19	6	25	22	4	23	7	4	15	16	8	13	18	8	17	17	5	17.2	16.5	5.8
1 Work group leader or supervisor	2	2	0	2	2	0	5	4	2	5	2	0	3	3	0	1	2	0	3.0	2.5	0.3
0 Operative or functional specialist	1	2	0	0	0	0	0	2	0	0	2	0	0	1	0	0	0	0	0.2	1.2	0.0

Number of decisions delegated to each level per enterprise

Sources: Data for 1984, 1985, and 1988, Child and Lu (1990: 339); data for 1992: interviews and documents in the enterprises, August 1993

director. Level 3 comprises persons heading several departments, such as deputy directors or chief engineers. Level 2 is the head of a single department be this a production workshop or a specialized functional department. Level 1 is a work group leader or supervisor. Level 0 is an operative or a functional specialist such as a buyer or a salesperson. Table 3.4 shows for each enterprise in 1985, 1988 and 1993, the number of decisions out of a total of 47 which were taken at level 5 or delegated down to other levels, together with the average for all firms taken together. Figure 3.1 charts the average number of decisions taken at each of these levels for all six enterprises.

What emerges from Figure 3.1 is the increase of decision making authority in the three large firms at level 5, where the board or industrial group headquarters are situated. Overall, the bureaux' intervention was significantly decreased across all the enterprises, and only two cases were identified at the bureau level. There is an increase in the average number of decisions taken by enterprise directors from 17.3 to 20.2 in 1988 and 1993 respectively, but this was much less than the rise from 12.2 to 17.3 from 1985 to 1988. There were also dramatic changes for deputy directors or other senior executives on the one hand, and department heads on the other hand. Many more decisions were taken at level 3 by 1993 than in 1985 and 1988. Conversely, department heads had lost their decision making powers. Finally, group leaders and individual staff, such as operators, had almost zero responsibility by 1993 for any of the decisions sampled.

A trend of centralizing decision making at the top levels was noted by Mintzberg (1979: 281–282), who argued that a hostile environment leads to more centralized control, as the speed and co-ordination of a centralized response is now required in order to survive. Compared to 1985 and 1988, 1993 was a more turbulent period in Chinese industry. The relaxation of the state planning and the imperfect market system had caused a degree of chaos and many state enterprises were facing a severe shortage of working capital.

From 1986 onwards, an increase of production costs, caused by the inflationary prices of raw materials, threatened the performance of industrial firms. A report drawn by the Municipal Planning Commission pointed out that the realized profit in its 14 industrial bureaux was reduced from 2.7 billion Yuan in 1985 to 1.1 billion Yuan in 1989 (Municipal Planning Commission 1991: 74). From 1985–1989 the costs of raw materials and energy rose by 87 per cent, employee salaries by 135 per cent, and administrative costs by 151 per cent (Municipal Planning Commission, 1991: 76). The decline of profitability was also evident in the six enterprises. In spite of their rapid growth of sales over the period 1988–1992, most enterprises were faced with a decrease of profit margin, except for audio-visual and audio, as indicated in Table 3.5. This was in sharp contrast to 1988 when the data in this research identified an increase of retained profit due to the expansion of enterprise autonomy.

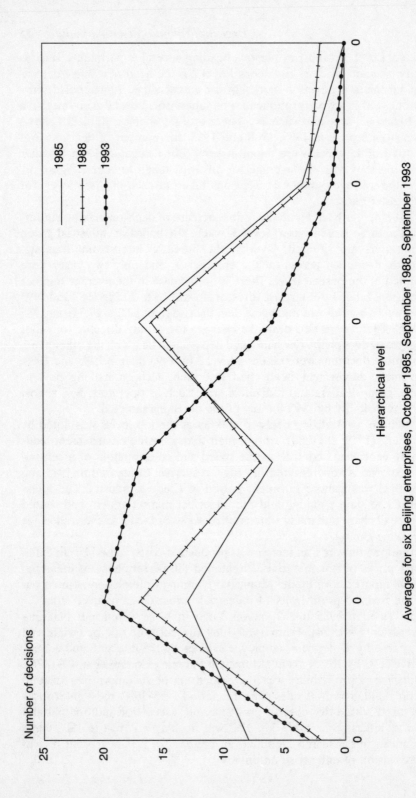

Figure 3.1 Distribution of 47 decisions by hierarchical level

Averages for six Beijing enterprises, October 1985, September 1988, September 1993

Table 3.5 Profit margins and percentage of retained profit in the six enterprises in 1985, 1988 and 1992

Enterprise	Profit margin (%) (net profit before tax/sales turnover × 100%)			Percentage of profit retained (%) (net profit after tax/ net profit before tax × 100%)		
	1985	1988	1992	1985	1988	1992
A Automotive	25.9	18.4	11.5	12.3	24.5	19.1
B Audio-visual	7.1	3.1	12.0	24.4	31.6	6.5
C Heavy electrical	20.5	19.5	5.6	19.4	19.8	3.1
D Pharmaceutical	14.8	19.9	7.0	20.9	35.4	2.8
E Audio	18.9	3.8	4.2	37.0	32.7	24.0
F Electrical switchgear	24.6	25.3	8.1	13.3	19.9	11.5

Sources: Data for 1985 and 1988: Child and Lu (1990: 330); data for 1992: interviews and documents in the enterprises, August 1993

From Table 3.5 it can be seen that between 1988–1992, profit margins declined in the enterprises, except for audio-visual and audio. The percentage of profit retained by the enterprises also declined for each of them in 1992 compared to that in 1988. Both external pressures from the problematic environment and the decline of economic efficiency pushed senior managers to take over most decisions. For instance, purchasing decisions were now taken in many cases by directors or deputy directors. This was the result of the government austerity scheme in July and August 1993 which caused uncertainty regarding external resources and shortage of capital. Therefore, directors and executives had to exert strict control over expenditures, especially in purchasing.

Another cause of the hostile environment was the question of tight internal discipline. As Tisdell (1993) noted, Chinese economic development requires an effective internal disciplinary context, in which managers can exert control over activities, as well as the advanced external market institution. It was evident that with organizational development, particularly in the case of large firms, the necessity for an appropriate management control mechanism was needed. In heavy electrical, sales people determined prices, and such decisions were made at the lowest level of the six enterprises. In an interview, the deputy director stated that this power was going to be given to the director, because delegation had resulted in a sharp profit decline. The audio-visual group experienced a loss of control over its subsidiaries in 1991, when decision making was delegated to supervisors and service companies. Therefore, from 1992, the group headquarters decided to resume control. An internal banking centre was established to impose cost control measures.

DISCUSSION AND SUMMARY

The comparison of decision levels in the years 1985, 1988 and 1993 supports the previous conclusion that granting enterprises autonomy manifested the progress of the Chinese economic reform. The surveys revealed that in 1985 and 1988 the six enterprises were still dependent in some degree upon the bureaux for resource mobilization and approval of important issues. In 1993, this reliance on bureaucratic co-ordination for supplies of raw materials had largely gone. However, state control over the enterprises remained in place and two institutional mechanisms were deployed as substitutes.

The first are the so-called 'soft budgetary constraints' (Kornai 1980, 1986), which were attached to the vertical relations between the state and the enterprises. Strategic issues required approval by the bureaux and the latter had power to determine personnel issues, such as the appointment of the directors, and also to assess enterprise performance. Such constraints were a result of the vertical hierarchy created by the ownership structure, in which the bureaux behaved as the principal representing state ownership. As Eggertsson (1990) argued, managers were assumed to have some delegated 'rights' in their operation, but they should represent the owner's interest in return for payment of some kind. Thus, the decentralization programme was undermined by the ownership control imposed by the state, which limited managerial decision making when the bureau acted as a shadow governor. As Nee (1992) also noted, state enterprises in China, due to their state ownership, were constrained by non-market factors, such as labour regulations. Consequently, these institutional constraints eventually caused problems in enterprise decision making. Child (1994: 101) showed that even though the relationship between state enterprises and the bureaux had changed from direct administrative intervention to one based on contract, the elements of the system, in which the enterprises were dependent on the bureaux, remained.

The second institutional mechanism is an emerging mixed form of state control and imperfect market that creates a hybrid economy (Nee 1992; Boisot and Child 1994). This hybrid economy, in various forms, such as long-term contracting, reciprocal trading, regulations and franchising, relates to the hierarchies and markets that are two polar co-ordinating mechanisms in economic relations. It displays intermediate values of weak administrative measures and the limited adaptation of firms to the environment (Williamson 1993). In the case of China, a hybrid was created when the state monopolized the infrastructure, such as resource mobilization, channels of financing and a national distribution network. In such circumstances, the state could exert an influence through its austerity schemes set by policies and regulations, and could also impose direct measures on the infrastructure which eventually affected enterprises. Here attention is drawn not only to the matter of ownership, but also to the market structure and a firm's specificity in economic relations. Mun Kin-Chok (1985) categorized the market structure in China into four groups, namely a directly planned market, an indirectly planned market, an enterprise direct sales market and a free market. According to Mun, state enterprises were not in the free market, but mainly in the first three hybrid forms of the state plan and market, whilst the non-state owned firms had access to any of the four.

The findings of the study of the six enterprises appears to support Mun's argument and suggest that, in addition to the ownership structure, a firm's product or market specificity should be considered, because it determines the location of the product in the infrastructure through which the firm establishes a relationship with others, such as customers and suppliers. Whenever this infrastructure was under state control, for instance resource supply and output distribution, the context showed a hybrid feature and the firm was closely linked to state control. For instance, although automotive had its joint venture status with complete autonomy in its business dealings, it was still constrained by state monopolized distribution. In contrast, the three enterprises with consumer goods – audio-visual, audio and pharmaceutical – displayed a weak hybrid character, being closer to the free market.

In such an environment, the enterprises responded strategically by developing their organizations through merging with other small factories, investing in suppliers and retailers, as well as sub-contracting services to their own companies (cf. Oliver 1991). These interfirm collaborations were largely used to stabilize transaction relations (Borys and Jemison 1989), and such alliances have become quite common, as Boisot and Child (1994) indicated, to provide both horizontal and vertical integration for the assurance of supply and sales. They argue that China's economy, through the decentralization programme and economic reform, is a hybrid quasi-market. The unique characteristic of this quasi-market is the rise of business networks in which government agencies play an active role.

Decentralization in China has transferred management decision making from the bureaucratic approach to a more market-oriented one. This has exposed managers to the need to co-ordinate horizontally with customers and suppliers, since they can no longer rely on this being done by the bureaux. Therefore, their level of professional competence and knowledge is important. With the progress of enterprise autonomy, managerial decision making began to shift from a synoptic approach, in which the process was top-down and normative, to the strategic approach, as Lee (1987) noted. Such a strategic decision process is driven by market preferences and competitive advantage (cf. Andrew 1980). As described in the previous section, the enterprises applied various business development strategies, contingent on the internal and external contextual variables such as size, product-technology specification and the market situation. In large firms an industrial governance structure was established based on a corporate group headquarters or the board system, and this governance structure is in some degree similar to that in a joint stock company. In such a company, managerial authority was held at a level above the manufacturing units. The rapid growth of both organization structure and business scope required the establishment of an effective internal discipline mechanism. This, in turn, produced a return to centralization, with decision making becoming more concentrated at the director and deputy director levels. This trend grew after 1988 with the delegation of decision making to 'professional' managers, many of whom had received some formal training.

There was a growing emphasis on qualified enterprise management in the enterprises studied, and this accompanied the concentration of decision making at the senior level. Top enterprise management secured a greater degree of decision making autonomy from government, while at the same time it limited the powers previously held by work group leaders and middle managers. This suggests, as Harbison and Myers (1959) observed in the industrialization process, that a professional management elite develops when the owners are separated from management. Kerr and his colleagues (Kerr 1983; Kerr *et al.* 1960) argued that the professionalization of management, with its capability of organizing information and technological knowledge, plays a key role in the industrialization process. Chandler (1977) also argued that the real powers of industrial decision making moved into the hands of professional managers, who decided on the allocation of resources and determined long-term strategies. This study of six Chinese enterprises suggests that, as decision making has become more strategic in nature under the reform, and as more trained managers have become available, a professional management class is evolving in China.

ACKNOWLEDGEMENTS

The authors wish to thank the British Council and the European Commission for their financial support for the research reported in this chapter. The authors also wish to acknowledge useful comments from Professor Max Boisot and the editors of this volume, and the kind assistance of Patricia Wilson.

APPENDIX

Marketing

1 introducing a new product
2 the price of products
3 the type of market to supply

4 the geographical spread of sales (in China, exports, etc.)
5 the priority of different product orders and deliveries

Purchasing

6 the choice of suppliers of materials
7 the procedure for purchasing

Production and work allocation

9 the overall production plan
10 the scheduling of work against given plans
11 the allocation of work to be done among the available workers
12 which machines or equipment are to be used
13 when overtime will be worked

Quality control

14 what items will be inspected – inward supplies
15 what items will be inspected – complete products

Work style

16 which production operations will be studied

Maintenance

17 the maintenance schedule or procedure

R&D

18 what research and development work will be carried out

Investment and accounting

19 the level of expending on new capital equipment
20 the type or make of new capital equipment
21 what will be costed: to which items will the costing system be applied
22 what unbudgeted money can be spent on capital items
23 what unbudgeted money can be spent on revenue/consumable items

Staffing

24 the number of work group leaders/supervisors
25 appointing workers from outside the factory
26 appointing supervisors from outside the factory

27 appointing managers from outside factory
28 the size of the total workforce
29 the total numbers of managers above work group leaders/supervisors
30 the promotion of production workers
31 the promotion of work group leaders/supervisors
32 the salaries of production workers
33 the salaries of cadres
34 the methods for selecting new workers and cadres

Discipline

35 dismissing a worker
36 dismissing or demoting a supervisor or manager

Training

37 the type of training offered

Welfare

38 what and how many welfare facilities are provided

Organisation structure

39 altering responsibilities/areas of work of non-production department
40 altering responsibilities/areas of production departments
41 creating a new department
42 creating a new non-production job
43 creating a new production job

Office system

44 the design of office systems

Representation of management

45 who is the most junior person who can deputize for the director in his
    absence
46 in discussions with the party secretary
47 in discussion with the trade union leader

REFERENCES

Andrew, K. R. (1980) *The Concept of Corporate Strategy*, revised edition, Ontario:
    Richard D. Irwin.

Boisot, M. and Child, J. (1994) 'China's emerging economic order: modernisation through network quasi–capitalism?', *Working Paper, Judge Institute of Management Studies*, University of Cambridge: September.

Borys, B. and Jemison, D. (1989) 'Hybrid arrangements as strategic alliances', *Academy of Management Review* 14: 234–249.

Chandler, A. (1977) *The Visible Hand*, Cambridge, Mass.: Harvard University Press.

Child, J. (1987) 'Enterprise Reform in China', in M. Warner (ed.) *Management Reform in China*, 24–52, London: Printer.

—— (1994) *Management in China During the Age of Reform*, Cambridge: Cambridge University Press.

Child, J. and Yuan Lu (1990) 'Industrial decision making under China's economic reform', *Organisation Studies* 3(11): 321–351.

—— (1995) 'Institutional constraints on investment decision-making', *Organisation Science* (forthcoming).

China's Reform and Development Report: 1992–1993, Beijing: China Finance & Economic Press.

Eggertsson, T. (1990) *Economic Behaviour and Institutions*, Cambridge: Cambridge University Press.

Granick, D. (1990) *Chinese State Enterprises*, Chicago: University of Chicago Press.

Harbison, F. and Myers, C. A. (1959) 'An international concept of management', in F. Harbison and C. A. Myers (eds) *Management in the Industrial World* 3–13, New York: McGraw-Hill.

Kerr, C. (1983) *The Future of Industrial Societies: Convergence or Continued Diversity?* Cambridge, Mass.: Harvard University Press.

Kerr, C., Dunlop, J. T., Harbison, F. and Myers, C. A., (1960) *Industrialism and Industrial Man*, Cambridge, Mass.: Harvard University Press.

Kornai, J. (1980) *The Economics of Shortage*, Amsterdam: North-Holland.

—— (1986) 'The Hungarian reform process', *Journal of Economic Literature* 24: 1687–1737.

Lee, P. N. S. (1987) *Industrial Management and Economic Reform in China 1949–1984*, Hong Kong: Oxford University Press.

Liu Zishen and Sun Yong (1993) *Dialogue on Reform's Progress and Problems in 1993* (*1993 nian gaige yu fazhang wunti manhua*). Shougang Research and Development (*Shougang yanjiu yu kaifa*), 6: 24–28.

Lu Yuan (1991) 'Decision-making in Chinese enterprises', unpublished PhD thesis, Birmingham: Aston University.

Lu Yuan and Heard, R. (1995) 'Socialised economic action: a comparison of strategic investment decision making in China and Britain', *Organisation Studies* 16 (forthcoming).

Ma Hong and Sun Shangqing (eds) (1994) *Economic Situation and Prospect of China* (*zhongguo jingji xingshi yu zhanwang*), Beijing: China Development Press.

Mintzberg, H. (1979) *The Structuring of Organisations*, Englewood Cliffs, NJ: Prentice-Hall.

Montias, J. M. (1988) 'On hierarchies and economic reforms', *Journal of Institutional and Theoretical Economics* 144: 832–838.

Mun, Kin-Chok (1985) 'An integration of the socialist market and planning in China', *Marketing, Investment, and Management in China and Hong Kong* 207–219. Hong Kong: Kwang Jing Publishing Co.

Municipal Planning Commission (1991) *Comprehensive Economic Analysis*, (*zonghe jingji yanjiu*), Beijing: Beijing Science & Technology Press.

Nee, V. (1992) 'Organisational dynamics of market transition', *Administrative Science Quarterly* 37: 1–27.

Oliver, C. (1991) 'Strategic responses to institutional processes', *Academy of Management Review* 16: 145–179.

People's Daily (overseas edition) (1993) 'Reforming planning and investing/financing system, the State Planning Commission proposing practical programmes' (*jihua yu tourong zi tizhi gaige, guojia jiwei tichu juti fang'an*) 9 December: 1.

State Statistic Bureau (1993), *China Industrial Statistical Yearbook*, Beijing: China Statistical Press.

Tisdell, C. (1993) *Economic Development in the Context of China*, London: St. Martin's Press.

Walder, A. (1989) 'Factory managers in an era of reform', *China Quarterly* 118: 242–264.

Wang, R. L., Wang, C. and Gong, Y. (1991) 'Enterprise autonomy and market structures in China', in O. Shenkar (ed.) *Organisation and Management in China: 1979–90* 23–33, Armonk, New York: M. E. Sharpe.

Williamson, O. (1993) 'Comparative economic organization', in S. Lindenberg and H. Schieuder (eds) *Interdisciplinary Perspectives on Organisation Studies*: 3–38, Oxford: Pergamon Press.

Wu Jinglian (1991) 'Difficulties and exit of state large and medium-sized enterprises' (*Guoying dazhong xingqiye de kunjing he shulu*), in Wu Jinglian (ed.) 1993 *Planned Economy or Market Economy* (*jihua jingji haishi shichang jingji*) 13–29, Beijing: China Economy Press.

Wu Zhenkun (ed.) (1993) *Overview of China's Economic System Reform* (*zhongguo jingji tizhi gaige tonglun*), Beijing: Beijing Industrial Polytechnic University Press.

4 Politics, culture and decision making in China

Robin Porter

ABSTRACT

Decision making processes are key to the successful modernization of China, as the Chinese government itself defines that modernization. It will be the contention of this chapter that political factors, derived from the structures and ideology in place especially over the years 1949 to 1979, and cultural factors derived from China's Confucian past, combine to inhibit rational decision making on a very large scale, and will continue to militate against the achievement of a rational order both in management and in government in China for many years to come.

In order to demonstrate this, a simple model of decision making is used as a framework for analysis of several typical Chinese decision sequences. Three typical cases are then given in outline, and a variety of political and cultural factors which combine to make up the context for decision making in present-day China is examined. These factors are related to delays and interruptions in the decision sequences for the cases outlined, and it will be suggested that the continued widespread prevalence of these attitudes and conditions represents a significant retarding force in the campaign to modernize China. The conclusion to this chapter will reflect upon the suitability of Western models for application in non-Western societies, in which Western assumptions about rational processes to achieve rational goals may not be widely shared.

INTRODUCTION

In recent years China has embarked upon a programme to modernize every aspect of its economy and society. This follows a period of 100 years up to 1949 during which only the periphery of China was touched by modern ideas or economic activity, and a further 30 years up to 1980 when social need and political objectives were paramount in determining policy on most matters.

The new emphasis on economic development and the transformation of society using ideas from the West and from Japan has given rise to a need for management decisions to be taken to alter the status quo over a very broad range of issues both major and minor. In this sense, decision making processes are key to the successful modernization of China, as the Chinese government itself defines that modernization, and a study of decision making will help us to understand to what extent, and for what reasons, China will be able to achieve her goals.

An indication is first given of the wide variety of decisions in China associated with the task of modernization. A simple model is then offered incorporating the principal common elements of decision making models in Western literature over the years, to provide a framework for analysis of several typical Chinese decision sequences. Three typical cases are then given in outline, which are neither hypothetical nor wholly specific, but rather represent composites of similar actual decisions known to the author. The cases are:

1 the decision of two organizations within the motor industry on production of a new model of car;
2 the decision not to introduce new technology at a factory producing metal components;
3 the decision of the national news agency not to introduce press conferences.

Each decision process is traced in some detail, and a sequence of events sketched which, it is suggested, could have led to the final outcome. In each case the actual outcome is drawn from fact, while the means of arriving at it is informed speculation.

A note on methodology

Some further observation is appropriate on the methodology to be employed. The first two cases chosen are both in the manufacturing sector and relate to production for the automotive industry. The decision in each case is of a general management or strategic nature in that it has important resource implications, and is multifaceted. The third case, that of the news agency, is somewhat different; the decision is still strategic in that it impinges on the whole direction of the work of the news agency, and has been included to show how achievement of an organization's stated goal may be completely undermined by political undercurrents.

Normally, the approach to investigating decision making in these organizations would be to collect evidence through a combination of structured or semi-structured interviews, questionnaires and documentation. In this instance, however, the researcher has had a lengthy working relationship with the industry or organization concerned.[1] The material for these cases is drawn both from field research in China, and from the author's experience working closely with the Chinese motor industry over a number of years, and working inside the Chinese news agency Xinhua for a year. The outcome of this has been that the cases are constructed at two levels.

At the first level, there is a factual account of the progress of the decision over time, and the recording of various intermediate and final outputs. At the second level, an interpretation of the progress of the decision is offered by the author, based on a knowledge of the industry, and of the organization and particular individuals within it. In this sense, the approach is both informed and speculative. The narrative style seeks to offer a glimpse of what is happening under the surface, and how individuals shape events on the basis of their own values and agendas.

MODERNIZATION AND STRATEGIC DECISION MAKING

The nature and scope of the process of modernization under way in China in recent years will determine the types of decisions with which Chinese officials and managers are routinely faced. The programme for the so-called 'four modernizations' – of agriculture, industry, science and technology, and national defence – which began in 1979, envisages the complete transformation of the economic life of the country over a period of several decades. The prime mover behind the modernization campaign was China's Vice Premier Deng Xiaoping. Twice vilified during China's Cultural Revolution, on his reinstatement Deng determined that ideology must be set aside and the country must modernize at all costs, a view which he still holds.

The modernization programme is an epic process of construction and change comparable to that which took place in Victorian England and in other parts of Europe and North America following the industrial revolution. In China the task is immeasurably complicated by the size of the country and its population and the desire to compress the time period within which the process takes place.

The range of strategic decisions which such a process will involve must inevitably be very broad. All branches of manufacture will come under scrutiny, as will every aspect of the transport network, and the provision of services, as well as methods of organization and management of productive facilities of all kinds (see, for example, Spence 1990). Thus necessary strategic decisions might include anything, from which technology an infrastructural industry needs to buy, to how to reorganize a government department to make it more effective. Typically, a manufacturing industry might need to decide to reorganize production, find new products and new markets, import foreign technology, set up a joint venture, institute a technical training programme, for example. A service enterprise might need to decide to set up new branches or offer new types of service, establish a franchise, or employ an overseas agent. A government body, responding to policy initiatives, might need to decide to re-structure its operations to devolve or assume responsibilities, send a delegation abroad to seek specific opportunities for collaboration, or to set up a human resource management programme for its staff.

Very many decisions currently being taken in China are interdependent, though the relationship is not always recognized and taken into account. Decisions need to be taken at both the macro and micro level, especially as China is still a part-market, part-command economy.[2] Change and improvement will be a widely shared objective, although not universally shared, and resistance to change will in some cases be a major obstacle.

A variety of models has been put forward by Western management theorists over the past several decades for the analysis of strategic decision making processes. These include notably the work of Simon (1957, 1960, 1965 and 1976), Cyert and Welsch (1970), Mintzberg *et al.* (1976), Hickson *et al.* 1986, Bennett *et al.* (1990), and Johnson and Scholes (1993). The principal advantage of using a model is that it can help the analyst to make sense of strategic decisions made in an organizational context. Some models can also take account of the interrelationship of related decisions bearing on a single project, for example, rather than focusing purely on individual behaviour.

Most Western models assume an underlying rational progression through a number of stages for any strategic decision, although there is often provision for non-sequential or intrusive activity which may not appear to be rational in terms of promotion of the project in view. Thus there may be additional routines of control, communication and politics (within the organization) which run throughout the decision process, as well as 'dynamic' factors – delays and interruptions as some would call them – which will affect the timing of the final outcome. Irrationality can therefore be accommodated to some degree in most recent Western models. Moreover most models can allow for iterative activity back and forth between stages.

Taken as a whole, this body of theory points to three distinct stages in strategic decision making: problem definition, in which the need for a decision is identified, and the nature of the decision defined; problem *analysis*, including identification of alternative solutions; and evaluation of alternatives leading to choice of a course of action. In practice, of course, the stages are highly interlinked and iteration around the total strategy formulation process would be commonplace, before a final decision is taken or emerges. Nevertheless, the stages provide a useful conceptual basis for the interpretation of the various cases.

The case studies which follow, representing a composite of actual experience, are typical of strategic decision sequences related to China's modernization programme over the past few years.

HYPOTHETICAL CASES

The decision to produce a new car

This decision involves two organizations, the Central Motor Industry Corporation (CMIC), and the Jiangsu Auto Company. The case describes circumstances obtaining in the mid-1980s.

The CMIC is part of the central government structure, a corporation under one of the industrial ministries, with residual responsibility for directing manufacturing plants in the automotive industry around the country, and an obligation to give technical advice on automotive priorities to the State Planning Commission. Jiangsu Auto is an up and coming branch of the CMIC, located in a major city, with the aspiration of expanding and proving its independence from CMIC by taking the lead in a new project for car production.

Problem definition

Realization of the need for China to produce a new car, the stage of problem definition, comes about at roughly the same time in both organizations. In part, as with most major policy developments in China's infrastructural industries, the impetus to pay attention to this matter comes from sources outside the industry concerned: the public widely perceives the automobile as a totem of modernization, and a goal which both China and individual Chinese should pursue; a senior Chinese leader and member of the Party Central Committee has declared publicly that it is time China produced its own new generation car. Taking their lead from this statement, both CMIC and Jiangsu Auto start to hold their own separate discussions.

Other specific factors within CMIC and Jiangsu Auto give additional impetus. CMIC has been told by the State Planning Commission that China is spending too much foreign exchange on the purchase of foreign cars for taxis and for official use, and has been required to draw up a strategy to solve this problem. Jiangsu Auto, which produces a model now 20 years out of date, wishes to diversify its production, and make something which it can both sell in greater numbers internally, and potentially export.

CMIC sets up an *ad hoc* committee to respond to the directive from the State Planning Commission to prepare a policy on car production. Whether car production in China is appropriate or not (up to now the industry has focused on truck production) is not an issue open to the committee to discuss; this decision has been taken by officials of the State Planning Commission, who have no expertise in automotive matters. In this sense a large part of the prerogative has been taken away from CMIC. What is left is whether China should design and produce its own car, adopt a foreign model in its entirety for production in China, or seek a measure of technology transfer for something in between.

The committee of three comprises two senior engineers and an administrator with no engineering background, but who is a high party official. One of the engineers is from Shanghai, and is mistrusted by the other two committee members because of his history of radical activity during the Cultural Revolution. Shanghai was noted for its radicalism at the time, and especially during the early years 1966–1969. Many young people were caught up in political campaigns, and some were clearly involved in violent excesses. The engineer from Shanghai is, however, the only one with any direct knowledge of car production. For his part the administrator is frequently unable to attend the committee's meetings because he must give priority to meetings to discuss the party's new campaign for discipline in the workplace.

In the light of these factors, the diagnosis or definition stage is very limited. There is no detailed analysis of the tasks likely to be involved in designing or producing a new car. Located as they are in Shanghai, where the taste for things Western is stronger than in other parts of China, Jiangsu Auto are clear that they do not want to design their own new model, but rather want to import a production line for an established foreign car. They believe that they know enough about car production not to have to conduct a detailed analysis of what would be involved in producing a new model. They feel that whatever new component technology will be required can be discussed in the course of business talks with a potential partner. These views prevail because they are held by the director and the chief engineer of the factory, who are long-time members of the party; they will not be challenged by their subordinates. There is therefore no real debate before business discussions with the potential partner begin.

Problem analysis/identification of alternative solutions

The analysis stage, involving identification of alternative solutions, is haphazard in both organizations, and in one of them at least is fraught with delays and interruptions.

In CMIC, one of the senior engineers has in practice been left to research and propose a solution to the car project. Mindful of the State Planning Commission's wish to conserve foreign exchange by producing a car in China which would substitute for imported cars currently used by officials and as taxis, the senior engineer has in mind a full six-seater, with a large engine. Because he is from the north-east, and also has friends in the auto industry in the north-east with whom he attended college, the engineer looks to some form of collaboration with the main factory in that part of China, Five Star Auto Works. He also favours an approach which would combine elements of technology transfer from overseas, with the use of local componentry wherever possible to save on foreign exchange. The senior engineer at CMIC is not fully aware of the discussions that Jiangsu Auto has begun to have with a foreign firm for what amounts to a rival project, even though Jiangsu Auto is notionally responsible to CMIC.

The engineer from CMIC travels to the north-east to explore the view of local factory managers at Five Star Auto Works. This and subsequent trips are difficult and time-consuming to arrange, not only because the engineer is needed for the new discipline campaign instituted by the party within CMIC, but also because CMIC does not enjoy a special relationship with the domestic airline, and finds it very hard to book air tickets for its officials. Travel by train, requiring 24 hours each way, is the only reliable method of getting there and back. The engineer discovers that the factory in the north-east already has a plan, for which negotiations are advanced, to buy the line and facilities to produce an American six cylinder engine. The body of the American model of car from which the engine came is considered to be too big for China's roads, and is rejected. In the course of several visits during which alternatives are screened out, the engineer from CMIC and the management of Five Star agree on a custom-made solution involving putting the engine into the body of another car from a European firm with which CMIC is in negotiation. The local factory would supply a range of components from the beginning, and would increase local content as rapidly as possible. The matter is referred back to CMIC for further negotiation with the foreign firms involved, and a decision.

Meanwhile, within Jiangsu Auto the routines of analysis and exploration are strongly influenced by exploratory meetings which have been going on for some time with a German firm which wants to transfer technology to China for production of one of its models no longer to be produced in Europe. A number of 'trial' cars have been donated to Jiangsu Auto for the use of its officials. The director of Jiangsu Auto is keen to conclude an agreement, as a prestige project of this nature with a world class company will boost his own position within the political hierarchy of the region. The chief engineer, who trained in Germany before returning to China soon after the liberation, believes the opportunity will arise for his daughter to attend university there if the deal goes through.

For these reasons, within Jiangsu Auto problem analysis and identification of alternatives comes down to negotiations with the German partner over matters of cost and degree of equity in a joint venture, the pace of localization of component production, elements of training and technical support to be provided by the German side, and so forth. There is no real search for alternatives, and overtures from other foreign firms are not welcomed. It becomes clear that *if* the project is to go ahead, it will be with this German firm. Negotiations proceed more quickly than those of CMIC, as under new party directives Jiangsu Auto has an allocation of foreign exchange to acquire its own technology, and believes it need not consult any other body on how to spend it. The right to an allocation of foreign exchange and the independence to decide how to spend it, up to a fixed limit, passed to certain major enterprises from the early 1980s.

Evaluation of alternatives and choice

CMIC now proceeds to the stage of selection of its new car project, through routines of evaluation and choice. The factory in the north-east is prepared to allow CMIC to take the lead in the project, because CMIC enjoys a close relationship with the State Economic Commission, which will have to approve the release of funds for it. The purchase of the engine line from the US is put to the leadership of CMIC, and following a meeting at which engineers from the north-east put their case, CMIC formally takes the decision to recommend its purchase to the State Economic Commission. After several months, authorization is granted, and foreign exchange released.

The contract is signed, and the engine production line is crated up and sent from the US to China's north-east. The American company concerned, which originally hoped to sell facilities for production of the whole car to China, and to develop a long-term business relationship with the Chinese factory, feels dissatisfied, and when delivery is complete cuts its ties with the factory.

Astonishingly, it is only at this stage that engineers from CMIC and the factory actually try fitting the engine, with modified transmission components, into the body shell of the European car. They discover that it doesn't fit. Even worse, they find that their experimental modifications to the body and transmission components make the car completely unsafe and unroadworthy. Negotiations with the European company over purchase of the bodywork production line are halted. The factory, after an inquest, turns its attention to producing a new model of truck, as a senior party leader has called in the press for an increase in China's capacity for truck production. The crates containing the engine line sit unopened in a corner of the factory for the next two years, before the line is assembled to produce engines to power a new van. When the factory eventually does turn again to car production four years after the failure of the first project, it sets up a much simpler operation to assemble limited numbers of kits of a whole car imported from Europe.

The collapse of the project has little impact on CMIC. The senior engineer most involved is due to retire shortly in any case. The engineer from Shanghai has gone back to Shanghai. The administrator has been promoted to a job in the shipbuilding industry, where he will be responsible for a project to build oil tankers.

Within Jiangsu Auto the negotiations with the German firm are speeded up, influenced by the personal agendas of the director and the chief engineer, and by the desire to make an announcement on or before China's National Day. At a time when party policy favours devolution, Jiangsu Auto is anxious to use the project to assert its independence from CMIC, to which in the past it has been responsible.

The negotiation process with one partner effectively displaces the normal routine of evaluation and choice; the choice has been made, and the object is to get the best possible terms and arrangements. Through reciprocal visits the two sides develop, in Chinese terms, a very good rapport. In the course of this, however, less attention is paid than should have been the case to certain aspects of the contract, notably the pace and content of localization of component production, and the prospect for exports of the finished vehicles.[3] The director, taking advantage of his new independence under the director responsibility system, signs the contract and announces it the day before National Day. He is publicly congratulated by the mayor of Shanghai, who himself is shortly to become a major national figure of influence.

Authorization for the deal is a formality, as most of the foreign exchange required has already been allocated to Jiangsu Auto, and an additional amount is to be made up by Shanghai Municipality. The arrangement is for a joint venture, and therefore also involves investment by the German side. Jiangsu Auto has succeeded in concluding its agreement for a new car project, without any significant involvement by the central government, or by CMIC, which previously would have been called upon to advise the State Economic Commission on the terms of such a proposal.

In the event, several years later problems have emerged. It has become clear in retrospect that the model of car chosen had been declared prematurely obsolete in the West because of certain design features which had undermined sales. The car could hold only four people in comfort, and was therefore not ideal as a taxi or an official car. The German firm has proved unsympathetic to the Chinese side's wish to increase local content of the car's components, claiming that quality levels achieved did not justify this. The same reason was used in opposing Jiangsu Auto's wish to begin exporting the cars, to bring in foreign exchange.

The director has become a top official in the Shanghai city government, while the chief engineer has become director of Jiangsu Auto.

The decision not to introduce new technology at an enterprise producing metal components

This enterprise, Lei Feng Metal Components Company, has its roots in a factory established in the countryside in 1967 as part of the policy to expand rural industry during the Cultural Revolution.[4] The factory has produced various things during its lifetime, but currently makes metal components of several kinds, including radiators, fasteners for the construction industry, parts for household appliances, and replacement components for the vehicle aftermarket.

The director was originally head of the revolutionary committee of the same factory, and has survived to control the factory for over 25 years, becoming in due course director of the enterprise. He is held up by the Provincial Party Committee as an example of a model manager, and a book has been written about him which is widely available in local bookstores.

Problem definition

As customers for the factory's products begin to modernize their own production, often with foreign assistance, the customer base for this factory's products is being eroded by reduced orders and cancellations; the factory's customers have introduced foreign technology and design in their manufacturing activity, and the Lei Feng factory has not upgraded its own component production to keep pace. The director believes he needs to find new customers, concentrate on one product line, and produce it in much greater numbers. He believes that if an export market can be secured for the item in question, this will preserve the prosperity of the factory well into the future. The director has come to this view through reading the official press and Chinese language publications from Hong Kong, which are full of accounts of joint ventures.

Problem analysis/identification of alternative solutions

There is effectively no detailed analysis of what a business strategy based on the need to concentrate production and to export would entail. Apart from the director, the enterprise is run by only two qualified engineers and an accountant, all quite young and inexperienced, while the director himself is in his fifties, and influential locally in the communist party. The director does not seek a detailed analysis from his management team, and they will not presume to offer one if not invited to do so.

In an enterprise in which the director rules unchallenged, the routines of analysis and exploration therefore are bound to be limited by his own contacts and inclinations. In this case the director has a friend in the automotive industry who knows of an American company interested in having certain aftermarket vehicle components made in China for sale through its extensive network of outlets in the US; the friend offers to effect an introduction. In the United States, the aftermarket for replacement parts for motor vehicles is big retail business, with nationwide retail chains supplying their own brands of parts. The director invites the US company to send a delegation to visit his factory. The visitors, two business managers who have diverted to China after a routine visit to their normal supplier in Taiwan, are shown the premises and wined and dined lavishly by the director. He assures them that the factory has over two decades of experience in producing castings of all kinds, and promises provincial government backing for any deal. They have no prior knowledge of China, and take back with them, along with a number of samples, a strong positive impression of the ability and willingness of the factory to meet the US firm's requirements.

Correspondence ensues between the US company and the director, in which the initial target items identified for possible collaboration are transmission castings and cylinder blocks. At a routine management meeting one of the factory's engineers expresses doubt about the ability of the factory to meet the technical and metallurgical requirements of the US firm; he is overruled by the director, who has already notified the Provincial Party Committee and government that a deal is in the offing. In the director's view the required items are of low technology, and well within the capability of the factory to produce. Preparations are made for a further visit by the US firm, and a large plaster cast of an American eagle is erected at the gate of the factory to celebrate what is firmly anticipated will be the signing of an agreement at the end of the visit.

This time, the American delegation consists of both commercial managers and engineers. Although the factory director wants to emphasize the ceremonial aspects of the visit, the engineers are determined to give the production facilities a thorough scrutiny; the samples received in the US proved to be of very poor quality, wholly unsuitable for use in modern vehicles in American traffic conditions. They have a brief to see whether or not production technology could be upgraded sufficiently to satisfy their requirements.

On their inspection of the factory, the US engineers find four major problems. There is a very high turnover of staff, as young people frequently move to the city to seek better prospects after a short period at the factory. The workers are predominantly unskilled and from a peasant background; there is no established regime of training for them and they are expected to learn on the job. The metallurgy and casting processes are primitive, and comparable to American technology from the 1920s. There is no regime of quality control, and even sight inspections are random and cursory.

Evaluation of alternatives and choice

When the two sides finally sit down to business discussions, these problems are put to the director. He has no knowledge of engineering, having himself come from a poor peasant background and risen through the ranks of the party. He is completely unable to grasp the technical points about the metallurgy, and cites a long list of local and provincial awards which have been won by his factory. He regards suggestions about staff management practice and training as a challenge to his authority as factory director. He insists that no new technology is necessary to produce the items the US firm require. The US side walk out of the discussions. As they leave, they are called aside by one of the factory engineers, who asks if they might sponsor him for study in the United States.

The decision by the national news agency not to hold press conferences

The national news agency in China, Progress News, derives originally from the communist party's propaganda arrangements during the period of struggle at Yenan in the late 1930s. Following the establishment of the People's Republic in 1949, the agency was given the dual tasks of disseminating news about events in China both domestically and internationally, and promoting the policy objectives of the party. It has its headquarters in Beijing, and branches in all major cities in China and throughout the world (see Porter 1992).

Problem identification

As China opens up to the outside world there is growing international interest in news about China. The news agency's previous practice has been to issue reports and statements about domestic developments broadly according to priorities determined by the communist party, and to treat reporting to the international audience in a similar way to domestic reporting. Formerly, these reports would be picked up on wire service by foreign news media at their overseas headquarters, interpreted and incorporated into news items about China. Now however there is an increasing number of foreign journalists resident in Beijing who use the agency's material as a starting point for their own investigative journalism. Frequently news agency reports give rise to further questions on the part of foreign journalists, but so far there has been no provision for two way communication between the agency and reporters.

Pressure for consideration of what to do about this matter has come from several sources. The agency's own research department, which records the pick-up of agency pieces in foreign publications, shows a high level of speculation about the content of agency releases in three distinct subject areas: conflicting policy statements by Chinese leaders; statistical information; and human rights matters.

The agency recently opened a Journalism Institute, and imported several foreign professors of journalism to teach Western journalistic techniques. Several recent graduates of the programme now work at the agency, and together with their foreign professor have begun to urge greater inter-action between the agency and foreign journalists on routine matters of work.

Finally, working foreign journalists have begun trying to contact the agency directly about aspects of its reports. One had actually managed to reach the external division by telephone. It becomes clear to the party cell of senior editors who direct the 'external' work of the news agency that the question of access will need to be addressed sooner or later.

Problem analysis/identification of alternative solutions

One possible solution would be for the news agency to arrange Western style press conferences to clarify and elaborate on the news agency's releases, using senior agency staff as spokespeople, or where appropriate bringing in China's political leaders to speak for themselves.

The trigger for consideration of this possibility is a suggestion made by a young foreign-trained journalist at a meeting of the daily work team, the small group of the most promising journalists who, with a senior editor, have the task of dealing with the most important news stories of the day. The editor, who is also a long-time party member, raises the matter with the chief editor of the external division of the agency at a private meeting that afternoon. It is put on the agenda for the monthly meeting of senior editors at which the direction and emphasis of news work is normally discussed.

In the event, other options are not considered, and the matter of greater access for foreign journalists will stand or fall on the press conference proposal. In a pattern that is characteristic of organizations strongly influenced by the party (the news agency is directly responsible to the Party Central Committee) there is a direct progression from theory to practice, from diagnosis to choice, without any extended attempt to weigh up alternatives.

Evaluation of alternatives and choice

At the monthly strategy meeting the proposal to introduce limited press conferences is put to the half dozen senior and chief editors assembled for their view. The senior party secretary present reminds the editors that the agency's principal task is to disseminate news of the party's policies on various issues, and to report the news in a positive way so as to mobilize people in support of those policies. To invite questions, even from foreign journalists, would compromise the message and undermine the party's news work. One editor believes that some allowance should be made for the different perspective of a foreign audience, but his colleagues remonstrate with him until he agrees to withdraw his objection in order to preserve the consensus. It is agreed that the proposal should be rejected.

Moreover, the party secretary then expresses concern that the fact that such a proposal has been put forward may indicate a slackening of party discipline within the external division of the agency. Several of the editors agree, and the chief editor of the external division is obliged to volunteer that measures will be taken to tighten up discipline. The party secretary reports on the views expressed at the meeting to the director of the news agency, who is in turn responsible to the Party Central Committee.

A week or so later, the young journalist who had made the proposal is taken aside and cautioned, and put onto routine feature writing away from the daily work team. The foreign professor of journalism is told that next term he will not have to teach so much, but will be asked to help with the 'polishing' of grammar and style of English-language news releases. The agency's switchboard is told henceforth to block any calls from foreigners to the external division.

POLITICS, CULTURE AND DECISION MAKING

The composite case studies presented above cannot, it is suggested here, really be understood unless they are placed against a background of very particular circumstances obtaining in China of both a political and a cultural nature. In this section, some general observations will be made about the context of decision making in China, and then specific political and cultural factors will be highlighted which, it is argued, have a major impact on the way in which strategic decisions are made.

The context

With respect to the context, in the first place it is important to appreciate that China is still a Marxist state in which parallel decision making structures of party and state exist (see, for example, Wang 1990). Most obviously, this means that at all levels organs of government are shadowed and monitored by corresponding organs of the communist party, which have until very recently tended to dictate policy on all essential matters, and supervise its implementation. It has also meant, however, that individual party members and sometimes party cells have performed a similar function within state run enterprises. Although many of these now have much greater, or even complete independence, party members are still active within them; despite the so-called director responsibility system, all too frequently decisions are still made with one eye on what the party might say if individual managers were called to account (see, for example, Blecher 1989). This both restricts the actual freedom of action of enterprise directors and, where they try to implement significant change, may cause a lukewarm response among middle managers.

It is also the case that there are still major conflicts over policy within the ruling communist party which are the residue of the extraordinary transition which has been under way since China started to open up to the West around 1980. The Tiananmen incident of 1989 served to underline these contradictions, and has raised renewed doubts about whether they will ever be finally resolved so long as the communist party remains in power. Among the most important of these dichotomies have been those between state and private ownership, centralized or decentralized administration of state sector enterprises, 'redness' versus expertise, skilled or educated versus unskilled or uneducated, and city versus countryside.

There may be, within the Chinese context, good reasons why a senior policy maker may advocate continued state ownership of certain industries, particularly those which are infrastructural in nature. In a similar way, there may be considerable logic in preserving a high degree of centralized administration of those particular state industries. Again, even in 1993, some older senior cadres continue to lament the loss of political instruction in the workplace, and will seek any opportunity that presents itself to promote 'redness' among the workforce above, or at least in competition with, technical expertise. Furthermore, while skills and training are in vogue among a majority of senior officials at the present time and are widely perceived as desirable, there is much less enthusiasm for the kind of tertiary education which encourages discussion of a broad range of new ideas, including those of a political kind. There is, moreover, a lingering doubt about the proper balance between city and countryside, and a lingering threat of reversal through policies of social engineering, of the massive movement of people and economic activity to the cities (Porter 1993).

A final point with respect to context has to do with Western assumptions about the purpose of decision making in business, and their applicability in present-day China. It is commonly assumed in the West, though this may not always prove to be the case in practice, that decisions are made in a business organization to improve production or sales or business methods in some way so as to increase the effectiveness and profitability of the firm. It is suggested here that in many enterprises in China this may only *apparently* be the objective, or may be only a partial objective. It is not only social interaction for pleasure that is ritualized in China; much of the interaction at work is ritualized too, and this includes the routines and processes of decision making associated nominally with improving production or methods. Hidden agendas exist at many levels, and the pursuit of them, while it may be rational for the individuals concerned, may not be in the best interests of the enterprise. Thus a sequence of routines nominally about importing technology and revitalizing production and profitability may in fact be a ritual whose real object is the adjustment of position in the local party hierarchy of several individuals, none of whom may really care about the project for itself. It should not be assumed therefore that the commitment to problem solving which is the *ideal* of so much management science in the West, and which is still the thread running through most decision making theory, necessarily exists in China. With these broad comments in mind, it is appropriate to look at a number of political and cultural factors which inhibit rational decision making in China.

Political factors

On the political side, there is first and foremost the need for enterprises in China when making decisions at the micro level, to conform to policies of the state and the party at the macro level. At a time when the country is attempting rapid modernization, and the economy is in transition from a command economy to a much more free market situation, it is often very difficult even for large state-connected enterprises to know where they stand. Frequently, policies are reversed in mid-stream, as when the move to decentralize decision making power in much of industry was suddenly reversed in the mid-1980s when duplication and waste made the government in Beijing feel it was losing control. Further relaxation was followed by a brief period of decentralization of control after the Tiananmen massacre of 1989.

Compounding this problem, and indeed running through all attempts to make decision making more informed, is the culture of secrecy and just plain vagueness which is a legacy especially of the 10 years of the Cultural Revolution.[5] A great many middle and senior managers in China still tend not to keep their staff or their colleagues fully informed, and themselves will not ask if they do not know something. For years it was simply safer not to know. Among some managers, the loss of education or training during the Cultural Revolution also means that they have never been taught to analyse problems for themselves, and this results in vague and imprecise answers being proffered or accepted where in reality a precise and detailed grasp of a problem is essential if an intelligent decision is to be made.

The primacy of the party, mentioned as part of the context above, is still reflected in a number of specific ways which impact on the role of an individual in a decision process. Perhaps most notably, it is still an important, possibly the most important, avenue of promotion in China, a sure route to power and privilege even if individual entrepreneurial activity has become the route to wealth.[6] A young party member working in an enterprise may therefore have divided loyalties; from the point of view of his or her career in the party it may be best to take a cautious view of a proposed business plan, for example, while what the enterprise may really need at that time is a more outward looking or entrepreneurial decision which may involve some risk. The discussion then will cease to be rational in terms of the information presented and the best interests of the enterprise, but will be hedged about with false premises and beset by straw men.

Cultural factors

On the cultural side, the need to satisfy imperatives which have their roots deep in China's Confucian past also impacts on decision making processes.

Among the most widely recognized in both sociological and Western business studies of China is the need to save face, preserve harmony, and to avoid conflict in social relationships (see, for example, selections from Confucius' 'Analects' in de Bary *et al.* 1964; see also Hwang 1983). Where strategic decisions need to be taken to secure the continued successful operation of an organization, such a cultural predisposition is likely to discourage the consideration of contentious information which may nonetheless be essential to an informed decision. The facts of the situation may be too embarrassing, or it may be claimed that reliable information is to hand when this is not the case. Moreover, the wish to avoid conflict may incline the decision makers towards an unsatisfactory or incomplete decision, or even towards no decision at all, where one is clearly required.

Another cultural imperative in professional or business life in China is the need to promote the interests of the family and even of the extended family. Under the dynastic system, which prevailed down to the early twentieth century, China was ruled by scholar bureaucrats who in practice sought to advance the interests of their extended families alongside the performance of their official duties. Even down to the lowliest peasant, comfort and favours were owed and could be claimed through the extended family (Yang 1967). The philosophical justification of this lay with Confucius (551–479 BC), who maintained that the family unit should be the foundation of all social and political life. Classical Chinese novels, such as *Dream of the Red Chamber*, also very frequently take the family as their theme. Thus, far more than is generally the case in the West, family interests may impinge upon professional life, and create hidden agendas which can detract from the rationality of decision processes defined in organizational terms.

Related to this is the phenomenon known as *guanxi* – broadly meaning having connections, or a special relationship, with important or influential people. Foreign business people have become aware of the usefulness of *guanxi* connections in recent years (see Hwang 1983; Campbell and Adlington 1988). Such a relationship may stem from personal friendship, from having attended the same college, from having once worked in the same workplace or having lived as neighbours in the same town, for example. The relationship strongly implies a willingness to 'help out', and acceptance of the right to ask favours, in return for which loyalty will be given. In a society which has always been heavily bureaucratic, both in traditional and in modern times, *guanxi* is the way most people get around red tape and solve day to day problems. The tendency to rely on and to function through the *guanxi* network undoubtedly influences strategic decision making, determining sources of information on which decisions are based, the scope and nature of routines followed in reaching a decision, and to a large extent the actual choice made. Once again, a systematic and objective approach to the decision will have been undermined.

Other culturally-rooted factors may also influence decision making. One is a widely felt dislike of rapid change, and its association in people's minds with *luan*, or chaos.

Until the twentieth century the notion of progress was unknown in China. The ideal was held to exist in the past, in a legendary 'golden age' that pre-dated both Confucius and historical record. When faced with difficulties China's rulers always invoked this golden age, and sought to put things right by restoring the ideal past rather than by seeking out new solutions (de Bary *et al.* 1964). Moreover, in social and political terms, change was much less obvious in China in the 2,000 years leading up to the twentieth century than it was in the West. There was no transition, for example, from feudal to early capitalist and then to modern industrial society. Change, when it did come, was traumatic and inconclusive in the half century before the People's Republic was founded in 1949, and chaotic through the policy shifts and political campaigns since 1949 (see, for example, Spence 1990).

For many decision makers, therefore, the worry may be that the consequence of novelty will be catastrophe. This fear of change, and of the chaos it may bring, undoubtedly imposes an additional constraint.

A final cultural factor which should be noted is a degree of xenophobia which still exists in China, and which is the legacy of 3,000 years of separate development during which China was seen as the centre of all civilisation.[7] While the need for China to look to the West and to Japan for advanced technology has become apparent in the past few years, there is a residual distaste among some people for the need to borrow from other cultures. In this, China is markedly different from, for example, Japan in the Meiji period.[8] This tendency affects managers and others in a position to make strategic decisions. A consequence of this may be a reluctance to accept technical advice, or to contemplate solutions to problems which may be seen to increase an organization's dependence on forces outside China, however temporary or tactically useful that may be seen to be. Once again, the options are limited and flexibility is reduced.

In sum, therefore, it is suggested in this chapter that in present day China in any case of strategic decision making there may be so many hidden personal or rival institutional agendas that it is frequently much more difficult than in the West to see the process as essentially rational, defined in terms of the goals of the organization. These hidden agendas are rooted in political imperatives outside the organization, imposed on all citizens of the Chinese state, and also derived from cultural influences and injunctions thousands of years old which have survived into modern times. These combine to straitjacket the decision making process, rendering it less amenable to objective consideration of objective choices. In the worst cases, strategic decision making becomes a lottery of external political imperatives, uninformed comment and vested interests. This is a harsh environment for expectations of Western-style decision making.

Western theory on decision making as a rule makes no allowance for a hostile political context outside the firm, where routines of politics in decision making have in recent memory resulted in dismissal, imprisonment and death. Nor it would seem can most Western constructs adequately allow for the influence of culture, and in particular of an all-embracing system of social relations, with its in-built provision for claim and counter-claim by individuals on each other, which can do so much to influence the decision making process. At a time of great transition in the world's economies, it may be worth reflecting that expectations in terms of broad management processes may not be readily transferable across political and cultural boundaries.

ACKNOWLEDGEMENTS

The author acknowledges the financial support of the British Council in carrying out part of the research on which this chapter is based. He is also grateful for insights offered by Paul Forrester, David Brown, and many Chinese colleagues and friends in the organizations concerned.

NOTES

1 The author is an historian and China specialist, who is also a Chinese speaker. He was one of two foreign sub-editors in the English language section of Xinhua news agency's external division in Beijing in 1979–1980, and was full-time adviser to the British automotive industry's SMMT China Trade Group from 1984–1988. Experience for the other case presented, that of the metal components factory, was gained during one of several research visits made between 1990–1993 under the auspices of the British Council's Academic Links with China Scheme.

2 Progress from a command to a market economy has not been linear, and throughout the period since the modernization programme began there have been influential voices within the party urging caution. A case can be made for continued central direction in some industries, notably infrastructural industries where normal market conditions do not obtain. See, for example, R. Porter (1990) 'Centralisation, Decentralisation and Development in China: the Automobile Industry', in N. Campbell and J. Henley *Joint Ventures and Industrial Change in China*: Greenwich, Conn. and London: JAI Press, 143–162.

3 These two issues have been critical in the negotiation of automotive joint ventures in China. The Shanghai Volkswagen project has experienced problems in this respect. So has the Beijing Jeep project. See Jim Mann (1990) *Beijing Jeep*, New York: Simon and Schuster. In the case of Beijing Jeep, both localization and exports were expected by the American partner, and the reluctance was on the Chinese side (see Mann 1990: 221–223, etc.)

4 The roots of attempts to establish rural industry in China lie in the work of social missionaries in North China in the 1930s to encourage self-help among the peasantry, and in the Industrial Co-operative Movement (known overseas as Indusco) during the Pacific War. The idea was revived during the Great Leap Forward in 1958, and again during the Cultural Revolution after 1966. In the latter case strategic considerations played a part, as concentrations of

heavy industry in the urban areas were felt to be particularly vulnerable to threat from the Soviet Union.

5 The Great Proletarian Cultural Revolution, invoked by Party Chairman Mao Zedong in 1966 to try to re-instil revolutionary vigour into the population, lasted technically until 1976, although its most active phase was in the two to three years from mid-1966. The Cultural Revolution was a complex phenomenon, embracing both genuine idealism and cynical struggles for power among its participants, with much random violence; it was also motivated in part by anxiety about external threats. For a thoughtful contemporary analysis see Franz Schurmann (1968) 'The Attack of the Cultural Revolution on Ideology and Organisation', in Ping-ti Ho and Tang Tsou (eds) *China in Crisis* 1(2): Chicago: University. of Chicago Press, 525–564.

6 In traditional China, down to the turn of the twentieth century, the route to power, through obtaining a place in the civil service by means of education and competitive examination, was also the route to wealth. While they were not usually well paid, it was expected of Chinese scholar bureaucrats that they would use their positions to amass wealth. A degree of squeeze and patronage was permissible, provided the tasks of administration were carried out with a sense of duty. See Ping-ti Ho (1962) *The Ladder of Success in Imperial China*, New York: Columbia.

7 The term used for China over the past 3,000 years, Zhong Guo, or Middle Kingdom, is an indication of the traditional attitude concerning the importance of Chinese civilization in comparison to those of other societies. Until the coming of the West to China in the nineteenth century, this view was reinforced by practical experience. To the north were nomadic 'barbarians', to the east was the sea, to the south and west were societies which had taken on aspects of Chinese culture and professed allegiance to China.

8 Japan's astonishing transformation in the Meiji period (1868–1912) from a small and insignificant society into a powerful modern nation able to assert equality with the West has been well documented. See for example, W.G. Beasley (1990) *The Rise of Modern Japan*, London: Weidenfeld and Nicolson. Size, social structure and political traditions may have had much to do with this rapid change.

REFERENCES

Beasley, W. G. (1990) *The Rise of Modern Japan*, London: Weidenfeld and Nicolson.

Bennett, D. J., Forrester, P. L. and Hassard, J. S. (1990) 'An Application of Decision Process Modelling to Manufacturing System Design', *Omega: International Journal of Management Science* 18 (1): 23–33.

Blecher, M. (1989) 'State Administration and Economic Reform', in D. Goodman and G. Segal (eds) *China at Forty: Mid-Life Crisis?*, Oxford: Clarendon.

Campbell, N. and Adlington, P. (1988) *China Business Strategies: A Survey of Foreign Business Activity in the PRC*, Oxford: Pergamon.

Cyert, R. M. and Welsch, L. A. (eds) (1970) *Management Decision-making: Selected Readings*, Harmondsworth: Penguin.

De Bary, W. T., Chan, W. T. and Watson, B. (1964) *Sources of Chinese Tradition* 1, New York: Columbia.

Hickson, D. J., Butler, R. J., Cray, D., Mallory, G. R. and Wilson, D. (1986) *Top Decisions: Strategic Decision-Making in Organisations*, Oxford: Blackwell.

Ho, Ping-ti (1962) *Ladder of Success in Imperial China*, New York: Columbia.

Hwang, K. K. (1983) 'Face and Favour: Chinese Power Games', unpublished manuscript, University of Taiwan.

Johnson, G. and Scholes, K. (1993) *Exploring Corporate Strategy: Text and Cases*, 3rd edition, London: Prentice-Hall.

Mann, J. (1990) *Beijing Jeep*, New York: Simon and Schuster.

Mintzberg, H., Raisinghani, D. and Theoret, A. (1976) 'The Structure of "Un-Structured" Decision Processes', *Administrative Science Quarterly* 21, June: 246–275.

Porter, R. (ed.) (1990) 'Centralisation, De-Centralisation and Development in China: the Automobile Industry', in N. Campbell and J. Henley (eds) *Joint Ventures and Industrial Change in China*, Greenwich, Conn. and London: JAI Press.

—— (1992) *Reporting the News from China*, London: Royal Institute of International Affairs.

—— (1993) 'The Impact of Recent Political Events on China's Trade and Development: A View from Europe', *Melbourne Journal of Politics* 21: 117–134.

Schurmann, F. (1968) 'The Attack of the Cultural Revolution on Ideology and Organisation', in Ping-ti Ho and Tang Tso (eds) *China in Crisis* 1, Chicago: Chicago University Press.

Simon, H. A. (1957) *Models of Man, Social and Rational: Mathematical Essays on Rational Human Behaviour in a Social Setting*, New York: Wiley.

—— (1960) *The New Science of Management Decision*, New York: Harper.

—— (1965) 'Administrative Decision-making', *Public Administration Review* 25: 31–37.

—— (1976) *Administrative Behaviour*, 3rd edition, New York: Free Press.

Spence, J. (1990) *The Search for Modern China*, New York and London: Norton.

Wang, J. C. F. (1990) *Contemporary Chinese Politics: An Introduction*, Englewood Cliffs, NJ: Prentice-Hall.

Yang, Lien-sheng (1967) 'The Concept of "Pao" as a Basis for Social Relations in China', in J. K. Fairbank (ed.) *Chinese Thought and Institutions*, Chicago: Chicago University Press.

5 Vision, mechanism and logic
Understanding the strategic investment decision making process

Mark Easterby-Smith and Gao Junshan

ABSTRACT

Decision making processes can be portrayed from different perspectives. The one applied in this chapter is to observe the aggregate behaviour of decision participants. A common pattern of strategic investment decision process is found in six cases from each of three British and three Chinese industrial companies. In general, the investment decision making is a fairly structured process due to its need to be incorporated with the routine budget planning and/or strategy review procedures and to get the sanction from an appropriate authority level in the organization. The top management team's view on the issue plays a key role in starting up and putting through the case, which is the result of a 'gestation' process before any formal procedures to deal with the decision have started; and an aggregate rationality appears in which the company tries its best to enhance growth and development potential. It is evident that in both the UK and Chinese contexts multiple criteria are used to evaluate and justify projects, rather than simple financial optimization.

INTRODUCTION

An industrial company makes two kinds of investments: those just for keeping the present operation going and those for introducing changes to the existing capacity, technology, product mix, or market position, etc. (Barwise *et al.* 1987). Being called 'important' or 'strategic' investments and often involving large amounts of capital, the latter have other distinct characteristics in that they contribute more to the company's future growth and development and in most cases appear to the company as open choices. The purpose of this chapter is to examine how a company reaches such a choice and commits itself to the implementation of a particular decision; it is based on six such investment decision cases from the three British and three Chinese companies. Part of the rationale for looking at both British and Chinese companies was to see whether similar processes occurred in the different cultural and political settings of the two countries – thus giving strength to any general observations that might emerge.

There are many different models, or interpretations, of organizational decision making processes. These include the early work on the concept of bounded rationality which explored the informational and computational limitations faced by individuals and organizations when making their choices (Simon 1947; Marsh *et al.*1988); the well known 'garbage can' model which focused on the coincidence of streams of choices, problems, solutions and attentions of participants (Cohen *et al.* 1972; March and Olsen 1976); the dual rationality theory which resulted from a large scale study conducted by the Bradford team, and which tried to connect the mode of a decision process with the political interests and complexity of problems raised by the decision issue (Hickson *et al.* 1986; Rowe 1989).

Although these general theories can apply to investment decision making, and indeed most of them did include investment decision cases to back their models, there were also studies specifically focused on investment decision processes. Examples include the often cited work by Bower, which argued that capital investment should be investigated as an organizational process (Bower 1972); King's six stage investment process model (King 1975); an extensive direct observation study conducted by a group from the London Business School (Marsh *et al.* 1988); and the recent work using the theoretical frame set out by the Bradford studies (Butler *et al.* 1991).

The study reported in this chapter adds another way of seeing the problem by focusing mainly on the aggregate behaviour of decision participants. The analysis is based on the data collected through field interviews conducted by a mixed team of British and Chinese researchers over a period of two years. Most interviews in China were carried out by one Chinese-speaking British researcher and by one Chinese researcher, and vice versa in the UK. Most interview sessions started with a general description by the interviewees of the decision procedures in their company before moving on to a description of the specific case. They were semi-structured in the sense that interviewees were invited to follow a checklist of questions with occasional prompting from the researchers. In general the degree of formality was greater in Chinese companies, although some of our informants in the UK companies insisted on detailed checklists in advance. In addition we found that the degree of formality reduced considerably in meetings with managers after the initial data collection visits had taken place (each lasting 10 to 14 days), and this was aided considerably if we met the managers off site. In all cases an effort was made to triangulate by talking to the main parties involved in the decision (including the presidents in each of the Chinese cases, and to senior general managers in each of the British cases). The average number of informants in the Chinese companies was 12, and we met with some individuals at least four times over the two-year period. All interviews, except in one Chinese company, were taped, translated and transcribed in English.

Table 5.1 gives a summary of the six companies and the decision cases; a more detailed description of the cases has been provided in the Appendix. The code used to identify the companies consists of the references of the national and the industrial sector, which is in accordance with other writings on the project. All six companies are large industrial undertakings, both Sino-Oil and Sino-Chem have been in China's top 50 companies list in terms of turnover in recent years, and Sino-Metal was among the top 500 companies in the country. A similar status is enjoyed by each of their British counterparts. Production levels in each pair were similar, although the number of employees in the British companies was between one-quarter and one-tenth that of each of the Chinese companies due to national differences in industrial and social organization. (Most Chinese enterprises operate as total communities. The work unit, *Danwei* as it is called, has responsibility for all social welfare functions including education, accommodation and health care for all employees and their families,

Table 5.1 Summary of the sample companies and decision cases

Company	Dependency	Main products	Investment for
Brit-Oil	Country company Regional HQ Group (Holding company)[a]	Petrochemicals	An installation to provide feed stocks for downstream products
Brit-Chem	Division Group	General chemicals	Another production line for a main product
Brit-Metal	Division Group (Holding company)[a]	Engineering steels	A second special furnace for high quality steel
Sino-Oil	National company SPC[b] State Council	Oil products and petrochemicals	Expansion to its major production line
Sino-Chem	PPC[b] SPC[b] State Council[c]	General chemicals	A new plant
Sino-Metal	Same as Sino-Chem[c]	General steels	A self-serving power station

Notes:
a It seems that the holding companies rarely exert any direct control
b SPC = State Planning Commission
  PPC = Provincial Planning Commission
c Sino-Chem and Sino-Metal are so called 'locally administered' enterprises which are under direct management of local economic administrations (in the case of investment, the major one is Provincial or Municipal Planning Commission). However, another line comes down from SC and SPC through the industrial ministries in the central government and local industrial bureaux, which mainly co-ordinate the business activities of the respective industries locally and nationally

and all employees of these associated service organizations are reckoned to be on the strength of the main enterprise.) As to the size of the investments, the three British ones are about 6 per cent, 11 per cent and 8 per cent of the total annual capital investment of their ultimate parents, with the company's size relative to the total organization in terms of the employee numbers being about $\frac{1}{36}$, $\frac{1}{7}$, $\frac{1}{5}$. All three Chinese investments were approximately one-tenth of the company's present asset value at the time when the decision was made.

In the following discussion all the six companies are treated as the operating units of other larger organizations. This gives no problems with the three British companies since they are so defined legally, and are practically treated as such, but some conceptual abstraction is needed to deal with the three Chinese ones. Although the three Chinese companies are defined legally as independent economic entities, they are subject to detailed supervision by ministries and other administrative bodies and therefore have only limited authority over capital investments. Thus for our present purpose there is a close parallel between Chinese industrial corporations when combined with the supervisory/sanctioning elements of higher administrative bodies and large industrial groups in the West. We use the term 'company' to refer to the operating corporations only, and other terms such as group, and higher level management/authority will be used to refer to the larger organizations.

Any sizeable investment needs to pass through formal procedures to be approved; the initiation of these formal activities provides a distinct point which divides the whole decision process into two phases: respectively before and after the formal procedures commence. The first phase tends to be rather informal and not very visible, but it is very important for the decision that is finally made. In the rest of the chapter we will first describe some features of this pre-formal phase, before moving on to the more formal and mechanistic stage of the process in which we shall try to understand the configuration of roles and procedures that seem to lead to 'good' decisions being reached. Following from this we examine the logic behind the process, and in particular the arguments that help an idea or a proposal to be accepted and/or which guide the tailoring of it. The chapter concludes with a brief summary of the model and its limitations.

STARTING UP: THE VISION

It is widely accepted that the process of decision making does not start from the moment when an issue or a topic is raised formally for discussion among the decision makers (Astley 1982). As Hickson *et al.* (1986) note:

> One of the most curious features of decision-making is not the time the deliberate process takes but what happens beforehand. There can

be conversations and speculations long before any definite steps are taken towards reaching a decision. ... This or something like it has been called the preconception period ... but this is inappropriate since the conception of a topic has certainly occurred.

(Hickson *et al.* 1986: 106)

This period, which Hickson and colleagues call the 'gestation period', is difficult to study since usually little traceable evidence can be found on how it proceeds, and the individuals involved either cannot recall what happened then or cannot link events to the decision made later. However, by tracing the story backwards it may still be possible to identify some of the key factors.

It is not difficult to find from the six cases summarized at the end of this chapter that when the investment proposal was formally raised in a company, there was already a consensus among top managers in the form of a shared or dominant vision on the situation the company faced, the direction along which the company should move, and a crude idea about what it was going to do. It is this vision which serves as the starting point and the base for the subsequent formal discussion, although it may not be very specific or in great technical detail, and it will vary case by case. In Sino-Oil, people knew that the aim was to expand the capacity of the present plant, but they did not know by how much to expand and in what way to achieve it. In Brit-Metal, both the technology and the required capacity were already known before the company formally started work on the investment proposal.

This part of the decision making process can be vague and complex, and managers may have great difficulty recalling with clarity what took place. For example a manager from Sino-Chem commented: 'The whole process was very complex, many events intersected with each other, you cannot draw clear lines between stages. A scheme usually formed as a natural result.' There was a similar comment from a Brit-Oil manager: 'I couldn't honestly swear as to who was the first person to say, "That needs to be done".' It happened very much along the line.'

But on the other side this lack of traceability shows the very informal character of the vision forming process. After the germ of an idea had started with somebody in the company, it might spread quickly around a circle of people and reach top managers in a range of unobtrusive ways such as: chatting over lunch or during tea breaks, linking the idea in with the transmission of news or gossip, providing hints embedded in 'pure' technical or professional information; or overtly, through notes, memos, or meetings.

To be effective, in the sense that it will be able to originate a specific proposal or raise a topic for formal discussion, the vision must be perceived and accepted by top managers, at least the major ones who hold the general responsibility for the organization or who are in charge of the specific area the project belongs to (i.e. the idea must fit in with the current rationales/strategies/recipes held by top people). Usually it will also be shared or accepted by the relevant lower level managers, because their detailed knowledge will be necessary in legitimizing the proposal. The origin of the vision may be anywhere in the company; it may even have been with the company when it was created, as in the examples of Brit-Chem and Sino-Chem (which were new organizations carved out of larger and older organizations). The internal and external changes and potential opportunities will be sensed by individuals because of their roles/ responsibilities, and then passed to the centre (top management) of the company through the variety of ways mentioned above. Personal motivations may vary, but are likely to include in varying degrees personal goals, concern for the company, etc. It seems that the closer the initiator is to the centre, the easier and quicker is the spread of the initial notion. This is illustrated by the contrasting examples of Sino-Metal and Brit-Chem: the rapid take-up of the idea in Brit-Chem may be linked to its origination with senior line managers; on the other hand, in Sino-Met the idea came from a relatively junior utility engineer, and adoption was very much slower.

However, the people involved in the process do not simply pass on whatever they receive, they normally add their own views, preferences, interpretations and judgments, and delete the parts they do not like; they might also impede, or simply stop, the transmission. It is a process of screening, enhancing, refining, and altering the original conception. Normally the aggregate result of this process is likely to be of benefit to the company so long as the individuals involved do not deliberately try to damage the organization and have adequate knowledge and experience in the relevant area. We believe that this process is the main reason why investment proposals are rarely turned down by the formal examining procedures: an inappropriate proposal would have been killed well before any formal discussions on it had started.

This is similar to the view of Mintzberg and Quinn (1991) who suggest that 'perspective' is one of five key features of strategy.

> Strategy is a perspective, its content consisting not just of a chosen position but of an ingrained way of perceiving the world. ... What is of key importance about this fifth definition is that the perspective is shared. ... In effect, when we talk of strategy in this context, we are entering the realm of the collective mind – individuals united by common thinking and/or behavior.
>
> (Mintzburg and Quinn 1991: 16–17)

This argument adds another way of understanding the vision and its forming process, especially the role in the process of strategic investment decision making. Whether the strategy is made up of the stream of decisions or individual decisions derived from overall strategy might be still in dispute (Barwise *et al.* 1987; Mintzberg *et al.* 1990), but there should be no doubt that the vision forming process during the gestation period is crucial to the decision made afterwards.

SANCTIONING AND CONTROL: THE MECHANISM

The latent gestation of the topic or the issue will surface when it is raised formally to be discussed. It usually starts with the inclusion of the project in the long-term plans for future development. Often a functional or business department, or a special working team is asked to undertake or co-ordinate the task, since a lot of technical work such as market forecasting, financial analysis and engineering calculations are needed. Once formally launched, the case is subject to a series of formal examinations and sanctions. Some of these procedures are stipulated in written documents and some of them simply kept as conventions, but in either case they are clearly understood and properly followed. In the light of this, the investment decisions could be classified as 'programmed' (Simon 1960) or 'structured' (Mintzberg *et al.* 1976) decisions; they are 'routine, repetitive', and 'definite procedures' do exist to handle them (Simon 1960) even for very big ones as in our examples.

In the introduction we emphasized that the six sample companies all can be viewed as the operating units of larger organizations. A distinguishing feature of these larger (or ultimate) organizations is that they theoretically have unlimited investment sanctioning authority. All of the operating units have investment ceilings beyond which any new proposal must be referred up to the larger organization. As shown in Table 5.1 there are also intermediate administrative bodies between the two ends. The terms used in this schema have had to be adapted a little because of the differences between Chinese and UK organizations with regard to context, structure and legal status. In some cases we have had to draw artificial boundaries around these companies because they are the logical units in which the particular decisions were considered, without necessarily being the legal entities.

Several observations are due from this conception. First, gestation mainly took place inside the operating unit, although sometimes there might be informal contacts with higher level management or even with people external to the organization. Second, each level of management had its own authorization power over investment (see Table 5.2). We were told that the distribution of this power was often adjusted by the higher level authorities. The point we want to make here is that the discretion of the authority must be kept at a level that would not cause any great trouble to the organization of that level if a mistake was made. Third, it was usually the operating unit which was the initiator and the owner of the project, and managers from this unit would have to push the case through all the intermediate levels until it finally reached the person/group/authority with power to give the final sanction. Last, different rationales were used to judge the project by different levels of management, a general trend would be that more consideration would be given to broad implications and less to technical aspects. Bower (1972: 80) included this effect in his process model of investment by identifying three phases as follows: 'the initiating phase of the process is triggered in product–market terms, the corporate phase in company–environment terms, and the integrating phase in terms of part–whole relationship'.

Bower further linked these to the five levels of management in the organization he studied:

> The corporate and group managers usually carry out the corporate phase of the processes . . . although the group occasionally performs an integrating role. The product group managers, and the area general managers both carry out the initiating phase of the process, although the general managers occasionally play an integrating role in the large multi-product divisions. Finally, the division accomplishes whatever integration is achieved.
>
> (Bower 1972: 81)

Although they do not usually have any direct responsibility, the functional departments and their personnel are always active participants in the process of making investment decisions. In the operating units they work out technical details and compile the proposal, at higher levels the chief executives rely on their analysis and advice to judge the proposal which has been put forward by lower level management – since they are the experts and specialists. So in a sense they are the real gate-keepers.

Table 5.2 Examples of investment controls

Body of authorization	Maximum investment authority[a]
British example: Brit-Oil	
Group[c] (ultimate owner)	> 40 (5,000)[b]
Region[c]	40
Country	20
Brit-Oil (operating unit)	1
Chinese example: Sino-Oil	
State Council (ultimate owner)	> 20
State Planning Commission	20
National company	6
Sino-Oil (operating unit)	1 (20)[b]

Notes:
a Although the exchange rate at the time of this study was £1 = 8RMB, the differences in costs and living standards between the two countries mean that figures expressed in sterling and Renminbi are roughly equivalent
b The figures in brackets are estimates of the annual capital investment at that level of organization measured by authorization limit given to the operating units
c They are described in the schedule provided by the company as authorized by country corporation with 'sound' support from these authorities

A manager from Sino-Oil made this point by saying: 'These functional departments are more serious than the ministers. If they don't say good things about your project, then the project cannot proceed.'

We found in our examples that the people responsible for pushing a particular case through seemed to know exactly what they were doing and how to ease its path. They regularly made use of informal and individual contacts, asking opinions and suggestions, sending a 'courtesy copy' of the draft proposal, and so on. This is how a manager from Brit-Chem summarized it:

> There is a general rule that you make sure that people feel that they have the opportunity to make comments and have influence, that you don't give them any surprises or put them in any embarrassing positions. . . . We involve them all as early as possible, even when it is still a vague idea. It is courtesy, good practice and strategic influencing at its best.

The functional departments have another important channel for influencing investment decisions, through their roles as monitor and regulator on issues in the specific areas across the organization. By formulating policies, standards and procedures, by organizing conferences, meetings and discussions, and by consulting outside agencies they can create and modify the decision context, which will limit greatly the range of choices and behaviour of the operating unit and its managers. The mechanisms vary a little from company to company. Within Brit-Oil there is an independent consulting company which must be consulted when evaluating any significant investment decisions, and this is similar to the use in China of specialist agencies which must be consulted in relation to the technical and commercial feasibility of major project proposals (as was the case in Sino-Oil). In Brit-Chem there are visits by the planners in the parent company every six months in which they check out the progress of strategic plans in each of the operating units. They have a particular remit to ensure the maintenance of standards across the whole organization in relation to technical quality, environmental protection and corporate image. Criteria for observing these standards are summarized in a booklet that is circulated to all line managers. In the Chinese cases the independent power of the functional departments is less because general standards such as these are pre-specified as national regulations and will apply to all organizations willy-nilly.

These formalities provide high level management with ways to influence and control the investment activities at lower levels. There are various reasons to argue that it is 'not just a ritual' (Marsh *et al.* 1988). We suggested an explanation in the previous section of why it is very rare for an investment proposal to be turned down by those people who hold the sanctioning power. Being aware that the case will be examined and evaluated later can make those who prepare it very careful in the first place. They will try to make it conform as far as possible to the strategy, policy, restrictions and rules already established, and/or they may try to introduce changes into the existing rules beforehand. So the real power is not just the final yes/no vote in the board room but the existence of such routine itself. Marsh *et al.* (1988) come to a similar conclusion which they summarize as follows:

> although projects were rarely turned down by Group, the threat of rejection was taken very seriously. Indeed, rejections were probably rare because Group was taken seriously and because the divisions had a fairly clear idea what would prove acceptable.
>
> (Marsh *et al.* 1988: 109)

There are other significant mechanisms built into the formal structure of the organization to enable top management to control and influence investment decisions, though some of them may still seem rather indirect. These include personal arrangements for maintaining control, for example, the so called 'wearing two hats' (Marsh *et al.* 1988). This involves the assignment of cross-level responsibilities to chief executives, which is a common practice in many large corporations, including some of our sample companies. Annual business reviews are used in most organizations and these can facilitate the monitoring of targets and objectives; and the removal and/or appointment of key personnel is a final measure that top management can take. A manager in Brit-Oil described it to the interviewers: 'It we do something really bad, then it will come through as part of the annual appraisal, and then our chairman will be kicked and he will kick down the line.'

SCRAPING THROUGH: THE LOGIC

Financial validity was a key criterion in the evaluation and justification of each of our investment projects, but it was by no means the only one. Even financial professionals are coming to recognize and agree on it, as reported by Romano *et al.* (1988) on the basis of two National Accounting Association studies:

> What really comes through is an emerging belief that 'if it's the right thing to do, our firm is going to do it'. Investment justification is now a broad subject, and top managers will not allow their firms to be undermined competitively simply because 'the numbers don't come out'.
>
> (Romano *et al.* 1988: 42)

The question is then what makes a project 'the right thing'. We found from this study that apart from financial considerations, there were three other aspects which attracted much of the managers' attention during the decision making process: the company's strategy, the technology to be used, and the public image effect of the project. Together with financial

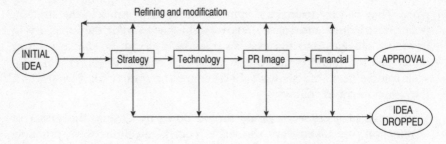

Figure 5.1 Potential sequence of considerations in investment decision making process

viability they served as the main criteria judging the project, and as guidelines for refining or modifying the initial idea and proposal (see Figure 5.1).

There is little agreement about the precise definition of strategy or on the relation between strategic decisions and strategy. We use it here, as did the managers in our field investigations, to refer to two things: the long-term plan, and the general policy towards activities in specific areas, which may or may not be in written form. It was recognized in each company that large investments must always conform to the wider strategy. We were told at Brit-Metal: 'The first thing you must have is the relationship of the proposal to the company strategy and the total sector strategy.'

The fate of Brit-Metal's VAR project spins the story in another way. The project got its high priority only after the change of the organizational structure, which in fact redefined the business area of the group and the company's position in the group. With changes of internal and external structures and conditions, decision makers have to change their ways of thinking and re-evaluate the directions they try to give to the company.

When making investment decisions, managers tried to assess how the projects would contribute to the long-term growth and development of their organization. This was the kernel of strategy from their point of view, however it was defined formally. The strategic significance of the six cases in this sense was: to increase market shares (Brit-Metal, Sino-Chem); to enhance positions in the industry (Brit-Chem, Sino-Oil); and to remove or reduce the impact of external constraints (Brit-Oil, Sino-Metal). This not only explains why the operating units compete with each other for funds and projects; it also suggests that top management will use their influence and control to ensure that this competition does not harm the overall organization. A Brit-Oil manager was very clear on the point:

We understand where our roles and responsibilities lie and how we should really be working for the common good. Whenever we have meaningful conversations rather than disputes, e.g. over transfer prices between oils and chemicals, we are always looking at the end of the day for what is the right thing for the Country Corporation.

Middle management and the ultimate authorities do not necessarily just wait and check proposals from the operating unit, as was the case in Sino-Metal. They will often actively help them to get the proposal through the system, especially when the project appears to fit with their own agendas.

There are sound reasons to perceive technological considerations as being another main component of the underlying logic of the investment decision making process. Since a majority of investments in industrial firms are technologically based, or even driven by technology, the decision process requires many participants from the technical area. This will undoubtedly affect both the course and the result of the process. It was also difficult, in our cases, to separate the evaluation and choice of technical aspects from the overall evaluation of the project. In the end the technology might look like simply a means towards achieving a higher level objective, but in fact the two streams were interwoven, resulting in a form of 'muddling through' (Lindblom 1959). As more technical details are explored and choices made, more precise financial predictions can be made and a clearer view of other impacts can be had. The 'snow ball' is rolled by many hands including some technical ones, and therefore its final shape is bound to have a technical dimension.

According to Brunsson (1989) the outputs of an organization need to be multiple, 'an organization's production and promotion activities need not be limited to physical products'. We found that companies were keen to create and keep a good public image and external relations, and took the investment opportunity as one means of achieving the goal. In describing the VAR decision process a Brit-Metal manager told the interviewers:

> We needed to ensure that the area had a certain PR image. In the first scheme the PR image, and still in this present scheme, was quite high up the agenda ... We are looking for a modern plant not only for the technical aspects that a modern plant would give us but also for the public relations.

Over half of the total expenditure in Brit-Chem's investment (56 per cent) went into peripheral equipment for treating the waste water discharged from the process, even though, according to the managers interviewed, the water authority was already satisfied with the environmental standards, and the company 'had and still does have permission to put it in the river' However, there was growing public perception that this was an unacceptable practice. Thus the company's main motivation was to improve its PR image and external relations, although this might also be seen as a protective measure anticipating further strengthening of environmental regulations.

While the British managers focus on the nice impression that a new plant would give to their customers and on showing the company's concern for the environment, their Chinese colleagues attempt to strengthen their companies' public images and external relations by emphasizing the contributions to the state's need and the fulfilment of their social obligations. Lu and Heard (1992) make the observation that in Chinese companies 'an investment project was painted with moral colours claiming its patriotic contribution to modernizing China'. We believe that this painting cannot be done without cost, and it should be seen as an investment in the company's PR image and external relations, as exemplified by this comment from Sino-Oil:

> The project is not very profitable for our company. But firstly it is of benefit for the state ... the country needs the product, and secondly it is good for society in terms of employment. There are therefore invisible benefits.

The financial evaluation and justification was made after the other considerations, and only those projects which passed them could reach it. There is no doubt on its key role in determining the fate of a project, especially because higher level discussions tend to be conducted more in financial terms, but it seems that the financial evaluation is more useful for internal reference than are cross-organizational comparisons, since different companies may use different sets of criteria, with different internal priorities and interpretations. Even where the same criteria and priorities were used, the parameters in the formulas and predictions on the uncertain variables needed by the calculations would hardly be the same in different organizations. In fact, as explained in the previous section, it is an important part of the control mechanism to impose through functional departments a consistent set of indexes, parameters and predictions against which to evaluate projects.

These four considerations existed implicitly in the minds of managers involved during the gestation period, and became explicit in the subsequent formal evaluation and approval stages. They functioned in one sense like a set of screens which block the weak cases from passing, and in another way like a set of rolling mills which mould the case into its proper shape. This means that the latter elements do not come into play until the earlier ones have been satisfied. A project might need to go through several rounds of this sequential examination before getting the final sanction, with more details being included at each round. Loops, short cuts, bypasses can exist but it is very unlikely that the order of the stages will be affected; in other words, passing through the previous justifications is a necessary condition for reaching the next one.

CONCLUSION

By attending to the aggregate behaviour of participants, three aspects of the strategic investment decision making process have been analysed: the underlying logic that affects the reasonings applied when initiating a project and scrutinizing the proposal; the sanctioning and control mechanism that helps to ensure that a rational or 'good' choice is made; and the gestation period during which the idea is cultivated and a common ground is prepared for a particular investment decision. These observations provide a coherent picture on how the strategic investment decisions are made and how managers behave during the process under 'the rules of games' which are 'expressed in the constitution and structure of the organization' (Hickson 1987).

Although the cases in this study have been drawn from large and mature industrial companies under normal situations, and the decision topics covered by the samples are limited to product and technology only, we expect that the pattern revealed would be generally applicable to any strategic investment decision making processes. More work needs to be done to test the allegation on a larger range of organizational types and sizes, as well as decision topics. It would also be interesting to see how investment decisions are made under more dynamic or critical situations, for example when the company's survival is severely threatened, or in companies which are in their early growing stages.

Due to the level of analysis chosen in the study, several aspects of decision process were covered only to a limited extent, notably the political and social interactions of the participants. Also, little effort has been made towards examining the effect on decision making processes of the culture and economic system differences of the two countries, which have been the main themes of many studies (Pettigrew 1973; Child and Tayeb 1983; Child and Lu 1990; Lu and Heard 1992). However, the study presented here might suggest that the political and social interactions during the investment decision making process, and the effects of cultural differences, are relevant mainly at the level of the individual, and they do not have a significant impact on the main stream of the process when considered at the level of the organization as a whole. Indeed, both the process and the results of decision processes are remarkably similar in Chinese and UK organizations.

APPENDIX: BRIEF DESCRIPTION OF DECISION CASES

Brit-Oil's PP Splitter investment

This investment greatly reduced the company's dependence on external suppliers for the feedstock of a strategic product. Brit-Oil used to have its own facilities to produce the feedstock but they were shut down in a rationalization of the production structure shortly after the oil crisis in early 1970s. Although this improved the company's economic performance, it resulted in a situation where it had to rely on external suppliers for all of this key feedstock. The company had been trying to solve the problem since then but no satisfactory measure had been found until this decision was proposed.

The suggestion came from a sister company in 1986. At the time this other company was in the process of renewing its oil refinery installation and associated processes, amongst which the main one was a gas separation tower. With careful maintenance the old tower would have been able to serve the new refinery installation, but many people did not like to see 'an inherently old process' stuck onto 'the brand new shining' installations. However, the straight replacement of the tower could not be justified on pure financial grounds. Thus the idea emerged of asking Brit-Oil to share the cost of replacing the tower in return for the inclusion of a 'PP Splitter' in the installation. This would provide Brit-Oil directly with the necessary feedstock (Brit-Oil's processing device and the refinery installation are in the same production site shared by the two companies). It was estimated that in this way Brit-Oil would save up to half of the investment that would have been required for it to build a separate facility for the same purpose.

The idea gained support from the country corporation and the group's headquarters. The two companies negotiated on how to share the investment as well as on the issues of the future operation and management of the plant. A preliminary estimate of the project was listed in Brit-Oil's budget plan for 1986 and a design fee of about 10 per cent of the overall estimate was approved in August 1986. The proposal went through country corporation, regional headquarters and was finally sanctioned in September 1987 by the international group committee of managing directors.

Due to the overall material balance, after the PP Splitter had been commissioned the company realized that it would have to stop the production of some other downstream products or buy their feedstock from external suppliers. The company made the second choice and the product selected was one that was to be given up shortly according to the company's product strategy.

Brit-Chem's MMA plant investment

MMA has been a major product for the group to which Brit-Chem belongs. Being one of the few producers of MMA, the group possesses a substantial share in its world market and enjoys a good profit from it. At the time the decision was made, the group had two factories producing MMA, one in the UK and one overseas. But they felt the company could benefit more if they further expanded their production capacity.

As the result of a major re-organization of the wider group, Brit-Chem was established in 1987 to take care of the group's industrial chemical business, including MMA. From the outset MMA and associated downstream products have been the main focus of Brit-Chem's business. It is said that the managing director of the recently formed Brit-Chem encouraged the general manager in charge of MMA business by saying 'You're not pushing this business hard enough'.

A proposal to build another production facility in one of the existing factories was quickly produced by this general manager for the company's annual autumn budget review. In the wake of recent disquiet from local residents and the press about environmental impact, the proposal also included an acid recovery plant to treat the effluent from both the new and the old production plants. After the budget meeting a brief proposal was prepared by the department in charge of MMA business, which was circulated among other functional and business departments before being discussed and approved in a weekly meeting of the company's chief executives.

The next step was for the general manager and one of his business managers to write a more detailed proposal and to gain support from functional departments in the group's headquarters. This took about four months to accomplish. In the summer of 1988 the general manager reported on the MMA business situation and introduced the idea of this project in his strategy review exercise with the group's main board, the highest authority in the organization, which agreed the investment in principle. Later, in that year's autumn budget review, the MMA project was formally included in the company's three-year capital programme.

A project manager was appointed in early 1989 and then a steering committee was formed to co-ordinate further work. The group's main board finally approved the investment in June 1990, according to the schedule that had been established three years previously. Before the final sanction about 10 per cent of the capital had been spent and 25 per cent of detailed design work had been completed.

Brit-Met's VAR furnace investment

Brit-Metal used to be a special steel plant under a large state owned steel corporation. In the late 1970s, its parent company at that time signed an agreement with another steel producer promising not to enter the vacuum arc remelting (VAR) product market in exchange for a concession in another product market. However, Brit-Met bought a second-hand VAR furnace in 1982 when the agreement expired, and the product proved successful in its main market, the USA.

The sales manager for VAR products in North America was enthusiastic about the technology due to his personal background of technical research in the field. It was also evident that there was an opportunity to increase the company's sales in the States. In conjunction with several other people in Brit-Met he started to push for another VAR in 1985, but initially did not get much support from above. The 'official' reason was that the market needed to be tested further, but some other factors existed, including the views of some functional departments of the parent company that 'it was a nuisance value' because of the relatively small quantity of the product.

The advocates continued their campaign until Brit-Met's managing director became convinced in early 1986. The sales manager was asked to write a preliminary proposal. Then came the privatization of the parent company in April 1986, and Brit-Met became the main constituent of a newly established company designated for special steel production. Following this change of ownership and the establishment of a new management structure, Brit-Met decided to continue the work towards another VAR furnace. The technical department was given the job of co-ordinating a formal proposal.

The formal proposal was finished and agreed by all relevant functional departments in August 1986. It was then included in the company's annual budget programme after approval by the operational director and the company's management committee. With the acceptance by the group strategic conference in October 1986 the project got the final approval from the group's board in December 1986.

Sino-Oil's ethylene plant investment

By introducing a major ethylene plant in the mid 1970s, Sino-Oil managed to reach the top of the Chinese petrochemical industry. The company wanted to build another ethylene plant after the first one had been commissioned, but failed due to the political and economic situation of China at that time. In a wide ranging internal discussion in 1985 on the company's future, especially on how to keep its position in the industry, some people raised the question of expanding ethylene capacity again but it was still not given a place sufficiently high on the agenda.

The issue was raised again in 1989, and this time the company was almost forced into a corner: the plant needed a main shut down for main-tenance due to its long service; indeed it had reached a point where there were serious concerns about its safety. In view of these circumstances the long-term planning department compiled a scheme to increase capacity by 20 per cent, but this did not win through. A significant criticism of the proposal was that it was 'not great enough', and that it would not make sure of 'keeping Sino-Oil on the top'. The top management of the company shared similar views.

Based on this feedback the long-term planning department revised, or more precisely, rewrote the scheme in February 1990 and proposed to increase the original capacity by 50 per cent. While further discussions were being carried on in the company, the top managers started to talk to the national corporation to gain their support. Six months later Sino-Oil sent the formal proposal through the national corporation to the State Planning Commission and State Council for final sanction. It was expected at the time of investigation that the State Council would grant this by the end of 1991.

Sino-Oil used three main arguments to back their case: first, that it would reduce the ethylene shortage in the domestic market and bring the company more profits; second, it would set an example and provide experience for other companies in the industry on the renovation of similar plants; and third, it would provide the extra ethylene with only half the amount of crude oil required by a normal plant for the same output, through the alteration of the product mix.

Sino-Chem's caprolactum plant investment

Sino-Chem is among the oldest of the major industrial firms in China and has faced recently the problem of updating its technology and product mix to retain its vitality. The company made great efforts during the 1970s to extend its business into petrochemicals with the hope that this would bring a bright future; but it turned out not to have a very happy ending. In 1983 Sino-Chem lost its petrochemical plants which had been built over the previous 10 years when the state carried out a substantial industrial management reform, which placed petrochemical manufacturers under another line of administration from the one to which Sino-Chem belongs. The company had, in a way, brought up a child for some one else.

The idea of the caprolactum could be traced back to the days when the company was developing its petrochemical capacity in the 1970s. It was proposed as a way of further processing a by-product of the ethylene plant that had been built at that time, but it had been kept only informally as an idea for future development up to 1983, when the petrochemical section was removed from the company's immediate control.

An understanding was achieved among the relevant parties when Sino-Chem was divided in 1983, that the caprolactum plant would be left to Sino-Chem and the new company would provide the old company with the main feedstock required by the plant. Reasons given for this decision include: that the old company should be left with some favourable opportunities; that it produced all other raw materials needed; that it had technical and managerial expertise since the company had run a small caprolactum plant for more than 30 years. An interesting point was that this plant had not been taken away in the recent restructuring because it was located inside the old site, which was about 10 miles away from the newly built petrochemical complex, and was fully ingrated into the processes of the old company.

Sino-Chem took the caprolactum as its first major investment project after the de-merger. The newly appointed president contacted the higher authorities to seek support while staff from the long-term planning department were working on a formal proposal. The proposal was finished and submitted to the Ministry of Chemical Industry and Provincial Planning Commission in July 1984. Then, with the approval of the ministry and the commission it was handed to the State Planning Commission who gave the green light in March 1985. The company then started the preliminary design and other preparations including the setting up of a joint venture company to be in charge of fund raising, and the management of construction and later operation of the plant. The preliminary design was finished in August 1986 and sent up through the same route, which was finally sanctioned by the State Council in March 1987.

Sino-Metal's self-serving power station investment

At least two background streams converge in this decision. The first one is that the company is located in an area where electricity is in short supply. On average the company can only get 80 per cent of its demand from the grid. The second one is that since the late 1970s the Ministry of Metallurgy has been encouraging steel works to adopt technology that can combine heat and power supplies, since this is more efficient economically and better for energy conservation.

The idea of a self-serving power station originated from a utility engineer in 1976, but it did not draw much attention from top managers until 1984, when the electricity shortage became worse and more complaints appeared about the performance of the steam-supplying boilers, with regard not only to their high coal consumption but also to some stability and reliability problems on account of their age and the technology used. The engineer's proposal was dug up and discussed, which resulted in the decision to replace these boilers with a self-serving power station.

A design institute was invited in April 1984 to join the company's long-term planning and designing department to work out the proposal and the preliminary design. It took them four months to finish the job. The Municipal Metallurgy Corporation, Sino-Metal's immediate higher authority, approved the proposal in October and sent it to the Ministry of Metallurgy and the State Planning Commission. It was soon found that the amount of foreign currency the company required for importing equipment was above the new authorization limit of the ministry, which meant more authorities would be involved in the approval process. Following suggestions from the ministry and the commission, Sino-Met revised the proposal, lowering the foreign currency application to just below the ministry's authorization limit. The project was formally sanctioned by the ministry in May 1985.

Subsequently it turned out that the real expenditure of foreign currency exceeded the approved level due to inflation and changes of exchange rate (the money spent was Japanese yen while the application was made in US dollars).

ACKNOWLEDGEMENTS

We are most grateful to the Economic and Social Science Research Council, the Chinese National Science Funding Council and the British Council for financial support of this project. In addition we would like to thank Dr Lu Yuan and Ms Rachel Heard who carried out the bulk of the field work and analysis associated with the case studies discussed in this paper.

REFERENCES

Astley, W., Axelsson, R., Butler, R., Hickson, D. and Wilson, D. (1982) 'Complexity and cleavage: dual explanations of strategic decision-making', *Journal of Management Studies* 19 (4): 357–375.
Barwise, P., Marsh, P. and Wensley, R. (1987) 'Strategic investment decisions', *Research in Marketing* 9: 1–57.
Bower, J. (1972) *Managing the resource allocation process*, Boston, Mass.: Division of Research, Harvard Business School.
Brunsson, N. (1989) *The Organisation of Hypocrisy*, Chichester: John Wiley.
Butler, R., Davies, L., Pike, R. and Sharpe, J. (1991) 'Strategic investment decision-making: complexities, politics and processes', *Journal of Management Studies* 28 (4): 395–415.
Carlisle, Y. (forthcoming) 'The concept of ideology and work motivation', *Organisation Studies*.
Child, J. and Tayeb, M. (1983) 'Theoretical perspectives in cross-national organisational research', *International Studies of Management and Organisation* 12: 23–70.
Child, J. and Lu, Y. (1990) 'Industrial decision-making under China's reform: 1985–1988', *Organisation Studies* 11: 321–351.
Cohen, M., March, J. and Olsen, J. (1972) 'A garbage can model of organisational choice', *Administrative Science Quarterly* 17: 1–25.
ESRC China Project (1992) 'A summary report: a comparison of investment decision processes in Chinese and British industry', Working Paper, Lancaster: Department of Management Learning, Lancaster University.
Hickson, D. (1987) 'Decision-making at the top of organisations', *Annual Review of Sociology* 13: 165–192.
Hickson, D., Butler, R., Cray, D., Mallory, G. and Wilson, D. (1986) *Top Decisions: Strategic Decision-Making in Organisations*, Oxford: Basil Blackwell.
King, P. (1975) 'Is the emphasis of capital budgeting theory misplaced?', *Journal of Business Finance & Accounting* 2: 69–82.
Lindblom, C. (1959) 'The science of muddling through', *Public Administration Review* 19: 79–88.
Lu, Y. and Heard, R. (1992) 'A comparison of investment decisions in China and Britain', paper presented at the 6th Annual Conference of BAM, Bradford: Bradford University.
March, J. (1989) 'Introduction: a chronicle of speculations about decision-making in organizations', in J. March (ed.) *Decisions and Organisations*: 1–21, Oxford: Basil Blackwell.

March, J. and Olsen, J. (1976) *Ambiguity and Choice in Organisations*, Bergen, Oslo, & Tromso: Universitetsforlaget.

Marsh, P., Barwise, P., Thomas, K. and Wensley, R. (1988) 'Managing strategic investment decisions', in A. M. Pettigrew (ed.) *Competitiveness and the Management Process*: 86–136, Oxford: Basil Blackwell.

Mintzberg, H., Raisinghani, D. and Theórêt, A. (1976) 'The structure of "unstructured" decision processes', *Administrative Science Quarterly* 21: 246–275.

Mintzberg, H., Waters, J., Pettigrew, A. and Butler, R. (1990) 'Studying deciding: an exchange of views between Mintzberg and Waters, Pettigrew, and Butler', *Organisation Studies* 11 (1): 1–16.

Mintzberg, H. and Quinn, J. (1991) *The Strategy Process: Concepts, Contexts, Cases* (2nd ed.), Englewood Cliffs, NJ: Prentice-Hall.

Morgan, G. (1986) *Images of Organisations*, Beverly Hills, Cal.: Sage.

Pettigrew, A. (1973) *The Politics of Organisational Decision-making*, London: Tavistock.

Romano, P., Kaplan, R., Riordian, J., Krowe, A. and Scott, J. (1988) 'The capital investment decision – how to make it', *Financial Executive* 4 (4): 40–47.

Rowe, C. (1989) 'Analysing management decision-making: further thoughts after the Bradford studies', *Journal of Management Studies* 26: 29–46.

Simon, H. (1960) *Administrative Behaviour*, New York: Free Press.

—— *The New Science of Management Decision*, New York: Harper & Row.

Part III
Enterprise challenges

6 An international perspective on China's township enterprises

Hong Liu, Nigel Campbell, Lu Zheng and Wang Yanzhong

ABSTRACT

Over the last decade, China has enjoyed the world's fastest growth and township enterprises (TEs) in China have been a key player. However, hitherto little attention has been paid to TEs by students of international business/marketing. This paper addresses TEs' development from an international perspective. Producing about one-third of China's total exports and about one-quarter of China's GNP, TEs have a number of distinctive characteristics: flexible and market driven, dedicated to human resources, innovation and quality, and having an international orientation. Many TEs are engaged in foreign direct investment. In many business areas, TEs can be an appropriate partner for Western companies to pursue a global sourcing strategy and penetrate China's domestic markets. The development of joint ventures with TEs enjoys numerous benefits, compared with SOEs. It is envisaged that joint ventures with TEs also have long-term strategic implications for global companies, as TEs are emerging as a strong competitor in China's markets.

INTRODUCTION

Over the last decade, China has enjoyed the world's fastest growth of both GNP and foreign trade. In 1992, China recorded GNP growth of 12.8 per cent and expects continuing growth of about 8 per cent annually to the end of the century (*Financial Times* 27–28 February 1993). Foreign investment in China in 1992 quadrupled, and the number of new investment projects exceeded 40,000, a figure equivalent to the total over the last 13 years (*Financial Times* 16 February 1993). This surge of foreign investment shows no sign of diminishing.

It may come as a surprise to many Western people that a new type of organization, 'township enterprises' (TEs), has been a key engine driving China's economy forward. In the coastal cities and areas, particularly in southern China, the main source of China's phenomenal growth, TEs have been strongest. In 1992, TEs' exports accounted for about 42 per cent of

China's total exports, and their production represented about 32 per cent of China's GDP (*The Economist* 28 November 1992). According to China's Township Enterprise Association, by 2000, TEs will generate 50 per cent of China's GDP and 55 per cent of its total industrial output.

Despite the important position of township enterprises in China's economic development, little attention has been paid to TEs by scholars in the fields of management and international business/marketing. This chapter examines the role of township enterprises in China's foreign trade, analyses their behaviour and development constraints, and discusses implications and the strategic choice for Western firms to develop a partnership with TEs in their global and China business strategies.

THE DEVELOPMENT OF TOWNSHIP ENTERPRISES

There are four types of township enterprises defined by a government document in 1984: county- and township-run enterprises, village-run enterprises, farmers' co-operatives, and individual or family-run businesses.

Many of the first two types, that is, county-, township- or village-run enterprises, followed on from the 'commune- and brigade-run' enterprises, at the time of the Great Leap Forward, which started at the end of 1958. During this period the whole nation became involved in industrial development led by steel making, and rural enterprises mushroomed. Many were closed by the government at the beginning of the 1960s, because of a lack of technology, supplies, and funds, or simply because of unsaleable products. In 1960 there were 117,000 commune- and brigade-run enterprises, whilst in 1964 only 10,600 remained (*The Almanac of China's Statistics 1991*).

Recognising the importance of rural industry in providing employment for an emerging surplus labour force and for the generation of capital for agricultural development, in 1966, the State Council came out with a new plan in order to prevent mistakes similar to the Great Leap Forward. As a result, a number of new regulations were issued. For instance, only organizations at or above the commune level were encouraged to run the 'five small industries': iron and steel, fertilizer, agricultural machinery, cement, and energy (including coal and hydroelectric power). These organizations were required to be self-financed, to employ local labour, utilize local materials, and produce products which satisfied local needs.

A substantial rural industry is a uniquely Chinese phenomenon. The shift of farm labour from agricultural into non-agricultural sectors is a common trend during the process of industrialization in any country. It usually leads to a build up of labour and industry in urban areas. However, in China, this has not happened because of the large surplus urban labour force. Furthermore, China's urban resident registration system, whereby every urban citizen has to be registered at the local police station to be able to live in the urban area, restricts the mobility of the labour force.

Instead, the surplus labour on the land was channelled into the development of rural industry. This has helped to reduce the huge gap between rural and urban areas and improve farmers' living standards. Rural industry has also helped agricultural development, such as infrastructure construction and the provision of agricultural supplies.

These advantages stemming from the development of rural industry helped to ensure the smooth implementation of the 1966 regulations, despite their introduction at the same time as the Cultural Revolution. The number of enterprises in the 'five small industries' grew rapidly. For example, in 1965 (before the Cultural Revolution started), there were 12,200 commune-run enterprises, whilst in 1977 (when the Cultural Revolution ended), the number of commune-run enterprises reached 133,000. By 1977, the 'five small industries' produced 50 per cent of China's nitrogenous fertilizer, 64 per cent of cement, and 33 per cent of hydro-electric power.

Despite this growth, the real potential of rural industry was restricted by the priority given to heavy industry. Administrative measures were used as well as the so-called 'scissors pricing' policy of 'high price for industrial products and low price for agricultural products'. This shifted funds from agricultural to industrial sectors. In short, the development of commune- and brigade-run enterprises was constrained by government policy, inadequate financial resources and a lack of real incentives.

At the end of the 1970s, the 'contract responsibility' system replaced the 'people's commune' system, and commune- and brigade-run enterprises began to enjoy greater autonomy. At last they had an incentive to increase production, improve productivity, and develop new businesses. In addition, the government adopted various policies and measures encouraging and supporting the development of commune- and brigade-run enterprises such as favourable loans (low interest, interest subsidies or exemption, priority provision of loans), tax reduction or exemption, and technical assistance. All these measures laid the foundations for the development of rural industries. In 1984, commune- and brigade-run enterprises were officially renamed as 'village and township enterprises' (township enterprises for short).

At this time, it was decided that the label, township enterprise (TE), which applied to about 1.3 million enterprises emerging from the commune system, would also apply to individual enterprises and those based on farm co-operatives. This meant that the number of TEs suddenly increased five fold to about 6.1 million. The additional 'farmers' TEs were mostly very small. Because of the family quota contract system, farmers produced an agricultural surplus and found themselves with some free time. They were encouraged and supported by the government to use the time to develop certain new businesses. In these TEs, government support and farmers' desire to become rich have been the driving forces behind recent growth.

Township enterprises (TEs) are controlled by local government at different levels. Unlike state owned enterprises (SOEs), TEs' finance, supplies, sales, production, and personnel are not subject to state planning. They are dealt with by enterprises themselves or by the local government, with which TEs are intimately linked.

The growth of all types of TEs led to a proliferation of new 'towns and counties', together with their infrastructures, and thus promoted urbanization in rural China. Between 1978 and 1990 the proportion of farmers in China's population decreased from 82 per cent to 74 per cent (*The Almanac of China's Statistics* 1991).

Greater autonomy, financial support, freedom from bureaucracy and entrepreneurial drive resulted in a stunning rate of growth. In 1978 there were 1.5 million TEs, which employed 28 million people, accounting for 7 per cent of the total labour force. By 1991 the number of TEs was 19 million, employing 96 million people, which amounted to 17 per cent of the total labour force. The output of TEs in 1991 was 24 times higher than in 1978. The average growth rate of TEs' output between 1981 and 1991 was 30 per cent, compared with 10 per cent for GNP, during the same period. In 1990 the industrial output of TEs represented 30 per cent of total industrial output (*The Abstract of Chinese Village and Township Enterprise Statistics* 1992). Table 6.1 shows the position of TEs in China's economy.

THE POSITION OF TOWNSHIP ENTERPRISES IN CHINA'S FOREIGN TRADE

In 1977, China's exports and imports totalled $15 billion, and accounted for a small fraction of world trade. The major exports were farm produce and minerals, particularly oil. In 1992, the figure reached $166 billion, with exports of $85 billion and imports of $81 billion (*Beijing Review* 18–31 January 1993). The export of manufactured goods represented 80 per cent of the total in 1992 (*Financial Times* 16 February 1993).

Table 6.1 Position of township enterprises in China's economy

Items	1978	1980	1985	1990	1991
No. of enterprises (million)	1.5	1.4	12.2	18.5	19.1
No. of employees (million)	28.3	30.0	69.8	92.6	96.1
% of total work force	7.0	7.1	14.0	16.3	16.5
% of rural work force	9.2	9.4	18.8	22.1	22.3
Total output (billion rmb)	49.3	67.0	275.5	958.1	1,162.2
% of China's GDP	7.2	7.8	16.6	25.2	26.6
% of total rural output	24.3	24.0	43.5	57.7	59.2
Industrial output (billion rmb)	38.5	52.2	184.6	709.7	870.9
% of China's industrial output	9.1	10.1	19.0	29.7	—

Source: The Abstract of Chinese Village and Township Enterprise Statistics 1992: 31

During the period 1978–1992, foreign investment reached about $87 billion, with foreign direct investment accounting for 34 per cent. Foreign-funded enterprises (including wholly owned, equity and co-operative joint ventures) numbered 84,000. Their exports of $17 billion in 1992 represented 20 per cent of China's total exports (*People's Daily* 19 February 1993).

Until 1984, exports from TEs were negligible. Starting from 1985, TEs' exports have increased rapidly. In 1986, TEs' exports of $5 billion accounted for one-sixth of China's total exports. In the same year, about 20,000 TEs specialized in production for export, 2,400 TEs were involved in equity and co-operative joint-ventures, and about 10,000 were engaged in compensation trade and production according to clients' requirements or samples.

In 1987, China's new policy of accelerating the economic development of coastal regions gave 14 cities the status of 'coastal open cities', with extra freedoms and tax breaks for foreign trade and investment. This gave a further impetus to the development of TEs. From the second half of 1988 to 1991, both central and local governments put great emphasis on the development of export-oriented businesses to acquire capital, technology, and raw material from Western companies and international markets. Although during the same period the central government was tightening money supply and controlling investment in domestic markets, export-oriented TEs began to take off. They succeeded because of their operating flexibility and customer-oriented approach.

The position of TEs in China's foreign trade is becoming increasingly important. From 1987 through 1992, TEs' exports and imports grew by an average of 60 per cent per year. Their exports of $20 billion in 1992 accounted for a quarter of China's total exports ($85 billion) (*Chinese Township Enterprise Bulletin* 5 February 1993). At present, about 80,000 TEs are engaged in export-oriented production. Table 6.2 summarizes the statistics relating to TEs' position in China's foreign trade and international business.

Many TEs started with the characteristics of 'three localizations': local supplies, local production, and local distribution. At an early stage of their development, many TEs relied largely on farm produce or farm-related by-products. Gradually, labour intensive manufacturing has become dominant, with some TEs engaging in high-technology business. Table 6.3 displays the composition of TEs' exports.

As seen from the table, the proportion of minerals, foodstuffs, native produce and animal by-products decreased from 21.6 per cent in 1987 to 16.7 per cent in 1991. Textile and apparel have been TEs' leading exports, as they are for the Chinese economy as a whole. While in 1991 textile and apparel accounted for 10.8 per cent ($7.8 billion) and 12.5 per cent ($9.0 billion) of China's total exports respectively (*Business China* 22 June 1992), TEs' exports of textile and apparel represented 25 per cent and 20 per cent of China's exports of textile and apparel.

Table 6.2 Position of township enterprises in China's foreign trade

	1986	1987	1988	1989	1990	1991	1992
Exports (\$ billion)	3.1	4.4	7.2	10.0	10.3	12.7	20.1
% of China's total exports (rmb)[a]	9.2	11.0	15.2	19.0	16.3	17.3	22.6
No. of equity and co-op. JVs	2,400	2,000	4,600	5,400	7,000	8,500	—
Output values of JVs (\$ million)	220.6	320.4	741.0	1,589.0	2,031.9	3,702.6	—

Sources: The Statistics of Village & Township Enterprises 1978–85; *The Abstract of Chinese Village and Township Enterprise Statistics* 1992; *The Almanac of China's Statistics* 1991 and 1992; *Economic Reference Information* 6 January 1993

Note: [a] Calculated in rmb, the Chinese currency

CHARACTERISTICS OF TOWNSHIP ENTERPRISES

In general, successful TEs have the following characteristics in common.

They are small, flexible, and market driven   From the outset, TEs had to rely on markets for sourcing supplies and selling products. Most TEs started business with inadequate capital and human resources, and used second-hand equipment, acquired from state owned enterprises (SOEs). Hence, in the face of market pressures, many TEs have positioned their businesses in areas where there have been severe shortages, or where SOEs have been weak. Others have taken advantage of unique access to certain agricultural supplies. The majority of TEs are small and autonomous compared with SOEs, and thus have flexibility to respond to market changes quickly, as the following three examples show.

In Shanghai a small TE started its business as a bulb manufacturer, with 100 employees. In the first year, it only produced 73 bulbs. Later the enterprise targeted the gaps in SOEs' product lines: where SOEs produced high-power bulbs, it focused on low-power bulbs; where SOEs specialized in standard bulbs, it manufactured bulbs with special specifications. With this strategy, it developed four product lines with 300 different types of bulbs which are used in the decoration of new flats and houses, shops and theatres. Now the TE has become the leading producer of bulbs in the country.

A few years ago, a large American company contracted with a Shanghai foreign trade company to produce women's dresses to a special design, requiring delivery within 15 days. Because of the complicated production process and urgent delivery, SOEs were unable to undertake the production due to their rigid planning system. The foreign trade

Table 6.3 Comparison by sector of township enterprises' exports (value unit: US $100 million)

Items	1987 Export	%	1988 Export	%	1989 Export	%	1990 Export	%	1991 Export	%
Total	43.8	100.0	72.0	100.0	100.0	100.0	102.8	100.0	126.4	100.0
Chemicals	2.2	5.0	4.0	5.6	5.6	5.6	5.2	5.1	6.1	4.8
Machinery	2.1	4.8	3.0	4.2	4.8	4.8	5.8	5.6	7.2	5.7
Minerals	2.0	4.7	3.7	5.1	5.2	5.2	5.1	5.0	5.3	4.2
Light industrial goods	—	—	7.7	10.7	10.4	10.4	13.5	13.1	19.2	15.2
Foodstuffs	4.3	9.2	7.3	10.1	9.4	9.4	8.8	8.6	10.0	7.9
Native produce	1.0	2.4	1.3	1.8	1.8	1.8	1.4	1.4	1.8	1.4
Animal by-products	2.3	5.3	3.1	4.3	4.0	4.0	3.8	3.7	4.0	3.2
Textile	8.6	19.7	11.5	15.9	16.5	16.5	17.2	16.7	20.2	16.0
Silk fabrics	—	—	3.5	4.9	5.3	5.3	6.2	6.0	6.5	5.1
Apparel	4.7	10.9	8.1	11.2	13.2	13.2	13.5	13.1	18.3	14.5
Handicrafts	6.8	15.4	10.1	14.1	13.0	13.0	13.0	12.6	15.4	12.2
Others	9.8	22.6	8.7	12.1	10.8	10.8	9.4	9.1	12.4	9.8

Source: The Abstract of Chinese Village and Township Enterprise Statistics 1992: 31

company came to a TE for rescue. Although it was harvest time and most employees were busy with farming work, the TE accepted the sub-contract. When the work had started, the TE was suddenly told that the American company required the delivery five days ahead of schedule. Even so, the TE mobilized day and night shifts and made the delivery on time.

In Guangdong province in 1986, two fan manufacturing companies, one a TE and one an SOE, recognized that plastic would substitute for metal in making fans. They were competing with each other to bring the new generation fan to the market, and both were trying to change their existing metal fan production lines into new plastic ones. The TE went ahead and invested immediately. In six months the products were successfully launched and exported to North America, whilst the SOE was still in the process of getting permission to change its production lines.

They are dedicated to human resources, innovation and quality Many TEs put a special emphasis on human resources, innovation and product quality. With their autonomous and flexible systems, it is their usual practice to recruit highly competent engineers and technicians from SOEs, to pay them attractive salaries and actively pursue innovation. At the beginning of the 1980s, they mainly targeted and sought retired technicians and engineers from urban areas. Since the mid-1980s, their attention has shifted to scientists and technicians, working in research institutes and SOEs, who are discontented with their working conditions. Currently they are competing with large and medium sized SOEs for talented staff and trying to attract foreign experts. The following are some examples:

A village in Tienjin achieved an output of $831 million in 1992, as a result of its special policy of attracting three types of human resources: professors and senior engineers, managers and marketers, and overseas Chinese and 'foreign friends' (*Economic Daily* 7 January 1993).

Having been established for two months, a village-run machine tool TE with 90 employees attracted the chief economist, chief designer, chief assistant accountant and 50 other leading technicians from a large machine tool SOE, which was established 50 years earlier with 6,800 employees. This incident caused a nation-wide debate (*Economic Daily* 3 February 1993).

Aside from attracting talent from SOEs, TEs also stress on-the-job training. In 1986, 29,600 TEs' employees graduated from open universities and part-time colleges, and 118,600 people from TEs obtained special technical certificates through training. In 1991 these figures were 85,200 and 342,900 respectively.

TEs maintain a close link with research institutions. About 60 per cent of inventions and innovations developed by China's scientific and technological institutions have been put into production by TEs. In 1988 about 1,000 of their products were awarded prizes for their high quality at national and provincial levels, and 16 products won international gold and silver medals for their quality (*People's Daily,* Overseas Edition 12 August 1988).

They have an international orientation   TEs, particularly those in coastal regions, are actively pursuing co-operation and joint ventures with SOEs, with other TEs, and with foreign companies. By developing joint ventures and sub-contracts with foreign firms, TEs have gradually upgraded their technology, and many became involved in foreign direct investment. As can be seen in Table 6.2, the equity and co-operative joint ventures between TEs and foreign companies have grown rapidly in the last few years. In 1992 the Fujian government approved 1,139 joint ventures and wholly owned firms.

In addition, more and more TEs have begun to make foreign direct investments. For instance:

A TE from Wu Xi in southern China developed a joint venture in Australia to run a sheep station, and ship the wool back to Wu Xi as raw material for its textile industry.

In 1987, a TE from Jiangsu province joined with a research institute and a small county factory to develop a joint venture in Thailand. They invested about $3 million in the form of technology and equipment for a 49 per cent share holding. In 10 months the joint venture company not only recovered all the investment and expenditures but also made $30,000 profits.

In 1992 TEs from Beijing established five subsidiaries overseas.

Despite these favourable characteristics, a significant number of TEs still suffer from limited funds, obsolete technology and poorly educated employees.

They have limited funds and supplies The growth of TEs has had to rely chiefly on re-investment of any surplus. Although the Chinese government has implemented favourable loan and taxation policies to support TEs, it has not directly invested in TEs, as it does in SOEs. Nevertheless, state bank loans have played an important role in sustaining the high-speed development of TEs. Another difference between TEs and SOEs is that the former have never benefited from supplies, at low cost, being provided by the central plan.

They have obsolete technology Many TEs are still using obsolete technology, partly because their businesses are small and newly established and partly because their managers and employees have only recently stopped working on the land. In fact some still work part time as employees and part time as farmers. Hence, they are incapable of pursuing R&D activities and developing new products. Apart from some TEs in the southern coastal regions, most still rely on mechanical or semi-mechanical technology, and quite a few on manual work.

Low level of employees' education One of the major problems in TEs is the employees' very low level of education. In 1991 only about 200,000 employees in TEs had a degree of higher education and only 420,000 held a medium level of technical qualification. The two figures together come to less than 1 per cent of employees (*The Abstract of Chinese Village and Township Enterprise Statistics* 1992).

REGIONAL DIFFERENCES

Although China's TEs have shown an exponential growth in the last few years, there have been substantial regional differences. TEs in eastern China or in coastal regions, specifically Liaoning, Beijing, Tienjin, Hebei, Shandong, Jiangsu, Shanghai, Zhejiang, Fujian, Guangdong, Guangxi, and Hainan, are more developed and better managed than those in other parts of China. In 1991, TEs in eastern China accounted for 66 per cent of TEs' total output, those in mid-China amounted to 30 per cent, and those in western China only represented 4 per cent (*People's Daily* 14 March 1993). In 1990, coastal regions, which accounted for 42 per cent of China's population, generated 52 per cent of China's GNP and 66 per cent of TEs' output. In 1981, GNP and TEs' output in coastal regions was 1.2 and 2.1 times greater than those in middle and western regions, while in 1990 those figures were 1.5 and 2.7 respectively. This indicates that differences between the two parts of China grew larger, as a result of economic reforms.

The difference is even more distinctive in foreign trade and international business. In 1991 southeast provinces accounted for 80 per cent of TEs' exports and 80 per cent of the foreign investment TEs attracted.

Historically the southeast was more developed than other regions, because it was there that Western influence first arrived. After the communist government took over, large and medium sized industrial complexes mushroomed in the mid-west regions and reduced the differences between the mid-west and the coastal regions. However, since the economic reforms began in the late 1970s, TEs in coastal regions have grown much faster than those in the mid-west region.

The recent faster development of TEs in coastal regions is due to better industrial and agricultural infrastructure, education, and entrepreneurship. Other important factors are as follows:

Geographical location and government policy   Coastal regions enjoy favourable conditions to conduct foreign trade and international business. Since the mid-1980s, the Chinese government has pursued the strategies of promoting foreign trade and international business in the coastal regions, with various supporting policies and regulations. As a result, TEs in the coastal regions actively introduced Western advanced technology, management, and investment, and thus became a major business player in China's foreign trade and international business.

A more open, far-sighted, and pragmatic business mentality   People in coastal regions are not constrained by ideological dogmas and avoid any political or philosophical debates on issues such as socialism or capitalism. The priority of business/economic development has been firmly established among local governments and people. For instance, during the 1988–1991 period of 'adjustment' and 'tight money supply', many enterprises found it difficult to maintain the existing pace of growth and many stopped construction projects. However, TEs in Wu Xi, Jiangsu, and Shanghai acquired funds from various sources, continued to invest in new projects, and achieved a 50 per cent annual growth rate, during this period. In addition, TEs in Wu Xi, Jiangsu, and Shanghai have developed new strategies in anticipation of China joining GATT, and gradually re-oriented their businesses towards international markets. Now about 30 per cent of their products are exported.

A few studies indicate that the overseas Chinese in Hong Kong and elsewhere have a strong business mentality (Ryan 1961; Redding 1990). This characteristic may be linked to residence in southern China. Redding (1990) has contended that the pragmatic mentality of the overseas Chinese may derive from their peasant and artisan origins in southern China.

Development of export and international oriented businesses/economy
The development of export businesses has been the policy of most TEs in coastal regions. In 1991, the ratio of TEs' industrial goods exports to their total industrial output in Guangdong province was 27 per cent, whilst the figure in the Zhujiang River Delta was over 50 per cent.

In 1991 Guangdong and Fujian saw the fastest growth of TEs' industrial output, as a result of their successful introduction of foreign investment and development of foreign trade. Guangdong's exports accounted for about a third of China's total exports in 1990 (*The Economist* 5 October 1991), while the output value of export-oriented TEs represented the half of Guangdong's total output value in 1991 (*The Chinese Township Enterprise Bulletin* 1 October 1992). Because of TEs' above-average growth rate in the coastal regions, the industrial output increments of Jiangsu, Zhejiang, Fujian, Shangdong, Guangdong, Guangxi, and Hainan provinces have accounted for 60 per cent of China's total industrial output increments between 1991 and 1992. The industrial output increments of TEs, together with other non-state owned enterprises, amounted to 61 per cent of China's total industrial output increments during the same period (*People's Daily* 19 January 1993).

The development of TEs' international business presents different patterns in different areas. In the past, foreign investment was largely concentrated in southern China. Since 1992 foreign investment has begun to shift from southern China towards the Yangtze river basin to provinces such as Shanghai, Jiangsu, Shangdong, and Zhejiang. For instance, last year 6,715 contracts were concluded between TEs and foreign firms in Jiangsu, involving $7.2 billion. This made Jiangsu the second fastest growing province after Guangdong. In Shanghai the number of contracts signed in 1992 was five times greater than 1991 (*Economic Reference Information* 23 February 1993). Particularly, in 1992 joint venture contracts in Shangdong reached 5,655, introducing foreign investment of $2.2 billion, also five times larger than the previous year (*People's Daily* 10 February 1993) .

CHINA'S BUSINESS STRATEGY AND PARTNERSHIP WITH TOWNSHIP ENTERPRISES

Western firms can use TEs as business partners or sub-contractors to pursue strategies for global sourcing and to penetrate China's domestic markets.

At present Asia's Four Tigers (Hong Kong, Taiwan, Singapore and South Korea), Japan, and the United States account for about 70 per cent of China's foreign trade, and overseas Chinese from Taiwan, Hong Kong and Macao account for 60–70 per cent of foreign direct investment (*The Almanac of China's Statistics* 1992). In recent years, investment from Japan, the United States, South Korea, and Western Europe has been increasing rapidly. Much of this investment has gone into joint ventures with TEs.

Before 1990, China's foreign trade was almost monopolized by the state owned specialized foreign trade corporations. Most TEs' exports were handled by these corporations, with only a small part exported through joint ventures, or through provision of parts and raw materials to large SOEs or foreign funded firms. Out of $10.3 billion of TEs' exports in 1990, 62 per cent were handled by state owned foreign trade corporations, 13 per cent were directly exported, and 25 per cent were indirectly exported. By developing direct business contact with TEs, Western companies can pursue their own sourcing strategies more effectively. Many TEs are now able to produce goods which are acceptable in international markets.

Other advantages are that TEs are less influenced by bureaucrats. They are more flexible, compared with state owned enterprises (SOEs), and hence they can respond rapidly to market changes. Since they have been operating in a quasi market context, they are more sensitive to market signals, and more conscious of efficiency. In addition, they are eager to develop partnerships with Western firms. In many cases, local governments encourage, support, and reward those TEs which have developed co-operation or joint ventures with foreign firms.

Through co-operation or entering into agreements and joint ventures with TEs, foreign firms can enjoy the benefits of lower taxation and fewer 'social expenses'. For instance, no pension or employees' medical expenses; no obligation or commitment to provide accommodation, nursery, health care, dining-rooms, or schools; and flexibility in recruiting or firing employees when demand changes.

TEs have greater autonomy to choose employees as their recruitment is not included in the state labour force plan. Since there are no 'iron rice-bowls' in TEs, their productivity is generally higher than that of SOEs. Also the sense of crisis felt by TEs' managers and employees is much stronger than in SOEs, and thus hard work and greater entrepreneurship are often the norm.

Land and labour in townships, counties, and villages are cheaper than in urban areas and salaries in TEs are 20–30 per cent lower than in SOEs. Thus by developing a partnership with TEs, Western firms' products are able to achieve competitive cost advantages in China and in international markets.

For all the above reasons, therefore, Western companies which want to have products manufactured to their own designs and specifications and to source supplies/components, may find TEs ideal partners. Products which require frequent changes in design and specifications and whose production batches are relatively small would be particularly suitable for TEs. However, as mentioned previously, a large number of TEs have limited financial, technological, and human resources. Do these problems place serious barriers in the way of developing partnerships with TEs?

In the Zhujiang River Delta and coastal regions, foreign direct investment (FDI) linked to TEs has already been significant. Although in the last few years most investors have come from Hong Kong, Macao and Taiwan, companies from the USA, Japan, Western Europe, and Australia have begun actively to seek co-operation or joint ventures with TEs. The location of FDI is gradually shifting from the Zhujiang River Delta and coastal regions to inland areas. Share holding by foreign investors has gradually increased from 25 per cent to 50 per cent, and the contract term has extended from three–five years to 10–20 years. This suggests that innovative Western companies are realizing the potential benefits that collaboration with TEs can offer and there seems little doubt that TEs will pay an increasingly important role in China's future industrial and foreign trade development.

FUTURE PROSPECTS OF TOWNSHIP ENTERPRISES

TEs' average growth rate in the last decade is far greater than that of the national average. Between 1979 and 1991 the average growth rates of GDP and industrial output in TEs were 30 per cent and 26 per cent, whilst those at the national level were 10 per cent and 12 per cent. It is estimated that between 1992 and 1995 TEs' total output, industrial output, and exports will have doubled, continuing to grow at a much faster pace than the national average.

In addition to continued rapid growth, other important changes are likely to emerge:

1 The gap between the developed coastal and backward inland regions will widen since TEs in coastal regions attract and introduce far more FDI than inland regions.
2 More and more TEs will turn to exports, including processing and manufacturing based on clients' samples and specifications, processing clients' raw materials, and direct export. Joint ventures between TEs and foreign firms will increase.
3 TEs in coastal regions will gradually develop their own R&D capacities. More and more capable technicians and scientists will be attracted to TEs in coastal regions, where they enjoy a higher living standard than inland areas and have autonomy and funds to pursue research.
4 A kind of conglomerate between TEs will develop to help them

compete in international markets and invest overseas. Co-operation and joint ventures between TEs, trading companies, SOE manufacturers, and research institutes and universities will grow.

CONCLUSION

China is emerging as one of the largest economies and markets, and TEs are becoming increasingly important to China's economy and foreign trade. TEs represent or reflect China's unique manner of industrialization and economic development. Hitherto, studies of TEs have largely been left to economists. Since TEs can be customers, partners, and suppliers to Western companies, research into TEs would be highly relevant and important to scholars in the fields of management and international business/marketing.

Although a large number of TEs are still using obsolete technology, and are poorly managed, many have been growing from strength to strength. TEs are not only China's major exporter, but are also becoming a major foreign direct investor. In many business areas, TEs can be an appropriate partner for Western firms to pursue a global sourcing strategy and penetrate China's domestic markets. The development of joint ventures with TEs enjoys a number of benefits, compared with SOEs, such as flexibility and faster response to market changes, higher productivity, lower land and labour costs, fewer 'social expenses', and easy labour relations. Such benefits have an immediate appeal but their long-term influence is likely to be significant as China's internal and external markets become increasingly competitive.

REFERENCES

Osgood, C. (1975) *The Chinese: A Study of a Hong Kong Community*, Tucson, Arizona: University of Arizona Press.

Redding, G. S. (1990) *The Spirit of Chinese Capitalism*, De Gruyter Studies in Organisation, Vol. 22, Berlin: Walter de Gruyter.

Ryan, E. J. (1961) 'The value system of a Chinese community in Java', unpublished doctoral dissertation, Cambridge, Mass.: Harvard University.

Reference note

The majority of statistics presented in this chapter are sourced from news based publications and the convention of incorporating the reference into the text has been adopted.

7 The challenges facing manufacturing managers in Chinese factories

Paul Forrester

ABSTRACT

This chapter considers the effects of economic reforms in China on the management of production. Modernization, decentralization of decision making and increased foreign investment are seen as being major imperatives to change in the technologies, production methods and management practices employed in manufacture. It explores the extent to which contemporary Western operations management theory explains management practice in Chinese enterprises. The main conclusion is that Western management literature and analytical frameworks only provide a partial explanation of manufacturing management practice in China. The context of production within Chinese organizations and society in general is very important in order that the constraints impinging upon manufacturing decisions might be identified, and possibly removed. Further empirical studies at the factory level are therefore required in order that we might better understand the process of manufacturing decision making within the modern Chinese enterprise.

INTRODUCTION

The transition from a centrally planned to a decentralized form of market economy is a recurrent theme in many of the nations of the world today and, most significantly, in Eastern and Central Europe (ECE), the former Soviet Union and China. In many ways there are parallels between these cases, but only at a fairly superficial level. Certainly, in all these economies, managers are finding they have greater autonomy in their activities and are now expected to assume greater responsibility for the decisions they make. There is a movement away from perceptions of success based merely upon the achievement of set quotas of production output, and towards market- and customer-focused success factors such as quality of product design, conformity with product specification and customer requirements, and delivery performance and reliability. This change in approach addresses the need to secure sales in the market, as opposed to merely matching output levels to the designated quotas imposed by the relevant state ministry. However, the challenges now faced by Chinese manufacturing managers are, in many ways, unique. Whereas many of the former communist countries of the world have seen economic change coincide with (or pre-empted by) substantial political transition, this has not been so in China where the pace of political reform has been far more gradual. Additionally, despite the label of 'communism', the cultural, social, political and historical circumstances of ECE, former Soviet states and China are exceptionally dissimilar. The specific conditions in each of these countries means that the impact on decision making at the level of the enterprise, and for the manager of operations within the factory, varies considerably. Each situation therefore warrants detailed, factory-based study. This chapter therefore considers the case of China.

In order to develop new mechanisms for operating production there has been an inevitable tendency for managers in transitional economies to look both West (to the USA and Western Europe) and East (to Japan) in an attempt to glean some of the lessons of successful companies in the market economy. One of the specific ways in which Western manufacturing companies seek to compete and succeed is through the design and management of 'appropriate' operations systems which support the corporate and marketing strategies of the company. It has been recognized that operations can be used as a 'competitive weapon' (Skinner 1978) in achieving corporate objectives, which contrasts markedly with the traditional Fordist view that the main goal of production should be the achievement of economies of scale. Other researchers have demonstrated the poignancy of Skinner's argument, many using the Japanese exemplar in the quest to identify the factors underlying the success of manufacturing companies in contemporary global markets (see, for example, Pascale and Athos 1981; Hayes and Wheelwright 1984; Schonberger 1986; and Womack *et al.* 1990). This body of literature, however, relates only to companies operating in a market economy. There is little relating to the management of production in the planned economies of the world, or of those organizations in countries currently undergoing a state of transition from centralized to market-driven decision making. China is currently undergoing reform whereby manufacturing enterprises have been increasingly subjected to market forces and so have needed to undergo restructuring in the way they market and supply products. The challenge for Chinese managers centres around how they might take advantage of new market opportunities as they continue to arise whilst, simultaneously, taking into account and addressing the cultural, social and institutional constraints inertia that constrain the development of manufacturing operations in the country.

Literature on the economic changes in China, in particular the economic reforms from central control to market economy, is now generally available (see, for example Lee 1987; CBI 1989), but is rather more limited in the area of manufacturing and technology management. Wacker (1987) discussed the state of Chinese manufacturing management and provided some conclusions on competitiveness, production management, supply management and personnel practice. Events in China have developed during the period of this study and it is now timely to re-evaluate these issues. A later study of Chinese competitiveness addressed the issue of market-oriented strategies in planned economies, but was restricted to the area around the city of Tianjin (He Jinsheng and Steward 1991). A study of manufacturing flexibility in Chinese enterprises by Bennett and Wang (1992) has highlighted the need for increased flexibility as a result of the industrial reforms, but suggested these demands were unique to China and the flexibility literature developed in the West has little to offer in explanation.

Based upon empirical investigations in a number of Chinese manufacturing enterprises in Shanghai and Zhejiang Province, this chapter considers the effects of economic reforms on the management of production. Some background to the programme of research is provided before describing the framework of analysis adopted, within which manufacturing decisions are classified into four types: operations strategy, design, production planning and control, and quality. Within each of these areas the chapter reviews the extent to which theory and practice developed in the West and Japan explains management practice and manufacturing activities in Chinese enterprises. Particular reference will be made to the processes of modernization, decentralization and increased foreign investment, and their combined impact upon manufacturing management practice. Finally a perspective of Chinese manufacturing management is presented in which the key points from the above analysis are summarized and conclusions given.

THE RESEARCH PROGRAMME

The programme of research conducted in China by researchers from Keele University has been a joint venture between Keele China Business Centre and the Department of Management. It has been funded by the British Council and has been conducted in association with faculty from the Department of Management at Zhejiang University, Hangzhou. The broad objective of this three-year project was to research management styles and corporate culture within Chinese enterprises and, more specifically, to investigate whether Chinese organizations, whose corporate culture reflects that of their market and environment, are more successful than those where there is a disparity. However, within this overall objective, there was scope to conduct research into the practice of manufacturing management. The aim, therefore, of the manufacturing management investigations was to explore the translation process and links between the environment, management strategies and the choice of operations systems in Chinese companies.

Table 7.1 The Chinese companies studied

Industrial sector	Company	Location	No. of employees	Ownership
Electronics	A	Shanghai	450	Chinese/UK/Singapore JV
	B	Shanghai	240	Chinese/Australian JV
Automotive	C	Hangzhou	3,600	Chinese (former USA JV)
	D	Hangzhou	2,500	Chinese
Domestic appliances	E	Shanghai	2,100	Chinese/Japanese JV
	F	Hangzhou	3,000	Chinese (part Korean JV)
Food processing	G	Hangzhou	1,000	Chinese
	H	Hangzhou	1,800	Chinese/Hong Kong JV

The primary data which forms the basis of this paper was conducted during three research visits to Zhejiang University which took place in 1991, 1992 and 1993. Fieldwork was conducted in companies located in the vicinity of Shanghai and Hangzhou, where a total of twelve companies were visited over the three research trips. This chapter draws on the findings from eight of these organizations (see Table 7.1 for more information). These eight companies comprise pairs of companies from four industrial sectors, namely the electronics, automotive, domestic appliance and food processing industries. The companies ranged from wholly Chinese owned organizations to those which were heavily financed by foreign capital. Joint venture partners in the foreign funded businesses included finance companies from Hong Kong and Singapore and manufacturing corporations from Japan, the United States, the UK, Australia and Korea. The spectrum of companies visited by the research team reflect some of the diversity, disparities and contradictions that occur in the running of manufacturing companies in the Chinese economy. The empirical work relied upon interviewing techniques using a purpose designed semi-structured questionnaire. The intention was that the questionnaire should not necessarily be rigidly adhered to, but should act as an *aide-mémoire* and be appropriated to elucidate the principal concerns and issues at each of the case study firms. The original questionnaire has been incrementally adapted to ensure better understanding and a lack ambiguity for respondents. The questionnaire was constructed in such a way that it traced the major decision processes for manufacturing operations throughout the life cycle of identified products. Translated into Chinese to facilitate greater understanding by respondents, the questionnaire was found to provide valuable insight to the market and operations strategies, design choices, production planning and control and quality management practices within Chinese organizations.

THE FRAMEWORK OF ANALYSIS

In order to capture the completeness of manufacturing management decisions at all levels of the business, the analysis of Chinese production practices was performed within a pragmatic framework for examining manufacturing management whereby decisions were classified into four types: operations strategy, design, production planning and control, and quality.

Operations strategy

Within the context of operations, strategy refers to the important and far reaching decisions which impinge, constrain and often dictate the nature of manufacturing. Such decisions include the translation of corporate and market strategies into technological and organizational choices in manufacturing, the consequent investment choices, and (particularly pertinent in the Chinese case) the advent and impact of joint venture agreements with foreign companies.

Design

Design relates to the conception, development and choice of new processes, products and work organization within the enterprise. This concept of design relies upon the model of innovation proposed by Utterbeck and Abernathy (1975) where the 'production unit' is seen as the unit of analysis for studying the design of products, processes, work organization, and the relationships between these.

Production planning and control

Production planning and control refers to operational decisions taken once products are in manufacture, processes installed, and work organization functional. In this context planning and control includes activities such as production scheduling, inventory control and labour management at the factory level.

Quality management

Finally, the important issue of quality is highlighted for special consideration. Quality pervades all levels of the organization and has been separately identified for analysis because of its critical importance to the future success of manufacturing in China. The achievement of quality standards comparable with those of competitive manufacturing nations is a key factor that will facilitate Chinese competitiveness in international markets. The chapter will therefore consider the strategically important area of total quality management and its impact on Chinese industry, in addition to the more day to day concerns of quality control and process maintenance.

The chapter now provides an evaluation of Chinese manufacturing management practice in relation to each of the identified areas in the analytical framework. In so doing a comparison will be drawn between observations made at the Chinese factories visited and the contemporary theories and practices of manufacturing management developed in the West and Japan.

OPERATIONS STRATEGY

Economic reforms in China are now resulting in increasing autonomy at the enterprise level especially in the areas of marketing, production and capital investment. The former centralized system, where the chief concern of companies was to comply with the production quotas determined by the relevant industry ministry is now being replaced by the right of enterprises to determine their own output level and markets. Over the last 40 years Chinese factory leaders and managers have not needed to concern themselves with such matters as to whom they should sell, the pressures of market competition, and decisions on which market segments provide the greatest opportunities. Instead importance has been attached to producing the quantity required for a single customer (the appropriate ministry) who will guarantee purchase up to the set quota. In such a bureaucratic environment only limited attention has been paid to assuring product quality and other conformity with the full range of consumer requirements. Centrally planned production has resulted in a legacy of poor and restricted customer contact for Chinese industrial management which has, in turn, created a void in the competencies now demanded of managers in manufacturing organizations. Historically Chinese manufacturing managers have had little or no involvement in the formulation of corporate, marketing, finance and product development strategies, whereas now there is an increased recognition that activities such as these are the very essence of the task for senior managers of manufacturing companies in the same way as they are for their counterparts in the capitalist economies of the world.

Chinese corporate managers now have more autonomy (and responsibility) in the way they deal with the market. But intelligent marketing and strategy formulation are not enough by themselves. The types of production systems, work organization and skills developed under the command economy are often inappropriate to satisfy the needs of the changing market. The formulation and implementation of new operations strategies at the level of the firm in China are therefore essential to act as a blueprint for the introduction of new processes and production infra-structures. However, judging from the interview data of the study in

Zhejiang and Shanghai, many managers do not feel fully equipped to deal with rejuvenation of manufacturing systems so that they might better match the emergent market-oriented strategies. The formulation of operations strategies in China, linking manufacturing decisions with the market, is therefore a critical area in which Chinese managers can learn from both the theoretical frameworks and management practices of the West.

Pioneering work on the role of manufacturing within corporate strategy was conducted by Skinner (1969, 1978). Skinner was concerned that, in the majority of US companies at the time, manufacturing was most often seen as a 'millstone around the neck' of the organization. He argued that a rather negative view of the operations function was taken whereby managers' concerns were directed towards limiting the damage that the manufacturing function could have on the success of the organization. He also identified that the role of the manufacturing manager was restricted to operational matters, so engendering a 'reactive' style of management where the manufacturing function responded to instructions and played no 'proactive' part in debates at a strategic level. He also pointed to the anachronistic (i.e. outdated) nature of many factories: both the technology and the management practices, he argued, were more suited to a period of world under-capacity, where the main task of manufacturing managers was to mass produce standardized products as cheaply as possible. Contemporary markets, however, are characterized by excess supply and increasingly discerning consumers. Technology-led production management, where the objective involves optimizing performance with respect to cost and productivity, does not always suit the demands of the modern market where attention to factors such as product design, quality, delivery speed/reliability and after sales service, in addition to price, has led to the emergence of market-driven operations management.

There is now a considerable body of literature which draws upon the approach to manufacturing taken in Japan and Germany (Hayes and Wheelwright 1984; Schonberger 1986). A key issue in these works was attempting to extract the lessons from the successful manufacturing economies of the world so as to apply these and rejuvenate the competitiveness of American companies. Rather than merely stating the malaise of Western manufacturers, Hayes and Wheelwright (1984) provided guidelines for senior executives wishing to compete through manufacture and so achieve levels of corporate effectiveness comparable to the best in the world. These are contained in their 'framework for analysing manufacturing effectiveness'. The framework presents four stages in the process of improving manufacturing effectiveness in a global context. As well as being descriptive and explanatory, the framework is intended to provide guidance to managers when evolving their manufacturing strategies and operations. The first stage (*internally neutral*) is where the emphasis is on minimizing manufacturing's negative potential and so is analogous to

Skinner's millstone effect. The next three stages are where the manufacturing function is seen as progressively proactive in achieving corporate objectives. Stage two is where an organization's manufacturing 'achieves parity with competitors' (*externally neutral*); stage three involves manufacturing 'providing credible support to the business strategy' (*internally supportive*); and stage four is where the organization 'pursues a manufacturing-based competitive advantage' (*externally supportive*). This fourth stage can be seen as comparable to world class manufacturing status as identified by Schonberger (1986) where senior executives see manufacturing capabilities as a significant influence upon overall competitiveness. So, in the externally supportive firm, manufacturing strategy is not merely determined by internal corporate and marketing strategies. Instead manufacturing executives have a meaningful role in contributing to the development of the company and its strategies as a whole. In some cases this will result in the realization that manufacturing is the key competitive weapon within the organization. Hayes and Wheelwright's effectiveness framework would seem to have relevance to the Chinese context as it demonstrates how an organization can establish and then further develop its links between manufacturing systems and market strategies.

Hill (1993) developed a framework for manufacturing strategy in which corporate and marketing strategy formulation is linked to decisions on process (i.e. facilities) choice and production infrastructure within the manufacturing function. Hill argues the need for 'strategic difference' in operations as well as in marketing strategy. This recognizes that different parts of the manufacturing system serving different customers or markets should be operated separately and involve distinctive process and infrastructure choices to initiate a high degree of market focus. Hill's objective was to link marketing and operations within an easily comprehensible framework so that strategies developed in both functional areas could support and complement one another. In order to achieve this Hill recognized the need to understand 'how products win orders in their chosen markets' by identifying and distinguishing between order qualifiers and order winners: qualifying criteria get a company's product into the marketplace or on to customers' short-lists and keep them there, while order winners give the product superiority and thereby an edge over the offerings of competing organizations. To be successful, the logic continues, companies should seek to convert the order qualifying criteria (that merely get them recognized as a competent supplier of manufactured goods) into order winners so that their products are more attractive to customers than those of their competitors. Typical order qualifiers and winners identified in the framework are price (cost), design, quality, delivery speed, delivery reliability, demand flexibility, product/service range, colours/patterns, economy of use, design leadership, technical support and after sales service. Not only are these qualifying/order winning criteria seen as being affected by the top-down imposition of corporate objectives and marketing strategy, but the features of the production process and its control infra-structure can also contribute and add to the order winning qualities of the company.

So what was found in the empirical study of companies in Hangzhou and Shanghai? Certainly, and fundamentally, the anachronistic nature of the factories visited in relation to the market was quite apparent. Much of the attention to research and development in relation to product and process design focuses upon deriving technology-led solutions to the relative neglect of improved manufacturing management practice and organizational development. The lack of market and strategic awareness was apparent in many of those organizations visited during the course of the research. One factory leader, whose company was hoping to export machined automotive parts to the USA, was asked about his company's research and development policy concerning the metallurgical aspects of product design. The reply was 'It is not really a big concern for us. After all, one piece of metal is very much like another'. Compare this with the stringent safety and testing requirements in the design of motor vehicles in the volume manufacturing bases of Japan, Europe and the United States, and one can see that the product being manufactured in this partic-ular factory would not achieve the desired standards.

In contrast to the above case, though, some companies were able to demonstrate evidence of market research and an awareness of how to access and penetrate export markets where they were seeking to develop business. For example, one wholly Chinese owned manufacturer of chains stressed the importance of maintaining high quality standards. Whilst identifying and stressing the extent of the organizational change required in the next two to three years, this company was nonetheless embarking on a realistic programme of progressive quality improvement towards quality accreditation to international standards and total quality management within the organization. Moreover the company had recog-nized the huge opportunities in one of the major markets for chain in the world, supplying the Japanese motorcycle industry, and the comparative cost advantage offered by the low factor costs in China coupled with the geographical proximity to Japan. This emphasis on low cost coupled with high quality standards seemed an appropriate strategy for this company. In other words the senior management of this company had identified the quality standards they needed to achieve (order qualifiers) whilst recognizing the low factor cost advantage they could exploit (price, there-fore, being the likely order winner). Indeed, by virtue of existing exports to Japan, South East Asia and the USA, this manufacturer was already achieving exports sales in excess of 50 per cent of the company's total revenue. This qualified the company for greater autonomy in developing its foreign markets because it was able to deal directly with overseas customers, rather than having to go through the central ministry which acted as the agent for all business.

When considering strategy in Chinese companies in the 1990s it is essential to make reference to the popularity of joint ventures with foreign companies. With just two exceptions in the eight firms considered, the companies were either actively involved in at least one joint venture, or else keen to develop such agreements with foreign partners. The reasons given for entering joint venture agreements usually centred around three considerations: the need to find new sources of investment; to gain access to new markets overseas; and to facilitate technology transfer of product and/or process technology. The first and third of these are important in that they increase the scope and discretion afforded to Chinese managers in making process choices. In the past substantive investments have always come from, and been granted by, the central ministry and the level of investment was often constrained for reasons beyond the control of individual companies. The injection of foreign capital is seen as a way not only to increase the level of investment, but to enable the company to secure funding for projects that the ministry might not approve of, or which might be outside its industrial domain should a company wish to diversify. The foreign partner often operates within the same industry and so can assist the Chinese company in the modernization both of its products and processes. Thus products are appropriated to the needs of discerning customers abroad and also within domestic markets, concurrent with changes in technology and management practice within the factory, the latter in order that the flexibility and quality demands of direct customers within the changing market environment are met.

Joint ventures were identified by one particular manager as having a number of caveats which, rather than facilitating change, could in fact hinder the transition to market-driven production. This manager was concerned that many factory leaders were seizing on economic reforms at the state level to increase their own personal power at the enterprise level. By developing joint ventures senior managers can gain autonomy from the central decision making apparatus of the ministry and, therefore, were exempted from many upward management reporting procedures. However, it does not naturally follow that the factory leaders match this with a devolution of authority within their own company. The fear is that some factory leaders are now taking on dictatorial proportions within their own organization. In some cases this would result in the choice of joint venture partners less likely to challenge the leader's power base, rather than those who would be most advantageous to the organization as a whole. Whereas, in an ideal situation, the injection of funds for investment from the foreign partner is complemented by technology transfer from abroad, this does not always happen in practice. Factory leaders may be wary about introducing partners with specific industry knowledge who might challenge the decisions made within the factory, and so are attracted to investment banks and the like who are less questioning about the companies' internal affairs. Decisions driven by these factors will, one might expect, have a severe effect on the development of operations to international standards and so cause the manufacturing function to restrict the feasible strategic options for the company.

A second caveat of joint ventures identified by this manager was the short-term view taken by senior Chinese managers in their establishments. A new joint venture company qualifies for important exceptions from central government, most notably a reduction in the basic tax rate from 55 per cent of profits made to 25 per cent, deferred until the third year of operation. Whereas the cash injection this provides has obvious attractions, some factory leaders have pursued this shorter-term advantage as the overriding goal, proceeding to sign joint venture agreements with extreme haste. In such conditions, little or no attention is paid to the longer-term goals of the business, such as product and process development, which could possibly be enhanced with a more considered choice of joint venture partner.

DESIGN

An organization's operations strategy will have implications for manufacturing design decisions. Companies in China are now facing the vexed question of how to adapt their products and production facilities to match the changing needs of the market. Design is, therefore, currently of particular interest in the Chinese context as the new market conditions and the related strategic response of companies' demands changes in product designs, process configuration and production organization at the shop floor level. However, changes in the design of either products or processes should not be seen or tackled in isolation. Indeed, models of design and innovation developed in the West emphasize the need for an holistic approach to change management. Of significance to the question of manufacturing change is the dynamic model of innovation proposed by Utterbeck and Abernathy (1975). This model is founded on the premise that innovations and manufacturing systems design should be evaluated and categorized using a three-part classification: product, process and work organization. By understanding the type of adaptation or innovation, it is argued, managers are better able to understand the full extent of the implications of design change. A number of studies have adopted the Utterbeck and Abernathy model and provide an interesting insight into organizational development and design innovation within manufacturing companies (see Abernathy 1978; Whipp and Clark 1986).

The design, development and eventual manufacture of new products, or the timely re-design of existing ones, is the very lifeblood of most manufacturing companies operating in competitive markets. Before the economic reforms in China the centrally planned system effectively detached the production organization from its environment and, as a consequence, dictated and determined the range of materials and products available for downstream customers and end-consumers alike. The advent of greater autonomy, exposure to market, increasing foreign influence, and the acquisition of new product technology (most notably through foreign joint ventures) has resulted in a rapid rate of product design change in Chinese companies. However, product innovation and intelligent marketing cannot, by themselves, guarantee success. If the characteristics of a new product render its production infeasible, require excessive process investment, or if the product is not transferred from concept to production in an efficient way, then there is a high probability of the new product failing to reach its potential in the market. Companies must ensure the concurrent development of new operations systems, so attention must be paid to the management of the design process not only for products, but also for the introduction of new production technologies and the re-organization of work within the factory (job design, levels of skills and labour flexibility). To ensure the smooth transition from product design to manufacture through 'design for manufacture' the manufacturing manager must, therefore, have timely inputs to the new product design process so that correct decisions are taken regarding its manufacturability.

There is evidence from Chinese companies that, whereas significant attention has been paid to the technical aspects of product and process design, significantly less importance has been attached to the management and organizational issues of design. From Western studies it has been identified that key organizational issues must be addressed during the design process, particularly with respect to the marketing, design and manufacturing interfaces. This causes considerable problems which frequently need to be overcome in the management of product introduction programmes. Oakley (1984) neatly observes the dichotomy that exists when people from different functional backgrounds are brought together on product development programmes. He uses the Burns and Stalker definitions of mechanistic organization to describe the qualities of what is traditionally seen as an efficient operations system and organic organization to illustrate the features of innovative design projects (Burns and Stalker 1966). The tacit qualities of a 'good' production manager and a 'good' designer often reflect these features in their work. Production managers seek order, stability and standardization, whereas design and marketing personnel see the need for change and frequent adaptation to customer needs. The distinction between mechanistic and organic organization would seem to explain many of the problems faced within Chinese companies. The command economy perpetuated the mechanistic form where production companies were directed by the relevant ministry and expected to follow the assigned plan. The technology-led approach to manufacturing was therefore induced, in which the objective was to optimize productive power and output. Compare this with the new emergent demands on Chinese production companies and one can identify the need to move towards more organic organizational forms and cultures in order to respond effectively to the need for change. This perplexed issue of managing and organizing for change is, indeed, one of the major challenges facing the manufacturing managers of Chinese companies during the transitional period.

Substantial and long-term capital investments are frequently involved when designing production systems and choices made are not easily reversed in the short term. Once funds have been committed to new process designs an air of entrapment will typically take grip, especially when the systems are finally installed. The cost of changing decisions once one has invested time and money in new capital projects is quite immense. In such circumstances it is important that the decision maker be aware of the consequences of specific process choices and has a thorough understanding of the process of developing new systems. Often a move to increase productivity will result in reduced flexibility and high capital outlay in advanced manufacturing technology. On the other hand, the desire to develop a truly flexible system, in terms of its response and adaptability to the market or in the range of items it can produce, can result in low productivity and high manufacturing costs, hence a lack of competitiveness. Process design, therefore, is frequently a process of adopting the appropriate systems for particular circumstances and of balancing the productivity/flexibility dilemma outlined above.

The caveats of batch manufacture and line assembly, where the emphasis is on mass production utilizing a high division of labour, are well documented in Western literature. In addition to the human and sociological impact of such work, a wider range of disadvantages have now been identified. Of particular concern is that such systems are not always the most effective designs to respond and react to the full range of customer demands and market change. Batch production will normally result in excessive queuing and excessive materials movement within the operations resulting in high work in progress, long production throughput times, slow response to market change and increased potential for poor product quality and damage. Line assembly has associated problems which centre around two main concerns: physical and human. Physical problems include the high capital costs (and, particularly, the fact that these are dedicated to a very restricted range of products), interdependency between work stations which can cause reliability problems for the line as a whole, and the general inflexibility of the process in terms of its ability to change to meet changing product designs.

As a consequence of the above, a wider range of factors is now being considered in the design and choice of processes in the West. Most notably, the design of production systems has been closely linked to the overall needs of the business. The new approaches to systems design tend not merely to consider the technical and volume/capacity aspects, but also to consider the wider strategic, market, organizational and human issues (see for example Bennett and Forrester 1993). This broader, more business-oriented approach to process decision making has resulted in the design and installation of innovative cellular forms of systems. Two of the most widely publicized systems designs are group technology (Snead 1989), a variation on batch production which seeks to incorporate the benefits of a sequential layout coupled with the work organization benefits of small group working, and autonomous group working where the long assembly line is replaced by small parallel cells of workers with longer cycle tasks and responsibility and authority for self-organization (Gyllenhammer 1977).

The evidence from the Chinese companies visited during the research is that many Chinese manufacturing managers are still committed to the achievement of economies of scale through high volume, mass production. This manifests in process choices of large-batch manufacture for components processing and upstream production activities (characterized by functional layouts, process oriented work organization, high work in progress and long production throughput times) or flow lines for final assembly with multiple stage build along sequential layouts, task oriented work organization, high capital costs and inflexibility in terms of product range and scope for design change. The technical imperative to systems design often overrides business, social and organizational considerations in Chinese manufacturing companies. However this does not necessarily mean that batch and line working are incommensurable with the needs of the Chinese market. The level and pattern of demand probably remains the key determinant of process choice in all economies of the world and there is no doubt that for volume manufacturers large batch and line systems remain as probably the most appropriate choices for mature products where the rate of product innovation and change is slow. For these companies the key order winners typically are price and continuity of supply, so low cost production and high productivity are the key performance criteria in manufacture.

China is widely acknowledged as having the fastest growing domestic economy in the world. The market potential for almost all products is immense and there are huge opportunities for companies which can produce a high volume of goods cheaply, and to a satisfactory quality. Additionally, when one considers the comparative factor cost advantages in global markets of manufacturing in China, one can again see that high volume manufacture is liable to continue to be a major factor of production in China where emphasis will remain on ways and means to increase productivity. Given the above, one might argue that many of the developments in process design and organization in the West, where the ability to cope with economies of scope is paramount, may not always be so appropriate to the Chinese manufacture where economies of scale remain the key concern. It is useful, therefore, to turn to the Japanese exemplar in order to glean some lessons to apply in the Chinese context.

The success of Japanese producers in world markets is well documented and has been the focus of attention of many researchers seeking the success factors in Japanese management (e.g. Pascale and Athos 1981; Schonberger 1982; Womack *et al.* 1990). Since the publication of the book *The Machine That Changed the World*, the Womack *et al.* concept of lean production has been the subject of considerable debate. The book is the culmination of a five-year study co-ordinated by the Massachusetts Institute of Technology (MIT) which had the objective of investigating the future of the world-wide automobile industry, but more specifically focused upon the factors underpinning the success of Japanese volume producers in world markets. Lean production is defined as being lean because

> it uses less of everything compared with mass production – half the human effort in the factory, half the manufacturing space, half the investment in tools, half the engineering hours to develop a new product in half the time. Also it requires keeping far less than half the needed inventory on site, results in fewer defects, and produces a greater and growing variety of products.
>
> (Womack *et al.* 1990: 13)

In the book the autonomous cellular approach increasingly adopted by Western manufacturers, most notably Volvo of Sweden, is subjected to some criticism. Terming the autonomous approach 'neocraftsmanship' (Womack *et al.* 1990: 101), proponents of lean production argue that increasing the cycle time and group autonomy are not the only ways in which the work can be made more fulfilling. Their view is that successful companies in the future will operate with low levels of slack at the factory level, where operations in the chain of manufacture (and reaching back to suppliers) will be synchronized. Manufacturing companies with de-coupling between processes and work design based upon neocraftsman-ship, they argue, cannot hope to survive in the high volume sectors of the market.

The above debate and the experiences of Western compared to Japanese producers certainly sends conflicting signals to Chinese managers who are seeking to adopt design practices appropriate for use in the market-oriented economy. It is important to note that both the group autonomy and lean production concepts aim to increase participation and work satisfaction of manufacturing employees to the advantage of the company as a whole. However, the ways in which they achieve co-determination towards improved business performance are distinctive. Companies who have adopted the autonomous approach, such as Volvo, have attempted to enlarge the inside work of production employees through job enlarge-ment, enrichment and rotation. Japanese approaches have concentrated more on retaining the task orientation of the work, but developing the outside work of employees, such as additional duties when production stops (problem solving and housekeeping) and the opportunity to be involved in improvement groups outside the normal working activities.

In truth the majority of Chinese factories visited in Hangzhou and Shanghai did not display many of the features of either autonomous production or lean production; rather they could best be categorized on the whole as traditional mass production. Production was either performed in large batches using functional layouts (i.e. for the component processing factories such as the automotive parts and chain producers) or else was characterized by assembly performed along long flowlines of workers (i.e. domestic appliance production such as televisions and refrigerators). In either case a sharp division of labour could be observed, and there were few attempts to increase the involvement and participation of employees in the decision making process. Progress towards autonomous or lean production systems would, one might conclude, increase the effectiveness of Chinese production operations. However, the choice of which approach to adopt is rather complex, given that arguments still persist as to the virtues of each form in the established market economies of the world. What can be said is that the choice of process and work design should be dictated by the basis upon which the company competes, and so comes back to the Hill (1993) argument that the way in which a company considers its products win orders in the market (e.g. combination of price, technical features, quality, delivery performance, demand flexibility or customer service) should govern the process and infrastructure choices made at the level of the factory. As has been mentioned, the fact that many Chinese companies compete in global markets on the basis of cost competitiveness and high volume manufacture might lead one to consider that the lean production approach might be most effective, particularly when linked with the emphasis on quality improvement stressed in the Womack *et al.* (1990) book. However, other companies, particularly those visited in the high technology electronics industry (PCB production and telecommunications equipment) see the advantages of a cellular approach with a high degree of group autonomy and market focus in order that they might cope with the dynamic nature of the market, especially with regard to the rate of product innovation, short product life-cycles and the customized nature of customer requirements.

PRODUCTION PLANNING AND CONTROL

Once a production system has been designed and organized, it will then need to be planned, monitored and controlled on a day to day basis. Debates in the West concerning approaches to operations planning and control are no less heated, however, than for process design decisions. Traditional planning and control has either relied upon rather unstructured approaches to production scheduling and inventory management and management control, or on statistical and algorithmic methods utilizing, where the objective is to optimize the utilization of resources. The unstructured methods include the use of manual planning boards and the engendering of a just-in-case style of operational management where more than adequate inventory is held or precautions taken to ensure (hopefully) the continued smooth running of operations. The optimization approach makes use of forecasting methods, scheduling approaches and statistical stock control theory (such as linear programming and least-cost economic order quantity determination) to optimize certain criteria (e.g. maximization of profit, revenue, or output and cost minimization) subject to identified and quantifiable resource constraints. Where strict optimization is not feasible, the optimization planner will turn to approaches based upon bounded rationality theory including scheduling algorithms and priority rules.

The central planning system in China has resulted in many conflicts at the planning and control level with factories. In some cases, most notably the automotive component factory, there appeared to be very little logic in the approach to operational management. One could observe high levels of raw materials, work in progress and finished goods stock, and very few measures appeared to be in place to address the excessive levels of finance-hungry inventory holding. Indeed, the very nature of the planned economy seemed to have instilled a siege mentality amongst the managers in the organization who were keen to hoard inventory as a buffer because, with few or no direct links to suppliers or customers, they had no confidence in the continuance of supply or in accurately forecasting precise future customer demand. Some of the more progressive factories, though, particularly those which were developing increased autonomy from the central ministry, were in the process of developing new operational management methods similar to the traditional Western forms of production planning and control outlined above. Assuming economic rationality, much of the investigative research attention in the more autonomous Chinese companies is currently being directed towards developing generic mathematical models and techniques to improve the operational planning and control of the company. Indeed, this builds upon a widely observable attribute of the Chinese character in general: that, historically, Chinese people have been very adept quantitatively and mathematically. Although held back to an extent by the lack of computing technology within the companies visited, production planners and operations managers were keen to demonstrate the models and techniques they had developed and were now using.

In the West and Japan, however, a number of alternative philosophies and techniques have been developed and are now in operation which challenge the logic underpinning the traditional forms of production planning and control. The advent of the computer in Western manufacturing has caused an explosion in the use of requirements planning systems where, instead of depending entirely on forecasts of expected future demand, the production and purchasing schedules for components and other materials are generated from the master production schedule, the plan for manufacture of the finished product. Using such materials requirements planning (MRP) systems parts and materials are planned to enter the factory or immediate work area as and when required, rather than being buffered in expectation of uncertain future demand.

Japanese approaches, loosely identified as Just-in-Time (JIT) management, challenge not only the more traditional optimization methods, but also the logic underlying the use of MRP. The chief concern is that planning and control of operations should be on the basis of demand pull rather than planning push. In 'push' systems, such as those operating under statistical inventory control or MRP systems, order times and anticipated start times are planned and production executed in expectation of future demand. This can create difficulties in production, particularly in the case of MRP where data accuracy is paramount and there can be discrepancies between schedules and quantities produced. Also, where situations change (e.g. costs alter, production and order lead times vary, or orders are cancelled), this can result in over-stocking or, conversely, shortages of materials. In contrast, Japanese inspired 'pull' systems are inventory (or usage) based systems whereby orders are placed when parts are required at the succeeding stage of production. Thus, a triggering effect occurs. Systems which pull their requirements from preceding activities 'just-in-time' to meet immediate requirements (as opposed to 'just-in-case' or 'just-too-late' ordering and receipt) are now viewed as an effective way of ensuring that manufacturing operations are responsive to market demands. Moreover, whereas push planning and control systems are liable to assume certain values when setting parameters for their operation (i.e. costs of ordering, lead times/set up times and holding costs), JIT/pull management actively attacks these assumptions and any other problems which prevent synchronization of the operating system and thereby encourage manufacture or purchase in large batch sizes. Therefore, in contrast to the optimization inherent in the more traditional planning and control management, JIT engenders an improvement approach which relates well with modern notions of total quality management and lean production. The Japanese philosophy of JIT is based around simple concepts of simplicity of control and operation, and techniques such as *Kanban* (the JIT production control system developed by Toyota for shop floor control) ensure that material is available in the right quantity and quality at the right time and in the right place (Schonberger 1982, 1986; Womack *et al.* 1990). Additionally not only are JIT systems straightforward in operation, but also can be extended to authorize and control ordering and movement of parts and materials between suppliers and vendors.

It was interesting to note an almost total absence of JIT/pull planning and control in the companies visited in China. Only in two joint venture factories where, in both cases, the foreign partner has played an active part in establishing the production facilities, was there any evidence of JIT operation. Most factories displayed symptoms of *ad hoc* or push-based planning and control within the factory, most apparent in the high levels of work in progress and poor co-ordination of facilities. Given the simplicity of basic JIT operation in comparison with the rather more complex methods of optimization and computer-based requirements planning, it is perhaps surprising that more companies in China have not adopted just-in-time in the control of their operations. A probable cause of the slowness of take-up is the technological fix apparent in many of the companies visited where senior managers run the risk of being distracted by the impressive product and process technologies of foreign competitors and joint venture partners. Attention then turns to how the Chinese company closes the technological gap, to the detriment of more simplistic and, often, more appropriate measures of improved control of operations which can give more immediate and far reaching benefits. The adoption the JIT philosophy and its associated practices seems to be an area for considerable take-up and resultant benefit for many Chinese companies.

QUALITY MANAGEMENT

Quality management has been separately identified for investigation during the study of Chinese organizations for two reasons. First, modern notions of managing quality in the industrialized market economies of the world see quality assurance as more than merely inspecting and testing through shop floor quality control. Instead quality is viewed as of strategic importance to the business: it is, at least, an order qualifier and, in many instances, is seen as a key order winner for business and therefore of strategic concern. The emphasis in quality management has therefore shifted from a sole reliance on quality of conformity, where goods in manufacture are expected to meet the design specification of the product, to an increased concern with quality of design, ensuring that possible sources of defects are removed in the design of the product and the development and control of production processes. The issue of quality therefore permeates all levels of the organization: strategy, design and operational planning and control. Second, quality is widely seen as a key area of importance for Chinese manufacturers. Chinese consumers have become accustomed to poor and unreliable products and, because of central state objectives in terms of production volumes, manufacturers have traditionally concentrated on quantity rather than quality. Now that companies are increasingly operating in a free market environment and/or are developing export markets for themselves, an increasing number are seeing the importance of quality as a key order winner and critical factor in business success. The achievement and maintenance of high levels of quality is therefore paramount should Chinese producers wish to further develop domestic markets, where customers are increasingly particular and demanding about product quality and reliability. Most significantly, the improvement of quality standards is critical if companies are to export successfully to overseas markets.

As expected, the management of quality emerged as probably the key issue raised by respondents in the case companies observed in Hangzhou and Shanghai. They were all keen to report the prizes and awards they had won for quality, so it was soon apparent that the improvement of quality was high on the agenda for manufacturing and corporate managers alike. However, it was also very clear that many organizations visited were not altogether sure as to the way forward. As a consequence, whilst attempting to promote a quality image of their organization, managers were quick to enquire of the researchers as to what they thought were the main lessons they might glean from the quality improvement approaches employed both in the West and in Japan.

The problem in many factories in China regarding quality has been quite simple to identify. Manufacturing performance under the quota system was primarily judged on achieving a predetermined volume of production. Thus the emphasis was on quantity rather than quality, and this was further extenuated by the fact that Chinese managers had little or no direct contact with either home or foreign customers, so there was a lack of feedback from the market. This lack of end customer focus resulted in limited knowledge concerning customer requirements and satisfaction. The introduction of economic and market reform in China has led to increased market awareness by Chinese manufacturing managers, and the identification of the need to get quality under control as a key operational concern. In the factories visited there was evidence that, in order to establish basic control over product quality and production processes, managers had introduced a great number of quality control stations at different stages of manufacture. Many factories had, as a consequence, increased the quality of goods leaving the factory by identifying defective work before it left. However, this reliance on mass inspection only serves to highlight the extent of the quality problem in many Chinese factories: problems of defective work, high scrap rates, defects and a lack of process control. The evidence suggests that, in many factories, the concept of quality management had not yet evolved from 'quality of conformity' to the right-first-time ethos of 'quality by design'.

A small number of the foreign joint venture companies visited, which were aware of the need to attain international standards of quality, were working towards the goal of achieving ISO 9000 quality standard accreditation. As in the West, this is seen as a way to improve the reliability and effectiveness of management practices and procedures such as design management, engineering change, documentation and quality control/ assurance activities, all of which have a bearing on the quality of the final product, and the level of service and consistency when dealing with customers. ISO 9000 was seen as a goal for these companies as it would signify a standard of quality management practice comparable with accredited companies internationally. However, the majority of companies visited displayed a lack of awareness of such international standards and quality audit systems. It is probable that continued ignorance of such standards, and the benefits of auditing the overall quality management system, could severely limit the competitiveness and market opportunities of Chinese manufacturers in the short term and, if such a situation continues, in the longer term as well.

CONCLUSIONS

Within the Chinese economy the number of companies obtaining the right to have increased degrees of autonomy in their decision making processes is increasing rapidly. This has implications and provides a major challenge for the management of production within Chinese factories and is seen as a major imperative to changes in the approach taken to factory management. This chapter has examined manufacturing management practice in Chinese factories using a four-part framework to structure empirical research data which was collected in interviews with Chinese managers, and the related fieldwork conducted in production organizations in Zhejiang Province and Shanghai.

At the level of operations the companies visited continue to grapple with the vexed question of how to reflect corporate and marketing decisions made within the context of an emergent free market with the choice of processes, work organization and operational planning/control methods within the factory. It has been demonstrated how the manufacturing strategy literature can provide some guidance for Chinese managers through the provision of frameworks to assist in the analysis of manufacturing effectiveness and the formulation and implementation of new, market-focused, strategies. The advantages and caveats of the popularity of joint venture agreements with foreign partners in relation to operations strategy were also considered. It was found that whereas these can provide necessary injections of capital and access to export markets, and facilitate the transfer both of product/process technology and management practice, there is a danger that they might be entered into by factor leaders keen to enhance their autonomy from the central ministries, and their power and authority within the company. In the latter situation, the improvements required at the operations level to support new marketing strategies may not be forthcoming.

Both design decisions and operational planning and control choices within many of the companies visited seemed to be constrained by a continued technological drive. Much of the developmental effort within China concentrates upon the issue of transforming science and technology into productive power. This is reflected in the research of the majority of Chinese scholars in the practical development of production management techniques. There has been little attention paid to organizational design and the work organization of employees. The evidence from the case companies, where the importance of technological change was heavily stressed, would appear to support this assertion.

The management of quality emerged as probably the key issue in the companies studied. They were all keen to report the prizes and awards they had won for quality and also questioned the researchers about any lessons they might learn from the West and Japan. Chinese consumers have become accustomed to poor and unreliable products and, because of ministry objectives stated in terms of production volumes, manufacturers have traditionally concentrated on quantity rather than quality. Now that some companies are operating in a limited market economy and/or developing export markets for themselves, an increasing number are seeing the importance of quality as a key order winner and critical factor in business success.

In conclusion, some theory and 'best practice' prescriptions emerging from the Western operations management literature are partially appropriate for Chinese enterprises. Notably the emergent literature on manufacturing strategy, which seeks to link corporate decisions to a market-focused approach to the management of operations, has relevance to the Chinese situation. The philosophies, tools and techniques of quality management also appear to have pertinence for Chinese manufacturing management. However, the models and frameworks for production system design appear to be more limited in their application at present. These tend to be rather market-deterministic in style which, from empirical observations at the companies studied, does not reflect the approach currently adopted by many Chinese managers, where technological advancement and improved productivity are often seen as the overriding priority. Indeed, given the comparative cost advantage of manufacture in China, there is some credence in the theory that the widespread pursuit of economies of scale is still a viable option for Chinese manufacturing managers, whereas Western producers are increasingly concentrating on high variety, 'economy of scope' production. There is some justification, however, for thinking that the Japanese exemplar may provide some guidance to Chinese manufacturing companies, given Japanese success in the volume markets of the world. In addition, Western operations management literature often displays a rather naive and rational perspective on the nature of decision making, one which largely overlooks the political influences on the processes of strategy formulation, design and operational management. The Chinese cases in this study, however, illustrate how the political context of the organization tends to have a critical bearing on the practices and style of manufacturing management adopted within the factory. The context within which manufacturing management decisions are made is extremely important and constraints upon the enterprise continue to inhibit the application of Western and Japanese-inspired manufacturing methods and techniques in China. Further empirical studies at the factory level are therefore required in order that we might better understand the process of manufacturing decision making within the modern Chinese enterprise.

ACKNOWLEDGEMENTS

The research upon which this chapter is based is funded by the British Council's Academic Links with China Scheme (ALCS). The author appreciates the support of the British Council in this work. Thanks also to my colleagues at Keele who have participated in the research, and Dr Robin Porter in particular for introducing me to work in China and jointly conducting the fieldwork with me, the data from which forms the basis of this chapter.

REFERENCES

Abernathy, W. J. (1978) *The Productivity Dilemma*, New York: Johns Hopkins University Press.
Bennett, D. J. and Forrester, P. L. (1993) *Market-Focused Production Systems*, Hemel Hempstead: Prentice-Hall.
Bennett, D. J. and Wang Xing Ming (1991) 'Manufacturing flexibility in Chinese enterprises', in Li Ming (ed.) *Transformation of Science and Technology into Productive Power*, London: Taylor and Francis.
Burns, T. and Stalker, G.M. (1966) *The Management of Innovation*, London: Tavistock.
CBI (Confederation of British Industry) (1989) *Opportunities in China: Who Will Benefit?*, Royston, Herts.: Rooster.
Gyllenhammer, P. (1977) *People at Work*, Reading, Mass.: Addison-Wesley.
Hayes, R. H. and Wheelwright, S. C. (1984) *Restoring Our Competitive Edge*, New York: Wiley.
He Jinsheng and Steward, F. (1991) 'An industrial competitiveness study in China', paper presented at *6th Operations Management Association Conference*, Birmingham: Aston Business School.
Hickson, D. J. *et al.* (1985) *Top Decisions: Strategic Decision Making in Organisations*, Oxford: Blackwell.
Hill, T. J. (1993) *Manufacturing Strategy* (2nd ed.), London: Macmillan.
Lee, P. N. S. (1987) *Industrial Management and Economic Reform in China 1949–1984*, Oxford: Oxford University Press.
Oakley, M. H. (1984) *Managing Product Design*, London: Weidenfeld and Nicolson.
Pascale, R. T. and Athos, A. G. (1981) *The Art of Japanese Management*, New York: Simon and Schuster.
Peters, T. J. and Waterman, R. H. (1982) *In Search of Excellence*, New York: Harper & Row.
Schonberger, R. J. (1982) *Japanese Manufacturing Techniques*, New York: Free Press.
—— (1986) *World Class Manufacturing*, New York: Free Press.

Skinner, W. (1969) 'Manufacturing: missing link in corporate strategy', *Harvard Business Review* 47, May–June.

—— (1978) *Manufacturing in the Corporate Strategy*, New York: Wiley.

Snead, C. (1989) *Group Technology*, New York: Van Nostrand Reinhold

Utterbeck, J. M. and Abernathy, W. J. (1975) 'A dynamic model of process and product innovation', *OMEGA* 3(6).

Wacker, J. (1987) 'How advanced is modern Chinese manufacturing management?' *International Journal of Operations and Production Management* 7(3).

Whipp, R. and Clark, P. A. (1986) *Innovation and the Auto Industry*, London: Frances Pinter.

Womack, J. *et al.* (1990) *The Machine That Changed the World*, London: Macmillan.

8   Changing patterns of collaboration between research organizations and business enterprises in technological innovation in China

Fred Steward and Charles Quan Li

ABSTRACT

This chapter reviews the changing relationships between research organizations and business enterprises in China. The three-tier Chinese research system is described and the top-down and bottom-up mechanisms which influence particular research programmes are outlined. The research focused on patterns of collaboration between enterprises and research institutions by examining data gathered from the scheme for National Awards for Scientific and Technological Progress which recognized domestic achievement in China. The findings suggest that closer linkage between research and production is being achieved by the extension of internal capabilities either within research organizations or business enterprises, rather than through the extension of formal collaboration between the two sectors.

INTRODUCTION

The relationship between research organizations and business enterprises in China has been a major focus of the reform process since the mid-1980s. This chapter explores the shifts in policy over this period and analyses some empirical data on changing patterns of collaboration between organizations from the research, business and government sectors. These organizations have all been officially recognized as engaged in successful technological innovation. Underlying the analysis is a recognition that innovation is an interactive rather than a linear process and that this has important implications for collaboration between different organizations in the Chinese research system.

The interactive model of the innovation process (Rothwell 1985) identifies the critical role of coupling a new technical opportunity with a market need in the successful management of innovation. It gives primary significance to the organizational capability required to achieve effective integration between research and customer. This capability is often concerned with the intraorganizational integration of different functions within a business enterprise. Increasingly the importance of interorganizational collaboration has also been recognized (Dodgson 1993). The model focuses on managerial capability embodied in specific independent organizations as the key asset for successful innovation.

The linear, science push model of innovation is quite different. It sees advances in scientific knowledge as the initiator for innovation. This model places emphasis on the creation of effective research organizations, adequate investment in them and project choice as the main focus for innovation management. It implies a hierarchy from ideas down to application. The business side of the process is limited to the commercial application of new ideas transferred from the research side. Empirical studies show the linear science push model to have serious limitations in the achievement of an innovative and competitive business enterprise sector (Langrish *et al.* 1973).

The expression of the science push model is found in market economies in the form of separate centralized corporate research laboratories and a distinct public research sector. However, it assumes its most extreme form in the research and development systems adopted in Soviet styled planned economies. The system originally developed in the People's Republic of China is such a case.

THE CHINESE RESEARCH SYSTEM

The Chinese R&D system is vertically structured on three levels. At the top level, the State Science & Technology Commission co-operates with other functional commissions to draft national science and technology plans and to supervise their implementation. Below this there are a number of industrial ministries, which are responsible for specific industries and where broad policy directives are translated into actual R&D projects. The third level in the hierarchy is that of provincial or municipal government where R&D plans reflect both tasks assigned from the central government and projects concerned with local needs. Research institutes are attached to both the second and the third levels, but not to the top one. Institutional arrangements differ between industrial ministries and localities.

R&D capacities are separately organized into five different sectors: the Chinese Academy of Sciences (CAS), the industrial ministries, the higher education sector, the defence research sector and the local research sector. These are all separate from the business enterprise sector. A linear sequence of innovation was envisaged. Universities provided technical manpower to research institutes; the academy generated basic scientific ideas; industrial research institutes supplied applied technologies; and production enterprises manufactured products. The primary role of industrial enterprises was considered to be production not innovation. As Conroy concludes:

The main generator of new S&T knowledge in China is the formal research sector. ... The main agent for transforming this knowledge into products/technology is the production sector. ... The state controls the development and orientation of research and development (R&D) through the planning of research topics and allocation of resources. It also largely controls the demand for new technology through decision making on what new products and processes are to be manufactured.

(Conroy 1984a: 2–3).

Centralized planning is claimed to provide more efficient and effective use of resources and research results. The two basic elements of the R&D system, hierarchical levels and sectoral compartments, are complicated, however, by the complex replication, fragmentation and inconsistencies of the system as it has evolved.

Replication is illustrated by features of the national R&D/industrial system being reproduced in different sectors and regions. Industrial ministries are equipped with their own universities, research institutes and production enterprises. Provinces developed their own versions of these structures to differing degrees. Since every ministry has its own universities, the State Education Commission only controls a proportion of Chinese universities.

Fragmentation is encouraged by a proliferation of separate administrative arrangements. For example, within industrial ministries, it is common practice for research, production and training to be supervised by different functional departments. Industrial enterprises are normally administered by the department of a particular product group; research institutes are administered by the department of science and technology; universities are supervised by the department of education.

Inconsistencies in the vertical chain of control become more apparent further down. Many local research institutes are subordinate to industrial bureaux at the provincial or municipal level. Since these industrial bureaux are local representatives of their respective industrial ministries, local research institutes are still controlled by central ministries, although local governments seek to assert significant influences and preferences. The difficulties are compounded by the relationship between defence and civil R&D spheres. Defence-related R&D undertakings are co-ordinated by the State S&T Commission for National Defence, but are largely performed by research organizations in industrial ministries and the Chinese Academy of Sciences.

TOP-DOWN PLANNING

The operation of top-down planning reflects these characteristics. The State Science & Technology Commission, in conjunction with other state commissions, holds meetings with technical experts in various fields.

Sometimes, a temporary planning team is formed. After consultation a preliminary plan is drafted which is examined by the State Planning Commission in relation to the national economic plan. Modifications are made and budgets are calculated. The plans for defence-related R&D drawn by the State S&T Commission for National Defence, and the plan for technical transformation in industrial enterprises prepared by the State Economic Commission (now incorporated into the State Planning Commission), are also integrated into a national plan.

The process is a complicated one, many parties are involved and it is of a political nature, rather than a simple rational selection process (Lieberthal and Oksenberg 1987). To resolve departmental conflicts in the planning process, super-commissional leading groups on S&T were created directly under the State Council and chaired by more powerful figures. These groups often consist of representatives from all state commissions and ministries concerned. These super-commissional leading groups, such as the State Council Leading Group on S&T, the Leading Group for the Development of Electronic Industry, and the Leading Group for Major Technical Equipment were set up as a temporary measure to assert stronger central control.

The State Science & Technology Commission is responsible for the final allocation of research projects and research budgets. This is not done directly to the individual research performers but through the existing system of industrial ministries, the academy, etc. (Conroy 1984b).

Within industrial ministries there have also been efforts to enforce co-ordination from above. The conventional approach primarily associated with civilian industries is a chain of command from the department of S&T of the ministry to its ministerial-level research organizations or its provincial bureaux, and down the system. The Ministry of Textile Industry and the Ministry of Light Industries are typical examples. Increasingly a strategic model has emerged, more related to defence industries. This involves the establishment of national research academies set up directly under the ministry which consist of a number of research institutes located around the country. Co-ordination is through the academies and often do not involve local bureaux. R&D and production are directly controlled and centrally planned by the ministry. Examples of this type are the Ministry of Aeronautic and Aerospace Industries and the former Ministry of Ship Building (now China Corporation of Ship Building). Through evolution, merger and break up some ministries possess characteristics of both conventional and strategic models. The Ministry of Mechanical and Electronic Industries is a good illustration in this regard. This super ministry was created from three big industrial ministries – Machine Building, Electronic Industry and Ordnance Industry.

Despite these efforts it has been argued that 'the vertical structure of the research system, promoted compartmentalisation rather than co-operation, communication and co-ordination'. Simon considered that this structure was suitable for national projects but not for the business enterprise sector generally:

> While a highly centralized task-oriented mode of organization was conducive to accomplishing such major projects as the development of atomic weapons, it was not appropriate for stimulating the type of innovative behaviour that leads to new and better quality products or more efficient production processes.
>
> (Simon 1985: 65–66)

BOTTOM-UP PLANNING

An alternative way of viewing the planning process is from a bottom-up perspective (Fischer 1983a: 76). Since the national plans for S&T only cover a selection of major projects there are many other projects in the ministerial and regional plans that originate in different ways. They may be formulated by the research units themselves and approved by the higher planning authorities.

This occurs extensively within industrial ministries. In the Ministry of Chemical Industry, for example, two important planning meetings are held annually by the department of S&T of the ministry. The first one is the meeting of representatives from major production units and local bureaux within the ministry. At the meeting, technical problems encountered in the production, problems concerned with production capacity, new products, etc. are raised. After preliminary screening of these problems by the personnel in the S&T department, sometimes in consultation with outside experts, the second meeting is held. This time the participants are personnel in charge of research or directors of research institutes in the ministry. The list of problems put forward by the first meeting is the focus of discussion. In addition, each institute also brings its own proposed research projects for the ministry to approve. These projects are not necessarily all production related; some might be basic research in nature. At the meeting, these research projects are discussed, assessed and roughly allocated. A preliminary plan is achieved at the end of the meeting.

However, such plans needs budget evaluation to ensure they are within the capability of the ministry's R&D budget. If some projects are too big for the ministry to handle, they are handed over to the State S&T Commission to be considered for inclusion in the national plan. Projects within the ministry's budget capability are allocated to research organizations after approval. Since nearly all of these projects are generated from below through consultations, the allocation can be regarded as a formality. Similar patterns occur at the regional level where the regional S&T commissions take the overall responsibility (Li 1991: Interview M).

Fischer argues a bottom-up process is a key feature of the Chinese system. Except for those projects of national priority, the S&T plans are actually initiated by factories' chief engineers, and then reported to the higher administrative level. The planning system is therefore seen principally as a fund allocation, negotiation and data gathering process (Fischer 1983b). It suggests that the role of central authorities in planning may be less important than the influence of sectors and regions.

DUALITY

There is a dichotomy in the operation of the R&D system in China. In some cases centralized control is exercised while in other cases decision making appears to be decentralized. In reality the two elements are interlocked in an extremely complicated manner. Lieberthal and Oksenberg argue:

> two popular concepts of the Chinese system that it is highly centralized (Beijing-in-command) or a cellular system with considerable local autonomy are both inaccurate. ... Negotiations, bargains and exchanges, in short, are essential ingredients of the Chinese system.
>
> (Lieberthal and Oksenberg 1986: 27–28).

This view is shared by Leung with the proviso that ultimate power resides with the centre. He argues that:

> both elements of centralization and decentralization are present in varied, uneasy combination at all times. Constant shifts can and do occur differentially, and in one direction or another. ... Whatever power the centre allows to be devolved to the local levels, it retains the ultimate right to intervene and take back whenever it feels necessary.
>
> (Leung 1984: 157–158).

As we have seen, the operation of both elements appears inimical to collaborative efforts by business or research organizations. In a vertically-chained system, as a result of lack of horizontal communication, the most achievable resources are either from superior level of administration or from subordinates. Because of competition over scarce resources, each organization tries to build up its own jurisdiction as independently as possible. With the establishment of such self-contained units, central control is sometimes sheltered from access to the lower level, or sometimes only has limited impact. This creates a situation where on the one side, the central government tries to control everything as a whole; on the other side, local organizations try to defend their own self-sufficiency.

The reform of innovation policy in China also expresses this duality. It is argued by Simon and Goldman that

> China's reforms are following a 'two-pronged' strategy for bringing about fundamental improvements in science and technology system. China has introduced 'market forces' as tools for stimulating scientific

advance and technological modernization. And, at the same time, it continues to rely on centrally directed control over research in key areas to promote rapid progress in important economic and military sectors.

(Simon and Goldman 1989: 16)

China's current S&T development policy combines elements of both market competition and state control. Nevertheless the state does retain a pervasive role throughout the entire innovation process, even with the introduction of market mechanisms.

Reforms introduced in the mid-1980s sought to re-organize the vertical structure. On the one hand, the lower levels were to be given greater autonomy; on the other hand, lateral links between horizontal units were encouraged, especially the co-operation between research and production organizations. The concepts of 'commercialisation of research' and 'joint research–production entity' expressed the trend.

Decentralization was hoped to bring a number of benefits. Greater operating autonomy of industrial enterprises and research institutes would eliminate a considerable amount of administration. Promotion of horizontal links between research institutes and industrial enterprises would create an environment of market competition. Through economic leverages and market mechanisms dependence upon the State would be reduced. By introducing direct contacts between the research and production sectors, technological innovation would become more one of 'demand-pull' than 'technology-push'. Avoidance of new problems, such as repetitive research, barriers to information sharing and risk-averse decisions was important. An appropriate balance between centralized co-ordination and market self-adjustment was the challenge for policy makers.

In spite of the emphasis on these changes Suttmeier (1989) acknowledged the ambiguities of the reform process:

China's political system has yet to find the 'right formula' for the relationship between centralization and decentralization of its political and administrative institutions. The reforms of the 1980s in the economy, in S&T, and in the political system more generally, while portrayed as decentralizing, also have the objective of increasing effective central power.

THE REFORM PROCESS

Since the Third Session of the 11th Congress of the Communist Party of China (CPC) in December 1978 there has been a commitment to link science & technology more closely to economic and societal development.

The post-1978 period can be considered to fall into three phases. The first phase (1978–1984), when the primary efforts were:

(a) to draw up a national plan for S&T development;
(b) to establish an award system for S&T achievements;
(c) to rationalize the S&T organizational structure.

The second phase (1985–1987) was marked by the issue of 'The Decision of the Central Committee of the CPC on the Reform of S&T Management System' in March 1985. Overall reforms of the S&T system were introduced in this period, including:

(a) the R&D funding system;
(b) new S&T legislation;
(c) the stimulation of commercialized technology transfer through a 'technology market';
(d) changes in the S&T personnel administration system;
(e) policies to encourage rational technology importation.

The third phase from 1987 was marked by more general reform of the economic system.

Managerial capability and organizational suitability were the focus of the mid-1980s reform of the science and technology system itself. A National Working Conference on S&T held in March 1985, marked the beginning of reform in the S&T management system. Deng Xiaoping and Zhao Ziyang addressed the meeting. 'The Decision of the Central Committee of the Communist party of China on the Reform in S&T Management System' emphasized three major areas.

1 Reform of the operating system, which entailed reforming the funding system, establishing a technology market and overcoming defects in the administrative control over S&T activities.
2 Reform of the organizational structure, which implied enhancing the integration of organizations under different jurisdictions and strengthening enterprises' capabilities to absorb and develop new technology.
3 Reform of the personnel system, which aimed to achieve optimum use of talented people by means of rational job mobility (White Paper 1, 1986: Appendix).

State expenditure on S&T was to be increased steadily, but allocated in a different way between three broad groups, developmental research, basic or applied research, and public services. Units engaged primarily in technology development expected to have practical value within a short term were to receive reduced government core funding for operating expenses for scientific research year after year during the Seventh Five-Year Plan period until a time when such funding would be completely suspended.

For units primarily doing basic research or applied research not expected to achieve practical value in the near future, their funding was to become gradually dependent on applying for specific funds, with the state giving only a limited amount of core funding for operating expenses.

Research institutes engaged in public services such as medicine and health, environment and standards, would continue to receive core funding (White Paper 2, 1987: 15).

Although units were encouraged to seek a diversity of funding sources the money removed from their budgets was reallocated to central government departments. Two thirds was to be retained by the competent departments under the State Council for technological work in particular industries or trades and for major national research projects, while one third was to be retained by the State Science and Technology Commission for use as funds for S&T credit loans (White Paper 2, 1987: 16).

The technology market was an important institutional change taking many forms, including exhibition fairs, technical services and horizontal research contracts. In essence, the technology market refers to the sum of the relations between exchange of intellectual commodities (White Paper 1, 1986: 237).

Technology markets were to facilitate the transfer of research results into production applications through contracts between research institutions and business enterprises, by bringing the market mechanism into S&T activities, and by the removal of rigid administrative barriers so that organizations in different administrative sectors could communicate easily.

Since the First National S&T Fair held in Beijing in 1985, various technology fairs have been organized all over the country. Over 1,100 exchange centres were set up, which diffused S&T information throughout the country. In 1987, over 130,000 technical contracts were made, amounting to a total of 335 million yuan which is a 60 per cent increase over 1986. Research institutes and enterprises were the major suppliers in the markets. The technology supplied by enterprises was mature and of quicker application. Enterprises were the major buyers, taking 42 per cent of the total, of which 53 per cent were bought by state run large and medium enterprises (*People's Daily* 23 February 1988: 1).

The technology market was considered to change attitudes 'It ... has helped people to acquire or realize the "sense of value", the "sense of orientation towards the economy", the "sense of market" and the "sense of operation [running a business]"' (White Paper 2, 1987: 66–67). Factors hindering the development of technology markets included: the irrational price system, legal responsibilities of contractual parties not clearly defined by law, but by administrative practices liable to change. Administrative interventions in many cases remained the most decisive method.

The reform of the organizational structure aimed to encourage close integration between research and production organizations from different sectors and localities. Four major types of co-operation were promoted:

1 between research sector and production units;
2 between developed regions and less developed regions;

3   between the military sector and the civilian sector; and in a broader sense
4   between advanced countries and China.

These types of co-operation were designed to facilitate technology transfer from more developed areas/sectors to less developed ones.

One important component was that greater decision making power was granted to research institutes. A system under which directors of institutes assume overall responsibility was introduced, while party branches in such organizations were recommended as only responsible for political or ideological work. This policy was further confirmed at the CPC's 13th Congress in November 1987, by the slogan: 'Separating party leadership from governmental administration and economic activities'. This proved to be a long process with only partial separation and delegation of power feasible in the early stages.

Obstacles to the fulfilment of the objectives of reform fell into two categories. One perspective saw the weakness of management capability as the major constraint. Fischer argued:

> introducing market forces ... will be far less effective in stimulating innovation and industrial change if the managers in that economy are not predisposed, through education and incentives, to recognize the opportunities inherent in such market influences and respond to the new operating environment.
>
> (Fischer 1989: 133)

Others stressed reform of the price system and the creation of an appropriate macroeconomic environment with rewards for innovation through market-type mechanisms as the most effective factor to encourage and support industrial innovation (World Bank 1985).

PATTERNS OF COLLABORATION

An investigation was undertaken to assess the changing patterns of interaction between research organizations and business enterprises during the reform process. Data were gathered from the scheme for National Awards for Scientific & Technological Progress which recognizes domestic innovation achievements in China.

Although there are other award schemes, the National Awards for Scientific and Technological Progress is the most broad and comprehensive in scope, covering some 30 categories of technology ranging across the spectrum of the economy. The basic criteria for the awards are similar to those used to identify significant innovations in other countries, i.e. the innovation is technically novel; and/or the innovation has delivered significant social or economic benefits. Items for nomination are based on peer review and evidence of economic success. Under the jurisdiction of the SSTC, a National Office for Science and Technology Awards is responsible for co-ordinating the award activities nation-wide. Provincial governments and industrial ministries play the most important role in the awarding process. Having been examined by experts and approved by the SSTC, the SSTC award committees announce the list of awards to be conferred. Announcements are normally published in the major national newspapers for public contention.

The scheme is primarily concerned with technological innovations, which have already been applied in industry. It offers an excellent opportunity for accessing patterns of technological innovation of economic significance. A list of National Awards for Scientific and Technological Progress was made available with the assistance of the SSTC for four award-conferring years of the scheme (SSTC 1985, 1986, 1988, 1990).

The time period of innovative activity covered is from 1978 to 1990, during which 1,800 award winning innovations were selected to cover the major manufacturing and consumer industries. This sample was used for the analysis of collaboration between research organizations and business enterprises. The sectors covered were: mechanical engineering, electronic industry, chemical industry, metallurgical industry, transportation, textile industry, light industries (consumer industries), medical equipment and pharmaceutical industry, health service.

Analysis of award winning innovations between 1978 and 1987 shows the relative role of different types of organization in the innovation process (Figure 8.1).

A primary role is fulfilled when the organization is the sole innovator or the lead organization in collaboration with others. A secondary role is played by organizations with a supportive function in collaboration with others.

Research institutes acted as primary innovators in the largest proportion (46 per cent) of cases compared with business enterprises which held a primary role in 31 per cent of cases of innovation. Universities held a relatively smaller share with 15 per cent. Business enterprises played the most important role as secondary innovators (45 per cent) compared to that of research institutes with 33 per cent and universities (10 per cent). Government agencies had a direct primary or secondary involvement in less than 10 per cent of cases.

This pattern confirms the 'science push' model of innovation with research organizations (institutes and universities) fulfilling the majority (over 60 per cent) of primary innovator roles. However, analysis of total involvement in either a primary or secondary role shows both research institutes and business enterprises to hold similar high levels. The volume of supportive involvements by research institutes and business enterprises shows a considerable degree of co-operation and joint activity in the process of innovation. Although many of these collaborative arrangements may have been arranged by government agencies, the low level of direct government involvement suggests that relatively

Type

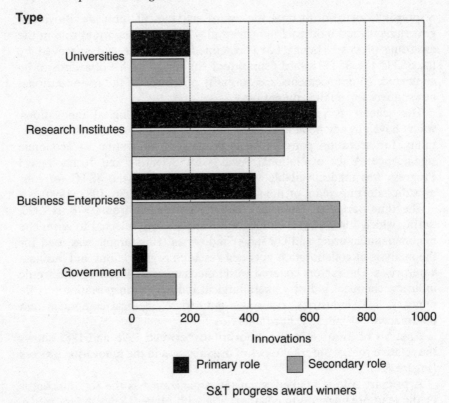

Figure 8.1 Innovating organizations (1978–1988)

independent co-operation between the research and business sectors may be fairly extensive.

One of the primary goals of the science and technology reforms of the mid-1980s was to facilitate a more interactive model of innovation. Analysis of the changing patterns of collaboration between organizations in the innovation process is therefore of particular interest. The sample of 1,800 award winning innovations can best be considered in three time periods 1978–1984 (awards made in 1985), 1985–1987 (awards made in 1987 and 1988) and 1988–1990 (awards made in 1990). Recognizing the lag between the innovation process and the receipt of award these three periods relate to three policy phases: the restoration of the traditional R&D system; the 1985 S&T management reforms; and the 1987 economic reforms.

Analysis of the extent of collaboration (Figure 8.2) shows that throughout the three periods over 50 per cent of the award winning innovations were based on interorganizational collaboration.

The proportion of collaboration initially fell during the 1985–1987

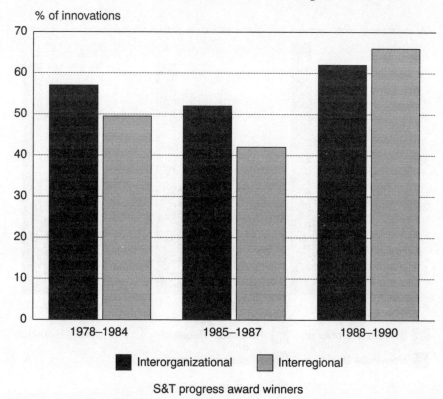

% of innovations

■ Interorganizational   ▨ Interregional

S&T progress award winners

Figure 8.2 Extent of collaboration (1978–1990)

period but then increased to over 60 per cent in the 1988–1990 period. The initial impact of the mid-1980s reforms appears to have been to discourage interorganizational collaboration. This was the opposite of the stated policy intention.

Investigation of the linkages between different types of organization (Figure 8.3) reveals a number of different patterns of change.

The largest category of collaboration, that between research institutes and business enterprises, falls during 1985–1987 and then remains stable at this lower level into 1988–1990. Collaboration between different research institutes, on the other hand, shows a steady and marked increase throughout the three periods from under 10 per cent in 1978–1984 to over 25 per cent in 1988–1990. Collaboration between business enterprises showed a decline in 1985–1987 which was then restored to just over the 1978–1984 level by an increase in 1988–1990. Collaboration between universities remained steady but very small in 1985–1987 and increased markedly in 1988–1990.

In summary, the initial fall in the overall degree of collaboration in

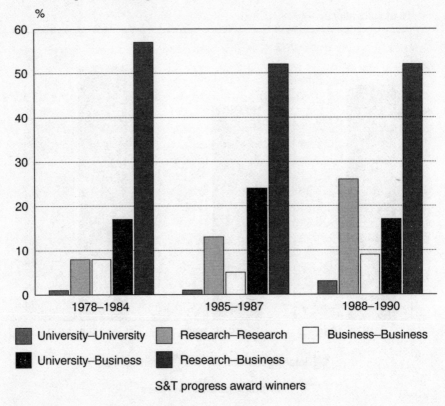

Figure 8.3 Types of collaboration (1978–1990)

1985–1987 was accompanied by a decline in the collaboration between research institutes and business enterprises. The subsequent marked increase in the overall degree of collaboration in 1988–1990 was not accompanied by any increase in this type of collaboration. Instead, the major increases in interorganizational collaboration have been between research organizations within the same sector (institutes or universities). A shift in collaboration between business enterprises themselves to one between business enterprises and universities appeared in the 1985–1987 period but was subsequently reversed in 1988–1990.

One factor which would be expected to influence the nature of collaboration is the technical novelty of the innovation. This is reflected in the class of award. Homogeneous co-operation between research institutes is higher in the special and first class awards than in the lower classes. In contrast, homogeneous co-operation between business enterprises was higher in the third class awards than in higher class awards. Universities and government agencies also figure more strongly in the higher class awards. This pattern would support the view that research organizations were more likely to be involved in innovations of high technical novelty than other types of organization. Strategic importance is probably a more important factor for government agencies and this may also be reflected in the class of award.

Another factor which needs to be considered is regional variation. The dominant role of research institutes in Beijing and Shanghai is partly because they are home to a large number of them, although the two national R&D centres do differ. In Beijing universities are more active than business enterprises while in Shanghai it is the reverse. In some industrially developed regions, business enterprises outnumber research institutes in involvement in innovation. These regions include Liaoning, Jiangsu, Shandong, Tianjin and Heilongjiang. This suggests that at the national level in key R&D centres research institutes play the principal role. As far as each individual region is concerned, business enterprises become increasingly important. In regions other than Beijing and Shanghai the roles played by research institutes and business enterprises are similar.

Also, in a few exceptional regions university performance as primary innovator is better than that of the business enterprise. These include Beijing, Shaanxi, Guangdong and Zhejiang. This is influenced by the absolute size of the sector.

As well as variations in the role of different types of organizations in different regions it is necessary to distinguish two patterns of collaboration. Intraregional collaboration is confined to organizations within one province. Interregional collaboration crosses provincial boundaries. During the whole period covered a majority of collaborative innovation is interregional. Comparison between the three time periods shows a marked drop of interregional collaboration in 1985–1987 followed by a striking increase in 1988–1990. (Figure 8.2). In other words collaboration became more confined within the boundaries of individual regions during the first phase of reform but the trend was radically reversed during the second phase. Interregional collaboration is more strongly associated with innovations of high technical novelty as shown by awards in the higher classes.

Analysis of the data on award winning innovations in China therefore shows a pattern which is deeply shaped by the science push tradition of the research system. The trends of change since 1985 suggest that the impact of the first phase of reform was the opposite to that intended. Rather than horizontal interorganizational interaction becoming more prevalent and extensive, collaboration, instead, became more restricted and localized. These trends were reversed during the second phase of reform.

Collaboration between different organizational sectors also diminished, principally that between research institutes and business enterprises. Collaboration between organizations within the bounds of the research institute sector increased through both phases of reform. Although, in the first phase of reform, collaboration between the business enterprise and university sectors increased, this was reversed in the second phase. By the end of the period analysed, growth in collaboration of business enterprises or universities was also confined to that between the same type of organization within its own separate sector.

Can these trends be explained by changes in organizational capabilities and the policy context? In 1985 research institutes were granted greater autonomy in their operations. Directors of research institutes were put in charge organizationally, financially and academically. Subsequently a new policy was introduced for applied R&D institutes to become self-financing within a specified time period, except those in the basic research and public service area. There was financial pressure to find research projects and institutes tended to take on projects with less risk and quicker returns. Although this may have been accompanied by new interorganizational contractual arrangements it was probably at the expense of longer term, more uncertain collaboration on projects with the degree of technical novelty that would be recognized by a national award system.

Related to this may have been a shift towards local partners, business enterprises or research institutes, which offered arrangements with assured commercial returns rather than technical novelty. Consultation and communication is easier with geographical proximity and interregional activities are likely to involve different provincial administrations resulting in sticky and slow procedures.

It seems to have been the case that the lack of an agreed legal framework for contracts along with the continuance of an arbitrary pricing structure during the first phase of reform, led to a retreat from interorganizational interactions rather than the reverse. Advances in these two policy areas in the late 1980s set a new broader context in which the intentions of science and technology policy reform for greater and wider horizontal interaction began to be fulfilled.

Nevertheless, although collaboration began to increase in the second period of reform (1988–1990) the pattern of interorganizational relationships was not expressed in more cross-sectoral links between research organizations and business enterprises as traditionally defined. Instead the growth appeared to be between organizations within the same sector, mainly between research institutes themselves but also between universities and between business enterprises.

CHANGES WITHIN RESEARCH INSTITUTES

Interviews were conducted with 38 research managers from the research institute sector to explore the institutional changes accompanying these patterns of collaboration.

Under the new competitive circumstances, there were a number of channels through which research institutes could generate their income.

First, the institute could still obtain research projects from the state, including both central and local governments, on a contractual basis through competitive bidding. This type of contract is frequently called a 'vertical contract'. Vertical research contracts are generally from the following sources: SSTC national plans, ministerial projects, defence-related projects from the State S&T Commission for National Defence, and local economic plans.

These vertical contracts remain centrally controlled in nature. This is reflected in two aspects: first, the centralized R&D planning process remains largely as in the past, and second, imperfect competition oper-ates in the allocation of research projects. Both aspects are determined by the planned nature of Chinese R&D systems. This is reflected by the fact that the position of a R&D institute in the R&D hierarchy deter-mines its degree of access to research projects and other R&D resources. It is commonly seen that projects are more likely to be granted to direct subordinate research units under the authorities, even though other research units may be more suitable or qualified.

Professionally, the centralized R&D system is designed in such a way that some research organizations are established as the centres for certain industry/technology, equipped with better research facilities and personnel. Naturally, when a competitive mechanism is introduced, these research units are in a much stronger position than other units in winning contracts. (Li 1991: Interviews G, J and K). Imperfect competition also exists sectorally in relation to government industrial/technology policy. When certain industrial sectors are chosen as priorities to develop, more projects are approved and more R&D resources are channelled to these sectors. As a result, R&D institutes in these sectors get research contracts much more easily.

Second, an R&D institute can look for research projects in the open marketplace, i.e. contracted research. This type of contract is often referred to as a 'horizontal contract'. Contracts of this type vary a great deal in their technical contents. Many of them are not necessarily tech-nically intensive, but are to provide technical service, consultancy or training.

In terms of competition, the market mechanism plays a greater role in horizontal contracts. However, due to the lack of effective and efficient infrastructure, such as a technical information network and a legal frame-work, many research contracts are not won through 'real' market compe-tition, but through personal or organizational connections. As admitted by an engineer from Beijing Academy of Iron and Steel, 'research groups look for horizontal contracts largely through personal contacts with factories and visits, not through technology markets' (Li 1991: Interview C).

Moreover, the ability of a R&D institute to attract research contracts is affected by its technical specialization. A R&D institute in applied industrial technology may find it more comfortable to adapt to the new competitive environment, but institutes engaged in specialized areas or basic research may find it rather difficult to do so. On horizontal research projects, a research assistant from Wuhan Research Institute of Physics, CAS, said, 'people don't like to do it, as it is not the same basic research people used to do before; and people simply don't know how to find contracts' (Li 1991: Interviews G, D and K).

Taking into consideration the existing technical levels of Chinese industrial enterprises and their motive for quick economic returns in the reform, research institutes who can offer appropriate and/or incremental technologies to increase short-term productivity and cut costs, are most favoured by business enterprises. In return, these projects bring quick economic income to R&D institutes and research individuals, thus helping the institutes to realize the target of self-financing. Consequently, in many research organizations, 'short, simple and quickly profitable' projects are most favoured.

Such a two-way demand cycle determines the presence of short-term behaviour in economic and technological activities in the reform. Many concerns have been expressed that if such short-term behaviours are to continue, China will lose its momentum of technological development in the coming century. Many researchers have urged the need to maintain a proper balance between long-term and short-term research and between basic and applied research (Li, 1991: Interviews A, F, K and C).

Many R&D institutes adopted a mixed approach in their innovation management:

(a) to fulfil a reasonable amount of vertical projects assigned by the state, or bid for, provided they carry enough funding
(b) to achieve as much 'real' economic benefit as possible by completing quick and profitable horizontal projects
(c) to maintain, if financial resources permit, the running of selected long-term research projects, in order to sustain technical competitiveness in the future. For example, Shenyang Research Institute of Metallurgy of CAS has a deliberate policy of funding research into frontier new material technologies. At the same time, developing horizontal links is positively encouraged (Li 1991: Interview A).

A third major source of research funding comes from the National Natural Science Foundation. The direction of funding is largely towards basic scientific research, with a reasonable portion towards technical research. Apart from the conventional provision of research funds, with state assistance, the National Science Foundation has set up a selection of national open laboratories attached to prestigious R&D institutes or universities nation-wide (Li 1991: Interviews G and L).

Finally, R&D institutes could develop their own research projects. At this level, due to financial constraints, self-initiated projects tend to be small in size. There are several incentives for R&D institutes to develop research projects on their own initiatives. First, R&D institutes regard some research projects as necessary long-term technological reserves. Some of the research results will either be applied directly or will lead to other innovations later. This largely happens in the area of new frontier technology, such as lasers, superconductivity, etc. Second, some projects are carried out with known market potential, although external finance cannot be obtained beforehand. R&D institutes initially have to finance the projects themselves (Li 1991: Interview I). Third, a R&D institute may recommend a research project to a production company or other potential users. Potential recipients then agree to support the research. Since the projects have secured both client and finance, the burden on the R&D institutes is much less than in the first two categories. But this requires close understanding between the R&D institute and its potential customers, so this type of research project normally occurs among old partners (Li 1991: Interviews I, J and L).

One fundamental problem of the Chinese reform is that on the one hand, the government realized the necessity of an independent market system to encourage innovation activities, but on the other hand, the government is extremely reluctant to release all the authority of control. The general feeling of R&D institutes as put by an engineer from Anshan, is that 'there are too many regulations to confine the operation of research institutes, but too few to really regulate the market' (Li 1991: Interview 11). The Chinese government speeded up the process of S&T legislation from the mid-1980s. Technology Contract Law, R&D Institution Law, S&T Foundation Law, etc. were drafted (White Paper 2, 1987: 82–94).

Industrial enterprises were granted more operational power over day-to-day running, finance and personnel matters. Enterprises could even retain a portion of profits and provisions of depreciation write-offs at their own disposal, provided they had met the responsibility targets agreed by the superior bureau and enterprises. However the amount which could be spent on in-house R&D or purchasing new technology from outside, was low. Horizontal contracts remained small in scale while there was a lack of sufficient financial resources. The State Economic Commission introduced the Technical Transformation Programme in industrial enterprises: first, to upgrade the technical level of industrial enterprises; second, to make enterprise managers realize the potential of technological innovation and its impact on product and process innovation; third, to provide additional funds for industrial enterprises to acquire new technology.

Funds for technical transformation come from central or local governments in the form of both loans and grants. These funds, however, are only to help enterprises absorb some of the start-up costs for taking advantage of emerging market opportunities. Just as the changes in R&D funding systems are designed to encourage research institutes to seek potential buyers for their technology, the Programme for Technical Transformation is aimed at motivating enterprises to look for potential partners in the R&D community, who can help them solve technical problems, develop a new product, or improve the quality of an existing product.

The lack of a rational price structure caused quarrels from the beginning of commercialized technology transfer. Both R&D institutes and enterprises complained about unfair pricing. On the enterprise side, company managers were used to a situation where new technology was transferred from R&D institutes under the auspices of central planning, free of charge. The transition from free transfers to commercialized transfers caused resistance, particularly where detailed price negotiations were concerned. On the R&D institute side, institute directors were under increasing pressure to achieve financial self-sufficiency, but they similarly were not used to the commercialized competition, and the prices they asked may not have been entirely rational.

One of the responses to the new environment was for organizations to extend the range of their activities rather than to seek cross sectoral collaboration. Some research institutes developed production activities. For example, the Shenyang Institute of Metallurgy became involved in 'the production of final products for sale to customers' in addition to their established R&D activities. The Beijing Academy of Non-Ferrous Metallurgy also 'expanded its capacity for small scale production'.

Similarly business enterprises developed research activities. The Research Institute of Grinding Machinery was located within the Shanghai Machine Tool Factory. Its research and design capabilities were principally oriented to the company's objectives and, interviewers were told, it 'doesn't co-operate very much with other organizations'. Nomenclature can be confusing when attempts are made to monitor these trends. For example, the China Ship Engineering Research Centre became part of the new China Ship Building Corporation but continued functioning as a separate research institute.

Universities have also become more directly involved in production and business under their own control. Huazhong University of Science and Technology through its National Centre for Laser Technology has developed and marketed several new laser products through the university owned Laser Equipment Factory and the Image Development Company (*Guangming Daily* 31 October 1993) 'High tech enterprises set up by universities' have become 'an important tool' according to the State Education Deputy Commissioner(*Guangming Daily* 31 December 1993).

CONCLUSION

The analysis of changes in the research institutes offers an explanation of the changing patterns of collaboration identified. It suggests that closer linkage between research and production is being achieved by the extension of internal capabilities within either research organizations or business enterprises rather than through the extension of formal collaboration between the two traditional sectors. Within this overall pattern it appears that commercialization of activities within the research sector has been the major change.

It is apparent that the reform endeavours of the 1980s did not achieve their stated policy goals in a straightforward manner. The institutional autonomy fostered by the mid-1980s' reforms led initially to less collaboration rather than more. When accompanied by wider economic reform in the late 1980s it did result in more collaboration, but one based on the diversification of existing organizations.

ACKNOWLEDGEMENTS

The authors wish to acknowledge the financial support of the British Council, the Chinese State Educational Commission and the State Science and Technology Commission under the Technical Co-operation Programme and the Academic Links with China Scheme. In addition we also wish to thank the Department of Science and Technology Policy of the State Science and Technology Commission for its assistance in the data acquisition and acknowledge the co-operation of Chinese research institute staff as interviewees during the research.

REFERENCES

Conroy, R. (1984a) 'Technological Innovation in China's Recent Industrialisation', *The China Quarterly* 1: 1–23.
—— (1984b) 'Science Planning in China', *Asian Exchange* 3(2 and 3): 7–32.
Dodgson, M. (1993) *Technological Collaboration in Industry*, London: Routledge.
Fischer, W. A. (1983a) 'The Structure and Organisation of Chinese Industrial R&D Activities', *R&D Management* 13 (2): 63–81.
—— (1983b) 'The Chief Engineer (R&D)', *The China Business Review* November–December: 30–34.
—— (1989) 'China's Industrial Innovation: The Influence of Market Forces', in D. F. Simon and M. Goldman (eds) *Science and Technology in Post-Mao China*, Cambridge, Mass.: Harvard University Press: 119–136.
Guangming Daily 1993 Beijing: Guangming Daily Publishers, 31 October and 31 December.
Langrish, J., Gibbons, M., Evans, W. and Jevons, F. (1973) *Wealth from Knowledge*, London: Macmillan.
Leung, C. K. H. (1984) 'Central–Provincial Relations in China: An Application of the Prefectoral Model', in M.Chen and L. N. Shyu (eds) *China Insight – Selected Papers from the Canadian Asian Studies Association Annual Conference Proceedings 1982–1984*, Toronto, Canadian Asian Studies Association: 136–168.
Li Quan (1991) 'Technology Policy and Technological Innovation in the People's Republic of China', PhD thesis, Birmingham: Aston Business School.
Lieberthal, K. and Oksenberg, M. (1986) 'Understanding China's Bureaucracy', *The China Business Review* 13 (6): 24–32.

Lieberthal, K. and Oksenberg, M. (1987) *Policy Making in China: Leaders, Structures and Processes*, Princeton, NJ: Princeton University Press.

People's Daily (Overseas Edition) (1988) People's Daily Publishers, Beijing.

Rothwell, R. (1985) *Reindustrialisation and Technology*, London: Longman Group.

Simon, D. F. (1985) 'China's S&T Intellectuals in the Post-Mao Era: A Retrospective and Prospective Glimpse', *Journal of Northeast Asian Studies*, 4 (2): 7–82.

Simon, D. F. and Goldman, M. (eds) (1989) *Science and Technology in Post-Mao China*, Cambridge, Mass.: Harvard University Press.

State Science & Technology Commission (1985) *Catalogue of National Awards for Science and Technology Progress*, Beijing (in Chinese).

—— (1986) *White Paper on Science and Technology* 1, Guide to China's Science and Technology Policy, Beijing: China Academic Publishers.

—— (1987) *Catalogue of National Awards for Science and Technology Progress*, Beijing (in Chinese).

—— (1987) *White Paper on Science and Technology* 2, Guide to China's Science and Technology Policy, Beijing: China Academic Publishers.

—— (1988) *Catalogue of National Awards for Science and Technology Progress*, Beijing (in Chinese).

—— (1990) *Catalogue of National Awards for Science and Technology Progress*, Beijing (in Chinese).

Suttmeier, R. (1989) 'Science, Technology and China's Political Future', in D. F. Simon and M. Goldman (eds) *Science and Technology in Post-Mao China*, Cambridge, Mass.: Harvard University Press.

World Bank (1985) *China: Long-term Development Issues and Options*, New York: Johns Hopkins University Press.

Part IV

Managing and developing people

9 Adaptive personnel management
Evidence of an emerging heterogeneity in China's foreign trade corporations

David H. Brown and Mohamed Branine

ABSTRACT

Within the state sector the Foreign Trade Corporations (FTCs) have been at the forefront of changes arising out of China's Open Door Policy. The FTCs have had to cope with deregulation, changes in scope and increased internal competition. Such pressures have brought about changes in personnel and management practices. What these changes are and how they relate to the Western development of human resources management (HRM) is the area of interest within this chapter. Structured into three parts, the first part focuses on reviewing concisely the recent debates around HRM and its origins in order to establish the characteristics as a basis of comparison with China's changing personnel practices. The second part is an account of these practices and here the literature is comple- mented by first hand empirical evidence from 18 projects undertaken by the FTCs. Finally, the third part seeks to interpret the Chinese changes. The research confirms increased emphasis in the FTCs on strategic aware- ness, individuality and flexibility. In two areas, however, namely worker representation and involvement, and the empowerment of line managers, there was no evidence of significant change. These developments in the FTCs, whilst far from being widespread throughout China's state owned enterprises, may well be a pointer to emerging personnel management practice.

INTRODUCTION

China's managers face an unenviable task. Since 1986 managers of state owned enterprises (SOEs) have been both the legal representatives of their enterprises and held responsible for their functioning. They have been asked to meet quotas, achieve organizational targets and be account- able for both profits and losses. The difficulties faced by managers in the foreign trade corporations (FTCs), part of the state sector, have been particularly acute. The introduction in 1979 of the Open Door Policy produced increasingly liberalized arrangements for international trade and the FTCs, which were the traditional conduit for import and export business, have undergone massive change. Numbers have grown from 12 national FTCs in 1978 to several thousand in 1993 (MacBean 1994). Provincial and township FTCs, with the power to deal directly with foreign firms, now compete for business with the once dominant national FTCs. And finally the scope of FTCs has been radically altered to embrace the Agency System (acting on behalf of domestic enterprises on a commission basis), the retention of profits, the payment of taxes and the rights to part of the foreign exchange earnings. Increasingly they are in competition with large companies licensed to trade directly with foreigners and with the wholly owned foreign, and Sino–joint ventures, which enjoy similar rights.

All these changes, which arise from the economic and general management reforms, have been accompanied by a raft of employee and personnel based regulations. A number of authors have now commented upon different aspects of these changes: labour law (Zheng 1987); labour contract system (White 1987); wages, bonuses and benefits (Guanghaw 1985; Hu *et al.* 1988); labour allocation (White 1982); labour relations (Littler and Lockett 1983; Lee 1986; Warner 1991); management decisions (Child 1991, 1993, 1994; Lu and Child 1994); management development and training (Warner 1985, 1987, 1992; Brown and Jackson 1991); and on employment policies (Han and Morishima 1992). Hence, in less than a generation the Chinese manager has been faced with the need to be both entrepreneurial and skilled in business decision making, but must do so within a context of demanding social and welfare obligations and within greater inherent constraints in employment, redundancy and reward systems. In aggregate the changes present major problems in managing people and increasingly the notion of learning from the Western development of HRM has attracted interest. For many SOEs changes in the traditional policies of personnel management are already underway, in many cases using the label HRM.

What are these changes and how do they relate to Western development of HRM? In the most recent contribution by Warner (1993) attention was drawn to some of the conceptual and definitional difficulties around HRM and concluded with a note of caution on the likelihood of convergence between Western HRM practices and Chinese management. In an account of very recent field research in China (Easterby-Smith and Brown 1993) a more open conclusion is drawn and evidences some career and manpower planning procedures at least as sophisticated as the most advanced in the UK. Clearly, different interpretations of the Chinese situation are possible (see Child 1994). In this account the approach taken is to try to shed light on this area by focusing on the conditions which have given rise to HRM as a meaningful concept in the West, and to examine to what extent such conditions are present or are likely to be relevant to the changing practices of managing people in China, especially in the FTCs. The stresses and strains which have been felt by these organizations as they deal daily with major changes are likely to emerge in other SOEs as their own agenda for change gathers pace.

To do this the chapter is structured into three main parts. The first part focuses on reviewing concisely the recent debates around HRM and its origins in order to establish the characteristics as a basis of comparison with China's changing personnel practices. The second part is an account of these personnel management practices, especially those that have undergone change. Here the literature evidence is complemented by first hand empirical investigations from a United Nations (UNDP) management development training programme, involving 18 'personnel projects'. These are described in more detail in subsequent sections. And finally, the third part seeks to interpret the Chinese changes, especially in the context of a Western analysis of the rationale underpinning the emergence of HRM as a means of exploring the likely development of HRM in China.

HRM: GENESIS, DEFINITIONS AND DRIVERS

In an ideal world the notion of HRM would not be problematic and this section would be superfluous. However, the burgeoning literature on the real or perceptive differences between traditional personnel management and HRM is ample evidence of the conceptual ambiguities and confusions. Given that a declared aim of this chapter is to make sense of and comment on the practice and management of human resources in China, then a clear understanding of HRM characteristics is needed.

One of the earliest contributions to the debate on personnel versus HRM is that of Watson (1977: 135) who asked whether HRM was a 'rose by any other name' or 'a more fundamental redefinition of personnel management'. Since then many commentators have sought to explain and define the emergence and substantive elements of HRM. In this respect the contributions by Guest (1987), Fowler (1987), Armstrong (1987), Legge (1988, 1989), Torrington (1988), Keenoy (1990) and Keenoy and Anthony (1992) are particularly helpful since they delineate the debate and provide a theoretical background.

In brief, personnel management can be seen as a set of activities related to people, as groups or individuals, at work within structured organizations. It is the process of attracting, holding and motivating people at work through the operation of specific functions ranging from employment (recruitment, selection, design, manpower planning and job allocation); compensation (determination of wages and salaries, job analysis and evaluation); training and development (the setting up of training programmes and running them, performance appraisal and management development); labour relations (communication, negotiation, participation and collective bargaining); administration (the creation and implementation of overall policies, record keeping and information networking); health and safety (the implementation of all procedures of health and safety at work); and discipline (taking disciplinary action against misconduct or non-respect of the organization's rules and practices).

Personnel management places primary emphasis on its traditional staffing function – the efficient fitting of people to jobs that have been designed to achieve specific objectives. Only when this function of personnel has been carried out can it move to functions such as employee appraisal and development. In terms of position, personnel managers, acting as 'personnel specialists', are often seen as playing a mediating role between employees and management, representing the interests of both by trying to resolve conflicts between the two.

By contrast, as Armstrong (1987: 30) states, 'Human resource management (HRM) is being promoted as a new approach which offers far more to chief executives than the conventional techniques of personnel management'. Human resource management is defined as 'a set of policies designed to maximize organizational integration, employee commitment, flexibility and quality of work' (Guest 1987: 503). It can be regarded as an attempt to achieve a unitary policy towards the management of organizations. This entails a widespread belief that all members of the organization, workers and management alike, are part of a team, individuals therein sharing common goals and interests (i.e. the goals of the organization). Models of human resource management are seen to be related to strategies of management that promote mutuality. That means mutual goals, mutual influence, mutual respect, mutual rewards and mutual responsibility in an organization. The argument is that strategies of mutuality will generate commitment which in turn will lead to both better economic performance and greater human development (Walton 1985).

Legge develops the distinction further by arguing the necessity to examine not only the practices of personnel management and human resource management but also their underlying normative models. She explains that,

> in theory, once a normative model of HRM is established and empirical research undertaken, several outcomes are logically possible: the normative models of personnel management and HRM might be similar but their practices differ; their normative models might differ, but their practices be similar; both their normative models and respective practices might be similar, or both, respectively, might differ. It is in the final case that we might be most confident that HRM and personnel management really are different approaches to managing employees.
>
> (Legge 1989: 20)

She goes on to argue that human resource management is not a single model, and that it is useful to distinguish between 'hard' and 'soft' versions (see also Storey 1987). To further explore this variation Legge suggests that the 'hard' version might be said to emphasize the management aspect, and the 'soft' version, the human resource aspect of human resource management.

A feature of the preceding analyses has been the concern with identifying the substantive distinctions between personnel management and HRM. The debate has been largely couched in terms of stereotypes. Recently, however, the practice of managing human resources has been looked at critically with the general outcome that making sharp distinctions between HRM and personnel management is somewhat futile. Keenoy (1990) makes the point that HRM

> is comprised of a variable mixture of three forms of management practice: (1) conventional operational personnel management: the acquisition, training, deployment, development and rewarding of staff together with the institutional management of employee relations; (2) the generic responsibility of line or general managers for the day to day 'people-management' activities; and (3) the strategic business policy decision-making activity designed to ensure a coherent and integrated approach to overall management of the organization.
>
> (Keeney 1990: 7)

The overlap between this account and a comprehensive personnel function is obvious. Guest and Hoque (1993) in their study of over 2,000 establishments found less than 3 per cent formally using the job title of human resource manager, rising to just 15 per cent if the sample is restricted to head offices. The point is made that good human resource policy and practice exists in many of these organizations and can do so under any labelling scheme. Finally, as if to emphasize the point, Goodhart (1993) draws attention to the views of senior personnel professionals who, whilst confirming the decline of big centralized personnel departments and the growth in importance of line management, note that in the main personnel as a function is changing to survive, but again without necessarily a name change.

These latter views are helpful since they divert attention away from the detailed definitional debate towards identifying the changes in practice which are taking place as organizations seek to cope with the stresses and strains of economic cycles and international competition. Without reverting to theoretical stereotypes there is, after a decade of change in the area of managing human resources, a growing consensus on the characteristics of sound organizational policy. In Table 9.1 we summarize the emerging policy principles of HRM as we now see them.

Whilst these five broad HRM principles can be viewed as a defensible set, to make progress in the understanding of the China situation requires an appreciation of the factors underpinning the development of such policies in the West and an assessment of their likely relevance in China. The rise of HRM has been commented upon by a number of authors,

Table 9.1 Emerging policy principles of HRM practice

Policy	Practice
Strategic awareness	A concern to integrate personnel management into organizational planning, especially within the strategic context. This requires supply chain perspective and in particular an appreciation of the environment in terms of customers and key relationships
Empowerment	A distinct move to empower line managers to enable them to both structure and resolve personnel based issues. The role of professional personnel managers therefore moves in the direction of expert facilitators
Individualism	A recognition of the importance of the individual and that an organization's best interests are served by developing practises in the areas of training, development and reward which reflect this view and raise personal commitment. Such a view requires effective organization-to-individual communication
Representation and involvement	A re-definition of the role of third parties, such as unions, in the representation of employees' interests and views. This is manifested through local rather than national agreements and the emergence of new kinds of forums of discussion-joint consultation, team-working, quality circles
Problem orientation and flexibility	A commitment to innovation and flexibility in the approach to and resolution of human resource based issues. Increasingly this results in a lessening of formal procedures and a willingness to act 'outside of contract' where this is seen to be in the shared interests of the organization and employees

notably Mackay and Torrington (1986), Guest (1987), and Legge (1989). From these authors it is possible to identify the following five main factors, or drivers for change.

The changing role for personnel managers

In an influential article by Guest (1987) he refers specifically to the 'failure' of personnel management. He argued that personnel managers had become marginally located and restricted to an administrative support task. The key function of industrial relations was no longer of high concern or non-existent, as line managers increasingly dealt with employees' problems which previously would have fallen within the responsibility of the personnel manager. In the words of Mackay and Torrington (1986: 161–162), 'the role of the personnel practitioner as the "in between" person seems to have gone. Personnel managers appear to be managers first and personnel people second'.

There has been a move away from what Legge (1978: 86) interestingly termed 'deviant innovation' towards 'conformist innovation' (see also Torrington and Hall 1991). Deviant innovation occurs when, for example, a personnel manager does not simply adhere to the consensus regarding organizational goals and interests, but rather seeks to challenge the consensus and promote new ideas. In contrast, 'the conformist innovator goes along with the existing organizational ends and adjusts his means to achieve them' (Legge 1978: 85). The combination of an increasingly competitive market situation with its attendant managerial difficulties and the increasingly support and administration centred role of the personnel manager has meant that such managers are much more likely to be conformist rather than innovators, in Legge's terms.

Competitive advantage and excellence

The search for competitive advantage and excellence has been a subtitle for many organizational policies through the 1980s. Convergence theory advocates such as Beer *et al.* (1985) and Tichy (1982) argued that industrialization on a global scale could not be achieved without better utilization of human resources. The increased competition from South East Asia, especially from Japan led many US managers to emphasize 'improved human resources management as a means of restoring the competitive position of their companies. By encouraging a culture of loyalty and mutuality it is thought that workers will prove to be more committed to the company and hence more productive' (Miles and Snow 1984: 36). Hence, the acquiring and developing of good human resources had become inextricably linked with increased competitiveness. A similar link was made by Peters and Waterman (1982) in which human resource management had become simply 'what the excellent company does'.

The decline of trade union power

A clear development throughout the 1980s has been the reduction in trade union influence. The reasons underlining this were both economic and political; economic recession and free enterprise policies created instability in the labour market. There has been a move towards the decentralization of collective bargaining and a willingness to explore new forms of collective agreements involving processes of joint consultation and co-operative relationships which reduce the employee's dependence on the unions (Guest 1987; Legge 1989; Jackson 1991). The development of this practice, involving more direct contact between employees and management, exemplifies the adoption of an HRM perspective.

The empowerment of line management

In parallel with the declining influence of the unions has been the strengthening of line management. This has manifested itself in the imposition of new working practices and tight discipline as managers took advantage of the relatively weak position of employees because of high unemployment. According to Purcell (1982: 3) 'a new breed of tough managers, almost contemptuous of unions and negotiating procedures seems to have emerged'. He goes on to describe such management as 'macho-management'. A strengthening of management control systems at all organizational levels has become evident and in many organizations the qualities associated with authoritarian macho-management have become synonymous with good management practice.

Changes in the workforce and the nature of work

It has been argued that today's workforce is better educated and has higher expectations (Beer *et al.* 1985), especially with the introduction of new technologies and the possibility of acquiring higher and more flexible skills. The latter mirrors the organizational pursuit of more flexible structure including flexible job content (Atkinson 1984; Atkinson and Meager 1986; Purcell 1987). The market dynamics which have led to the need for organizational flexibility in turn has led to the need for closer integration of human resource planning to meet an organization's strategic intent.

The extent to which these drivers have been, or are likely to be present in China is returned to later. Before doing so, however, it is necessary to look first at what managing people in China has involved and how this is changing.

MANAGING PEOPLE IN CHINA

Despite the reforms having been in progress for some 15 years there is evidence that in the field of personnel management practices adoption of the reforms has severely lagged behind the policy directives (Brown and Jackson 1991: 121). The cautious implementation of such changes is in part explained by the deeply rooted values and practices within Chinese organizations before the reforms. Hence to interpret the present it is necessary to revisit the past.

Before the reforms, it was notably the state, through the party committees, that was in charge of all important personnel decisions from employment to training and development, and to promotions and rewards. Directors of SOEs were selected, appointed, transferred and removed by the state and party committees. Ye (1987: 697) pointed out that despite the fact that 'the managing director was a member of the Party committee, he had only one vote and hence no more power than any other member; in short, this system of collective leadership meant that nobody was really responsible'. The function of planning was based on the state plans which were interpreted by the local authorities and ministries into organizational targets. The function of organizing '... was minimized, since the complex internal organization of simultaneous systems and parallel authority structures permeated and restricted the very essence of Chinese industrial enterprise' (Schermerhorn and Nyaw 1991: 13). The functions of leading and controlling were given to the party officials who sought to ensure that the state plans and targets were being met – frequently without success.

The belief in 'eating out of the same big pot' and having an egalitarian society has for a long time shaped the functions of Chinese management. Personnel decisions were often made away from the workplace by a small circle of leaders who were appointed either by themselves or by the party, virtually as 'caretakers'. They were there to ensure that the 'iron rice-bowl' was available to all who worked and conformed within the system. National procedures for centralized planning and personnel policies and regulations were in place but in the main proved too general as far as controlling the labour market was concerned since the criteria for recruitment, training and promotion were inappropriate or non-existent. Heavy emphasis was placed on loyalty and commitment, which could not be measured. Jobs were assigned regardless of aptitude or personal preference. Rules were very strict for those who wished to transfer or leave their jobs.

The above 'network of constraints', coupled with the lack of power and confidence, created idle managers. In this respect, Han and Morishima (1992: 235), reported that before the reforms 'labour management was the most rigid and furthest removed from market mechanisms. As the economy became more complex, the system became more and more unsuitable and central control of labour allocation proved unrealistic'. Pre-reform therefore, what was happening in China was not personnel management, in the Western sense, but controlled employment policies which were applied through a web of administrative bureaucratic procedures. Many of the administrators and personnel officials operating in that system are the same people who in 1993 found themselves managing within a decentralized, market economy.

From the perspective of managing people the key reforms occurred in 1986 and after when enterprise directors and their managers were given broad responsibilities. The role of party committees in enterprises was limited to the supervision of implementing the principles and policies of the party and government; to the provision of support to trade unions, youth leagues, and other mass organizations in their ideological and political activities; and to the help of party members in maintaining the spirit of socialism in enterprises (Ye 1987).

In theory under the reforms the enterprise directors had been given the right to recruit, select, promote, train, demote and dismiss their employees within the limits of the system. In practice the phrase 'within the limits of the system' is unlimited in its interpretation and prevents many of the difficult decisions having to be made. The state 'system' does not encourage redundancies (even though this is now beginning to happen). In an analysis by Han and Morishima (1992: 249) the objectives of the labour policy reform, which were the liberation and motivation of employees and managers, were only partially achieved. They pointed out that most of the employees and managers had become better motivated and consequently production had increased and productivity improved but they also argued that the reforms produced some unanticipated results which hinder rather than foster the reforms process such as unequal job opportunities and unfair income distribution, increasing conflict between fixed-term and contract-term employees, widespread corruption, high inflation, expectations of personal development vs willingness and ability to confront uncertainties and risks, weak protection of employees' interests, and growing frustration among managers.

What then is the reality for managers in the state owned sector, particularly in the area of managing people? On the one hand their responsibilities for overall enterprise performance, especially outputs and profitability, are highly visible; on the other their control of key input costs, such as labour and conditions of employment and social and welfare obligations, is very limited. Perhaps, not surprisingly, many managers have adopted a rather 'safe or middle' position. Child (1991: 97) noted a preoccupation with staff attitudes and behaviour and an emphasis on formality, for example the requirement of written authorization from general managers before proceeding with the implementation of decisions. Writing in 1993, Easterby-Smith *et al.* have provided additional observations. In a study of comparative HRM decisions between China and the UK, they noted that in China some of the career and manpower planning procedures were at least as sophisticated as the most advanced procedures in the UK. There were however significant differences – in particular the continuing influence of external agencies such as the ministry or the party in key appointments. In the following section further empirical evidence for the nature of these personnel based changes is presented.

EVIDENCE FOR CHANGE

The empirical work referred to below derives from a major UNDP funding management development and training programme for China (Brown 1993). A key feature of the overall training programme was the commitment to develop managers within the top trading corporations and the related departments within the Ministry of Foreign Economic Relations and Trade (MOFERT) who have responsibility for the traditional personnel functions. (Interestingly the term HRM is recognized in these organizations both in terms of referring to their activities and in some instances to defining the titles of post holders in organizational departments.) The main objective of the programme was for the Chinese managers to develop their understanding of Western management concepts in the areas of human resource planning, recruitment and selection, training and development and employee relations through a combination of lectures, cases, site visits in the UK and Canada and individual project work. Briefly the programme required the managers, aged between 25 and 55 and drawn from 20 organizations, to undertake four modules of training over a lapsed time of eight months. During and between the modules the managers were required to focus on a recent initiative that had been undertaken in their organization or on a proposed change which had received approval.

The projects were undertaken by the individuals on a self-selected basis. Western tutors became involved only after the choice of the projects had been made and their input was limited to responding to specific managers' queries about what their organizations were doing or proposing to do. Most frequently these queries took the form of comparisons with Western practice. In the final of the four modules the various projects were written up by the managers in Chinese and presented to other colleagues. The Western tutors were observers only. Each project resulted in a revised report and was published internally by MOFERT and distributed widely throughout the foreign trade sector. The projects on which these reports had been written, together with the discussions held with individual managers, are the basis of the initial empirical observations which we make below. The 20 organizations were the sources of 18 projects which could be classified in four areas: performance appraisal, reward and motivation, manpower planning and policy, and training and career development. The distribution of the self-selected projects is shown in Table 9.2.

From the comprehensive sample of 18 projects a further four, one from each category of initiative, are detailed below. In each case we have teased out the essential elements of the proposed initiative and we reflect on these in the final section.

Case 1: China National Complete Plant Export Corporation (COMPLANT)
Category: Performance appraisal
Title: Appraisal of cadre job performance

COMPLANT was founded in 1959 with responsibility for the implementation of economic and technical aid to foreign countries. After the provision of loans to targeted aid projects COMPLANT assists the recipient countries to carry out the whole set of internal and external activities

Table 9.2 Personnel oriented project initiatives in China's foreign trade sector enterprises

Organization	Original Chinese project title	Project focus
Chinese National Complete Plant Export Corporation	Appraisal of cadres' job performance	Performance appraisal
MOFERT International Trade Research Institute	Performance appraisal of professionals	Performance appraisal
China National Technical Import and Export Corporation	Inspiration – the lever to arouse the internal vigour of staff members	Reward and motivation
China National Light Industrial Products Import and Export Corporation	Improving bonus system: fairly reflecting the contribution of different departments	Reward and motivation
China Foreign Trade Development Companies	Enhancing the effectiveness of enterprises by integrating material remuneration with spiritual encouragement	Reward and motivation
China National Textiles Import and Export Corporation	Development of personnel administration	Manpower planning and policy
	Development in a foreign trade business	
China National Native Produce and Animal By-Products	The optimization of managers in medium sized import and export corporation foreign trade enterprises	Manpower planning and policy
China National Arts and Crafts Import–Export Corporation	How to improve employment management	Manpower planning and policy
MOFERT Technology Import and Export Department	Control of employee turnover and outflow	Manpower planning and policy
MOFERT Import–Export Department	Training new employees	Training and development
China National Export Bases Development Corporation	Training workers in an aimed way	Training and development
China Trust and Investment Corporation for Foreign Economic Relations and Trade	Training plan for FOTIC staff	Training and development
MOFERT Personnel, Education and Labour Department	Training of personnel managers in foreign trade enterprises	Training and development
China Conic Import and Export Corporation	How to enhance the self-management skills of high and middle level executives	Training and development
MOFERT Quota Licence Administration Bureau	In-post training of licence managerial personnel	Training and development
MOFERT Internal Audit Institution	Foreign trade training for staff	Training and development
China National Machinery Import and Export Corporation	To have young personnel in the enterprise well trained	Training and development
MOFERT Personnel, Education and Labour Department	The training of skilled workers	Training and development

necessary to take a project from design, through construction to final hand-over of operationally complete plant and post-implementation assistance. Since its founding COMPLANT has completed over 1,200 projects. In general the organization has highly educated and experienced staff. There are about 600 cadres of which a quarter have served overseas to implement projects. Supporting the cadres are a large and varying number of technicians and workers at home and abroad to support the individual projects.

In the personnel area COMPLANT faced a very difficult situation since it was estimated that some 70 per cent of managers would reach retirement age within 10 years. The need therefore to identify younger cadres to promote and develop to higher positions was a pressing one. The problem was exacerbated by the fact that in a fragmented organization such as COMPLANT, with many overseas branch offices, different regulations or expectations about employee advancement existed. The general scheme for appraisal of staff in COMPLANT was similar to that in other state enterprises, namely an individual's performance was evaluated in four broad areas – moral integrity, ability, diligence and achievement with an overall grading for cadres which went from 'excellent, good, pass to unqualified'. The mechanisms for such evaluation include the daily observation of staff by leaders, evaluation by colleagues, and interview by the leaders, leading to evaluation and recommendation. Difficulties associated with this appraisal scheme were two-fold. First, it has proved difficult to interpret the grades consistently, not least because the necessary detail within any single category is not specified. Hence making a judgment about 'ability' would require prior identification of personal qualities, which is simply not done. Second, the ongoing mechanisms referred to above are not systematically adhered to. For example when a vacancy occurred at the Yunnan branch for a senior position the personnel manager from headquarters visited to supervise the new appointment. The branch leaders recommended four candidates and all were seen. However neither the candidates themselves nor the branch leaders were able to provide substantiated and clear evidence of what the various candidates had achieved. There was a lack of written material about previous performance and the leaders were only able to provide subjective impressions of day to day job performance. Such incidences were commonplace and gave rise to this project, which was concerned with establishing a consistent basis for performance appraisal as an input to the process of promotion.

The proposed amended appraisal system seeks to tackle these problems by introducing an annual system based on more detailed categories and an associated weighting. The categories now include current achievement (30 per cent), policy comprehension and formulation (20 per cent), work attitude (20 per cent), personal initiative (15 per cent), political thinking (10 per cent), and organization and co-ordination ability (5 per cent).

Initial appraisal would be within a cadre's own department but would be subject to a comprehensive evaluation by the personnel department. Even though this process is more specific it will still require consistency of judgment by the managers.

Case 2: China Foreign Trade Development Company (CFTD)
Category: Reward and motivation
Title: Enhancing the effectiveness of enterprises by integrating material remuneration with spiritual encouragement

Situated in the Shenzhen special economic zone the company is only seven years old. It was set up as a MOFERT initiative as a direct result of the reform processes and the experimental economic policies. Its primary role is general export and import, acting on behalf of many of the new enterprises within the Shenzhen special zone. A secondary role is the development of industries by building up factories which have an export focus. Supporting both of these activities are additional activities in the field of storage and transportation, and in the organization of exhibitions, including hotel provision. The latter two are part of its import and export promotional role. At present the company has about 1,000 employees across eight departments. Whilst remuneration for employees is better than many MOFERT related organizations it is comparatively lower than that enjoyed by employees in the local enterprises. The company's policy is to try to develop commitment, initiative and responsibility throughout the workforce by developing a package of employee benefits. The aim is to create a motivated and effective workforce. The company recognizes that salaries and bonuses elsewhere in the Special Economic Zone (SEZ) are likely to be higher but attention has been paid to other motivators. These include: new residences for all employees; a revised bonus system which recognizes significant differences between good and poor performance; provision of free medical services and company visits to employees who are ill; industrial injury insurance and family asset insurance; revised old age pension arrangements. In terms of the working environment, decision making processes are designed to engender a sense of participation. Managers have adopted 'praising and encouraging' as the main working method in order to improve employees' performance. Further steps under consideration include flexible schedules and the provision of holidays for employees chosen as 'advanced' workers.

Case 3: China National Textiles Import and Export Corporation (CHINATEX)
Category: Manpower planning and policy
Title: The development of a personnel administration department in a foreign trade business

Established for over 40 years the company is part of China's largest export industry. The company sales amount to several billion pounds sterling with eight subsidiaries in China and a branch network of over 100 offices at home and abroad. The majority of exports are to Europe and the USA which make high demands on quality. The quality issue is pivotal and has replaced production capacity as a strategic issue. It is against this background that the company has had to readjust its personnel structures and educational levels. The priority task for the personnel department has been to review its manpower recruitment and adjust the training available in order to increase the enterprise performance. However, in order to do this the personnel department itself needed to look internally at its own processes and led to this project with the specific remit of improving manpower planning and policy within the department. The project focused on an analysis of the personnel administration function and the desirable characteristics within that function. The function of personnel administration was broken down into a number of sub-functions which include the monitoring of individuals as a basis for reward, promotion, etc., the identification and provision of development opportunities for individuals and 'the servicing' of the organization in respect of recruitment and dismissal, administration of office hours and the facilitation of good relations between leaders and staff. Against this analysis a profile of staff requirements for the personnel function could be determined. This led to specific policies under recruitment of personnel department staff which specified appropriate educational levels and language ability. Additionally a system of formal training plans was devised, aimed at developing personnel administrators effective across the full range of functions within the department.

Case 4: China National Export Bases Development Corporation (CANED)
Category: Training and development
Title: Training working staff in an aimed way

The China National Export Bases Development Corporation (CANED) is a specialist foreign trade corporation working in the field of investment to support the expansion of export production throughout the country. The organization is heavily committed to graduate entry with over 90 per cent of its employees having a university background. The corporation has built up co-operative business relations with more than 400 enterprises in China, has 33 branch companies and a network of overseas contacts. The quality of staff is crucial given the complex nature of the company's activities, and new graduates do not have the appropriate background in management of commercial subjects. The corporation perceive this as a critical weakness and a training programme was specially constructed. The programme consists of business related lectures mainly in the finance area, supported by case studies; a workshop on organizational theory; a seminar series on practical problems in business administration from experts within and outside China. Supporting this main initiative there is foreign language training, where the aim is to have 80 per cent of all new staff with commercial level English. The latter has involved the formal expansion of part-time education and self-study.

MAKING SENSE OF THE CHANGES

In this section we look at the evidence of change described in Table 9.2 and the four project descriptions, and seek to interpret it. Our approach is to pose three related questions. First, leaving aside the idiosyncrasies of individual enterprises, what general but significant observation can we make about these findings as a whole and how do these relate to other authors' views? Second, how do these findings fit with the broad policy principles for HRM which have emerged in the West and what is our interpretation of this fit? And third, how well do the accepted factors responsible for the development of HRM in the West explain the changes in China?

The complete list of projects reveals three broad level observations which generally were not anticipated. The most striking is the very considerable emphasis the managers have given to the area of training and career development – 9 out of the 18 projects were clearly focused on this area. This empirical evidence is insightful since it would appear to legitimize a focus on individuals and their needs in contrast to the pre-reform emphasis on meeting the organizational needs. The finding further supports earlier research (Wang 1986; Warner 1987, 1992; Child 1991, 1994; Lu and Child 1994) citing the importance of training and development as the means of successfully implementing the enterprise reforms. Child's conclusions in this area were unambiguous:

> the training of Chinese staff is an inevitable requirement for developing their technical competence to work with new methods and technologies. It can also be a very important means of showing recognition of individual worth and engendering a pride, neither of which were much encouraged in the typical Chinese enterprise.
>
> (Child 1991: 104)

The nature of the training evidenced across the nine organizations and specifically the advanced training on offer within the China National

Export Bases Development Corporation (Case 4) shows the broad scope of training and its importance within these foreign trade corporations. It may be that because of the important and exposed position they hold in the field of export promotion that their training need is particularly acute and explains the primacy given to this activity. But in the main we think not and believe that the importance of training and development highlighted here is likely to be reflected in other sectors. Our views here are in contrast to Warner's (1993) observation that training in China may be seen as narrowly defined when set against the longer staff development of Western HRM prerogatives.

The second observation is notable for the absence of any managerial interest. The area is that of industrial relations and given the size of China's union representation and the scope of the reform process we anticipated that this area would be a focus, if only because the role could potentially change. In the event this appears not to be the case and the role of the unions is non-problematic. Their function remains one of facilitation between cadres and workers and is essentially non-confrontational. Our findings here strongly support Warner's claim that 'there is little comparison between western collective bargaining and the Chinese model of labour management with the trade unions in a subordinate role in the enterprise' (Warner 1993: 49). Similarly in a recent paper by Easterby-Smith *et al.* (1993) which looked in depth at HRM decisions in three Chinese enterprises, the role of the union was not a significant issue.

Our final observation is the importance given by the managers to the related areas of performance appraisal, reward and motivation. Five of the FTCs were engaged in changing and bringing about improvements in these areas. In the case of COMPLANT (Case 1) the appraisal system was interpreted to specifically include an evaluation of personal initiative and would form part of any reward decision. The situation for China Foreign Trade Development Company is of even more interest. The range of non-salary inducements here would not be out of place in any ambitious Western corporation and shows a departure from the normal arrangements in state owned enterprises. It reflects the relative youthfulness of the company and the particular environment in which it is operating. In short, the corporation is effectively in competition with non-state enterprises for competent workers and has responded with a motivational package in which high pay – a MOFERT constraint – is not the principal component and which compensates for this with locally specific benefits. This finding has a wider significance and signals the potential and actual flexibility within the state sector. It suggests that as the reform process is maturing state organizations will increasingly be willing to adopt procedures which are appropriate to their particular context and not necessarily be constrained by national norms. This reinforces a similar finding of the ESRC (1993) study by Easterby-Smith *et al.* in which the Chinese enterprises were influenced by norms and cultures but were not bounded by them; they too adopted change in response to their particular context.

Turning now to the fit between the broad policy principles of HRM and the evidence from the projects, some interesting and contradictory findings emerge. A increasingly mature literature has focused and reflected on the nature of HRM as practised in the West (Guest 1987; Torrington 1988; Legge 1988, 1989; Keenoy 1990; Storey 1992; Blyton and Turnbull 1992). From these authors, whilst there are differences in emphasis, there is common ground on the basic characteristics of HRM, especially in its contrast to traditional personnel management. These characteristics include: empowerment; individualism; representation; strategic awareness; and problem orientation and flexibility. The greatest weight of evidence concerns individuality and the recognition of the importance of the individual as a means of enhancing an organization's effectiveness. More than half of the enterprises have shown increased commitment to the training and development of individuals through on job training and formal programmes. The UNDP programme itself is an example of a major formal training and development programme co-ordinated by MOFERT and on offer to the FTC sector. Importantly, however, complementing this general initiative there is evidence from the CHINATEX project that the identification and provision of development opportunities is taking place at the level of individual needs. The focus on individuals is further evidenced through the strengthening of performance appraisal and particularly through the reward systems. In both COMPLANT and CFTD the reward systems in place will recognize an individual's contribution and performance. This, whilst not yet a widely spread practice, is a particularly interesting development since it will cut across the more normal pattern of sharing bonuses, etc. across the individual work unit.

Further supportive evidence is provided in respect of problem orientation and flexibility and strategic awareness. For the former enterprise managers are under increasing pressures to be innovative in order for the FTCs to cope with the hugely changing competitive situation. This in effect legitimizes personal initiative elsewhere in the enterprise and is reflected in the amended personnel appraisal system in COMPLANT. In the area of strategic awareness the commitment to training and development is once again a powerful indicator of the FTCs' understanding of what is needed for long-term strategic development. In this sense the personnel management function can be seen as an integral element in the company's planning.

In contrast to the preceding paragraphs in which the evidence supports the adoption of HRM practices of strategic awareness, flexibility and individuality there is no or little support for the concept of empowerment or a redefinition of the representative role. Indeed the evidence on empowerment is compelling. The paradox is that whilst all the reform policy initiatives are in the direction of decentralizing authority and responsibility to enterprise management (Child 1994) this would seem not to extend to the personnel function. We found no evidence that the empowerment of the individual line managers had increased in the areas, for example, of promotion, pay and terms and conditions of work. Such managers were part of the decision process but the active involvement of the personnel department was evident in all the projects. Specifically, in COMPLANT headquarters personnel staff were significant participants in branch office promotion decisions; likewise, in CANED the influence of the personnel department on the recruitment and staffing profiles to service the 33 branch companies was dominant.

Concerning the redefinition of the representative role within Chinese enterprises, there was no evidence of significant change here. There always has been a long standing tradition of employee participation and in the case of CFTD a deliberate company aim was to encourage this. In doing so, however, there is no suggestion of a revised union role. Both these latter examples are themselves insightful and relate directly to the drivers underpinning the personnel management changes. These are referred to in our final observations. In respect of the overall analysis linking Western HRM characteristics with the evidence of changing practice in China it is evident that personnel management practice in China is beginning to change and that this change can be seen to be in the direction of Western HRM practices. However, the adoption of such practices is only partial. The role of personnel managers in China and the internal mechanisms within Chinese enterprises for participation and communication are different and, as we will suggest below, are unlikely to change significantly. Hence, what is happening in these FTCs is not HRM as we may understand that term in the West. Instead, one way of interpreting the situation in China is to see the changing role of the personnel function as *adaptive personnel management*. Such a term signals a move in these organizations from a conventional and institutionalized role for personnel management to a more responsive and integrated function, but at the same time retains its clear identity as a specialized function. This finding is significant but we would be cautious in generalizing. It needs to be remembered that the FTCs have been in the forefront of change and compared with the SOEs in the manufacturing sectors, for example, are likely to have a higher proportion of younger management and many of these will have been exposed to Western organizations. Warner (1994) in some recent research into labour reform in SOEs in north-east China draws attention to the slow adoption of many labour policy initiatives. This underlines the increasing heterogeneity within Chinese management practices.

Finally, we turn our attention to the five HRM drivers identified earlier (see pp. 196–198). Two of these, namely 'competitive advantage' and 'changes in the workforce and the nature of work' are powerful forces in bringing about the changes in the personnel management function identified in the FTC cases. At all times in the empirical work we were conscious of the priority given by the managers to the need to be competitive and that in the context of the FTCs there was a daily reminder of this in terms of world prices. This has led directly to a willingness to tackle the problems of retraining first managers and then workers. Recently, there has been increasing indications of the readiness of enterprises nationally to take the unpalatable personnel based decisions needed to ensure competitiveness. In 1992, for example, 104 SOEs were declared bankrupt with major job losses and no reassignment, and in the case of the Seagull watch factory in Tianjin half of the staff, some 2,500, were laid off (*Time, Special Report on China*, 10 May, 1993).

Other drivers felt to be important in the West are shown in this research to be relatively weak. In particular, 'the changing role of personnel managers' and 'the empowerment of line managers' are both areas in which the changes do not fit the Western trend. It has been argued by Boisot and Child (1988) that the aim of the government and the party was to introduce reforms in a way which minimizes any ideological orientation of the country and that control could be retained through bureaucracies. Child (1991: 100) developed this further and highlighted the personnel function, which remains an area of importance for the party, as the vehicle for preserving conformity in the organization. This is a view we share and explains the continuing active involvement of the personnel management function in all the 20 enterprises that formed the empirical base for this work.

For the future we anticipate that the sort of initiatives identified in this sample of FTCs will extend into many other state corporations, but the rate of change will vary considerably across different sectors of Chinese industry and even different geographical regions. It means there is unlikely to be a major convergence of personnel management practice in China and Western HRM. One reason for this is fundamental and lies within the nature of the state owned enterprise and its ultimate control. As the economy continues to grow at 10 per cent or more per year the new organizations underpinning this growth are the private, provincial, township and rural enterprises for which the concept of ownership is a grey or problematic issue. In this sense state control is inevitably being diluted and the formal SOEs, despite their lacklustre economic performance, will remain important as the manifestation of a modern industrial and socialist society.

ACKNOWLEDGEMENTS

The authors wish to acknowledge the co-operation of the Ministry of Foreign Trade and Economic Co-operation (previously MOFERT) and the many foreign trade corporations that were involved. In particular we wish to thank Zhang Zhifeng for his invaluable co-ordination role. In addition we are most grateful to Professor Donald Wehrung and his colleagues at the University of British Columbia for their insights and participation and to Brian Barclay and staff of the Office for Asia and Pacific Technical Co-operation, International Trade Centre UNCTAD/ GATT for their overall support for the UNDP project CPR/88/006 within which this work was done.

REFERENCES

Armstrong, M. (1987) 'Human Resource Management: a Case of the Emperor's New Clothes?', *Personnel Management* 19(8): 30–35.
Atkinson, J. (1984) 'Manpower Strategies for the Flexible Firm', *Personnel Management* 16(8): 28–31.
Atkinson, J. and Meager, N. (1986) *Changing Patterns of Work – How Companies Introduce Flexibility to Meet New Needs*, Falmer: IMS/OECD.
Beer, M., Spector, B., Lawrence, P., Quinn Mills, D. and Walton, R. (1985) *Human Resources Management: A General Manager's Perspective*, New York: Free Press.
Blyton, P. and Turnbull, P. (eds) (1992) *Revisiting Human Resource Management*, London: Sage.
Boisot, M. and Child, J. (1988) 'The Iron Law of Fiefs: Bureaucratic Failure and the Problem of Government in the Chinese Economic Reforms', *Administrative Science Quarterly* 33: 507–527.
Brown, D. H. and Jackson, M. (1991) 'Meeting the Challenge to Provide Effective Managers in the Changing Chinese Environment', in N. Campbell and D. H. Brown (eds) *Advances in Chinese Industrial Studies* 2, Greenwich, Conn.: JAI Press.
Brown, D. H. (1993) 'Briefing Note on the UNDP China Management Development Project', Internal Paper, Lancaster: University of Lancaster.
Burton, C. (1987) 'China's Post-Mao Transition: the Role of the Party and Ideology in the "New Period"', *Pacific Affairs* 60: 431–446.
Child, J. (1991) 'A Foreign Perspective on the Management of People in China', *The International Journal of Human Resource Management* 2(1): 93–107.
Child, J. (1987) 'Enterprise Reform in China – Progress and Problems', in M. Warner (ed.) *Management Reforms in China*, London: Pinter.
—— *Management in China in the Age of Reform*, Cambridge: Cambridge University Press.
Davies, D. (1988) 'Unequal Chances, Unequal Outcomes: Pension Reform and Urban Inequality', *The China Quarterly* 114, June: 223–234.
Easterby-Smith, M. and Brown D. H. (1993) 'Decision Making in UK and Chinese Companies', *ESRC China Project Main Report*, Lancaster: University of Lancaster Press.
Easterby-Smith, M., Malina, D. and Yuan, L. (1993) 'HRM in Chinese and UK Companies: a Comparative Analysis', Paper presented at the British Academy of Management Conference, Milton Keynes, September.
Fowler, A. (1987) 'When Chief Executives Discover HRM', *Personnel Management* 19(3).
Goodhart, D. (1993) 'Personnel Crisis? What Crisis?', *Financial Times* 27 October.
Guanghaw, Y. (1985) 'Employment, Wages and Social Security in China', *International Labour Review* 124(4): 411–422.
Guest, D. (1987) 'Human Resource Management and Industrial Relations', *Journal of Management Studies* 24(5): 503–521.
Guest, D. and Hoque, K. (1993) 'The Mystery of the Missing Human Resource Manager', *Personnel Management*, June: 40–41.

Han, J. and Morishima, M. (1992) 'Labour System Reform in China and its Unexpected Consequences', *Economic and Industrial Democracy: An International Journal* 13: 233–261.

Hu, T., Li, M. and Shi, S. (1988) 'Analysis of Wages and Bonus Payments among Tianjin Urban Workers', *The China Quarterly* 113, March: 76–93.

Jackson, M. (1991) *Industrial Relations*, London: Croom Helm.

Keenoy, T. (1990) 'HRM: a Case of the Wolf in Sheep's Clothing?', *Personnel Review* 19(2): 3–9.

Keenoy, T. and Anthony, P. (1992) 'HRM: Metaphor, Meaning and Morality', in P. Blyton and P. Turnbull (eds) *Reassessing Human Resource Management*, London: Sage.

Lee, L. T. (1986) *Trade Unions in China: from 1949 to the Present*, Singapore: Singapore University Press.

Legge, K. (1978) *Power, Innovation and Problem Solving in Personnel Management*, Maidenhead: McGraw-Hill.

—— (1988) 'Personnel Management in Recession and Recovery: a Comparative Analysis of What the Surveys Say', *Personnel Review* 17(2): 1–72.

—— (1989) 'Human Resource Management: a Critical Analysis', in J. Storey (ed.) *New Perspectives on Human Resource Management*, London: Routledge.

Littler, C. R. and Lockett, M. (1983) 'The Significance of Trade Unions in China', *Industrial Relations Journal* 14(4): 31–42.

Lockett, M. (1988) 'Culture and the Problems of Chinese Management', *Organisation Studies* 9(4): 475–496.

Lu, Y. and Child, J. (1994) 'Decentralisation of Decision Making in China's State Enterprises', Paper presented at the Conference on *Management Issues for China in the 1990s*, March: 23–25, Cambridge: St John's College.

MacBean, A. (1994) 'China's Foreign Trade Corporations (Export–Import Companies): Their Role in Economic Reform and Export Success', Paper presented to the Conference on *Management Issues for China in the 1990s*, March: 23–25, Cambridge: St John's College.

MacKay, L. and Torrington, D. (1986) *The Changing Nature of Personnel Management*, London: IPM.

Miles, K. M. and Snow, C. C. (1984) 'Designing Strategic Human Resources Systems', *Organisational Dynamics* Summer.

Peters, T. and Waterman, R. (1982) *In Search of Excellence*, New York: Harper & Row.

Purcell, J. (1982) 'Macho-Managers and the New Industrial Relations', *Employee Relations* 4(1): 3–5.

Purcell, J. (1987) 'Mapping Management Styles in Employee Relations', *Journal of Management Studies* 24(5): 533–548.

Schermerhorn, J. R. and Nyaw, M. K. (1991) 'Managerial Leadership in Chinese Industrial Enterprises', in O. Shenkar (ed.) *Organisation and Management in China: 1979–1990*, London: M. E. Sharpe.

Storey, J. (1987) 'Developments in Human Resource Management: an Interim Report', Warwick Papers in Industrial Relations, no. 17, Coventry: University of Warwick.

Tichy, N. M., Fombrun, G. and Devanna, M. (1982) 'Strategic Human Resource Management', *Sloan Management Review* 23(2): 47–61.

Torrington, D. (1988) 'How Does Human Resources Management Change the Personnel Function?', *Personnel Review* 17(6): 3–9.

Torrington, D. and Hall, L. (1991) *Personnel Management: A New Approach*, 3rd edition, London: Prentice-Hall.

Tung, R. (1993) 'A Comparative Perspective on Management and Industrial

Training in China: a Review of How Chinese Managers Learn', *The International Journal of Human Resource Management* 4(1): 241–245.

Walton, R. E. (1985) 'From Control to Commitment in the Workplace', *Harvard Business Review* 63(2).

Wang, N. T. (1986) 'United States and China: Business Beyond Trade – an Overview', *Columbia Journal of World Business* 15(1): 3–8.

Warner, M. (1985) 'Training China's Managers', *Journal of General Management* 11(2): 126.

—— (1987) 'China's Managerial Training Revolution', in M. Warner (ed.) *Management Reforms in China*, London: Pinter.

—— (1991) 'Labour–Management Relations in the People's Republic of China: the Role of the Trade Unions', *The International Journal of Human Resource Management* 2: 205–220.

—— (1992) *How Chinese Managers Learn*, London: Macmillan.

—— (1993) 'Human Resource Management "with Chinese Characteristics" ', *The International Journal of Human Resource Management* 4(1): 45–65.

—— (1994) 'Beyond the Iron Rice-Bowl: Comprehensive Labour Reform in State-Owned Enterprises', Paper presented at the Conference on *Management Issues For China in the 1990s*, March: 23–25, Cambridge: St John's College.

Watson, T. J. (1977) *The Personnel Managers: a Study in the Sociology of Work and Employment*, London: Routledge and Kegan Paul.

White, G. (1982) 'Urban Employment and Labour Allocation Policies in Post-Mao China', *World Development* 10(8): 613–632.

—— (1987) 'Labour Market Reform in Chinese Industry', in M. Warner (ed.) *Management Reforms in China*, London: Pinter.

Wong, T. T. (1989) 'The Salary Structure, Allowances and Benefits of the Shanghai Electronic Factory', *The China Quarterly* 117, March: 135–144.

Ye, S. (1987) 'The Role of China's Managing Directors in the Current Economic Reform', *International Labour Review* 126(6): 691–701.

Zhang, Z. (1990, 1991) *Report of the HRM Projects in the Foreign Trade Corporations* (in Chinese), Beijing: Ministry of Foreign Economic Relations and Trade.

Zheng, H. R. (1987) 'An Introduction to the Labour Law of the People's Republic of China', *Harvard International Law Journal* 28(2): 385–431.

10 Beyond the iron rice-bowl

Comprehensive labour reform in state owned enterprises in north-east China

Malcolm Warner

ABSTRACT

In this chapter the author first reviews recent developments in the management of human resources in the People's Republic of China. The debate
on the greater use of market mechanisms is discussed. He then traces the
impact of the latest reforms of the Chinese labour-management system in
the state owned enterprises mostly in the north-east (*Dongbei*). The introduction of a new system of labour contracts, wage and social insurance
reforms are examined and data from a recent field investigation is
reported. The author concludes that the pilot enterprises play a critical
role in the economies of the cities of the north-east, which constitute the
industrial heartland of China. The official goal is to extend these reforms
to all firms in the state sector. Nonetheless, caution should be exercised
in extrapolating too much from these experiments: in the PRC, there is
frequently a gap between intent and practice.

GENERAL

Introduction

This chapter reviews ongoing reforms of the management of human
resources in the People's Republic of China and the ongoing moves
towards greater use of labour markets. The main hypothesis is that the
system is moving towards a hybrid form 'with Chinese characteristics'
blending 'Western-style practices' with indigenous ones (see Child 1994;
Warner 1991, 1992, 1993). The theoretical basis for understanding the
above process is set out elsewhere (see, for example, Warner 1995) and
it must be stressed that we must be very cautious in applying conceptual
schema derived from Western behavioural and institutional frameworks
to very different Chinese cultural contexts.

Labour market reform

As a linchpin of the system, China's 'iron rice-bowl' employment policy (involving job security and cradle-to-grave welfare coverage) had its roots in the early 1950s (see Kaple 1994). It was based on a combination of a Soviet-style management system with full, direct urban labour allocation, adapted to Chinese circumstances. It was also influenced by Japanese employment practices in Manchuria pre-war and under the occupation, for Japanese personnel at least. It was originally intended to protect skilled workers in state owned industrial enterprises, but eventually spread to cover the majority of those in urban employment (see Schurmann 1966). Although in some respects, it exemplifies a 'lifetime employment system', comparisons with Japanese companies may be as misleading as they are illuminating, as the two country contexts markedly differ. The wage grade system had also been taken over and adapted from the Soviet model. For much of the time, an egalitarian wage payment system was common, and incentives were limited (see Leung 1988; Wedley 1992). Such a system, based as it was on a *danwei* (work unit), also had gender implications in that it provided infrastructural support and opportunities for women workers.

In the late 1980s, economists discussed proposals to create a labour market although they did not all accept that labour was a commodity under socialism. Currently, the official view employs euphemisms like 'labour service market', or 'labour force market' as the notion of a 'market' for labour has presented problems for Marxist theory (see Dong 1986). The Maoist proposition that 'distribution according to labour', conditional on 'each according to his labour', has been largely jettisoned. Chinese economists began to support the notion that the total wage fund of the enterprise ought to be a reflection of its performance on both macro and micro grounds (Hsu 1991).

As a result of such thinking, material incentives were slowly introduced in the 1980s. Bonuses became more important as a method of rewarding effort and productivity over the same period (see Takahara 1992). Whilst such new practices were welcomed by workers who stood to benefit, potential losers were likely to be resentful. The reforms saw a move away from the Soviet-style grading system to greater rewards for flexibility, edging towards an experimental model, albeit very much adapted to Chinese circumstances (see Table 10.1, column 2).

By 1987, the State Economic Commission had launched extensive wage reforms (see Korzec 1992). In future, state enterprises could decide their own reward levels. There would be a basic wage, topped up by bonuses and productivity deals. Such reforms were not welcomed by economic conservatives, whether lobbying at macro or micro levels, and were not at all well received in trade union circles (see Chan 1993). Under the old labour system, dismissals were very rare (Granick 1991). With the reforms

Table 10.1 Characteristics of the labour reforms

System characteristic	Status quo	Experimental
Strategy	Hard-line	Reformist
Employment	Iron rice-bowl	Labour market
Conditions	Job security	Labour contracts
Mobility	Job assignment	Job choice
Rewards	Egalitarian	Meritocratic
Wage system	Grade-based	Performance-based
Promotion	Seniority	Skill-related
Union role	Consultative	Co-ordinative
Management	Economic cadres	Professional managers
Factory party role	Central	Ancillary
Work organization	Taylorist	Flexible
Efficiency	Technical	Allocative

they have become somewhat easier in principle but in reality are not extensive, often less than one per cent per annum, with several forms of dismissal, varying in severity, and depending on the gravity of the offence. Sometimes workers are transferred to a 'labour service' company owned by the same enterprise group, or even to a plant on the same site. This may be referred to as 'one factory, two systems'. Redundancies are another novel feature of the economic reforms. As state enterprises are made more economically responsible, the less productive ones are shedding labour, often women workers, particularly on 'pilot' or 'experimental' sites selected to try out the most recent enterprise reforms. A new Labour Law (July 1994) has now legitimized this practice (*Renmin Ribao – People's Daily*, Overseas Edition, 7 July 1994: 2–3 contains the full text in Chinese).

The extension of the notion of contracts for jobs based on Western-style personnel practices has also been a feature of the changes in the labour market in the second half of the 1980s and is now sanctioned in the above new law. By the end of the decade, it was estimated that at least one in 10 workers in the labour force was employed on a contract basis rather than having jobs for life, perceiving themselves in effect to have a second-class status in a dual labour market (see White 1986; Korzec 1992). Whilst labour contracts had been implemented in the state enterprises only in varying degrees, and then until recently only for newcomers, since the mid-1980s they are now relatively common in many other forms of economic organisations, such as township industries, joint ventures and privately and/or foreign owned firms. The labour force in these instances is more likely to be young, and/or female, as well as of recent rural origin. Less high overhead social costs means lower labour costs for enterprises, but higher money wages may sometimes be on offer for such recruits to compensate for limited tenure and leaner benefits. Often poor salaries and harsh working conditions prevail. In effect, the 'iron rice-bowl' has been broken for such workers.

State industrial enterprises

A major policy shift signalled in early 1992, confirmed by the late spring and legitimated in the autumn of that year, has been the reform of the state industrial sector. This part of the economy had long been the favoured recipient of government support, heavily subsidized and staunchly protected. Over 30 per cent of the state budget was going into subsidies overall by the end of the 1980s but has now fallen back to half this amount. The reason for this special treatment was its vanguard role in the modernization process since 1949. It was also a major contributor to state funds, as tax revenues could be gathered from its more productive sub-sectors (Lee 1988; White 1991).

State-owned enterprises ('owned by the whole people', in the official jargon) have long been the work-horses of Chinese industry and are mostly found in large industrial cities like Shanghai, Shenyang and the like (see Leeming 1992). Since the late 1980s, it increasingly has been believed that the volume of state subsidy has become not only a drain on resources that could be best used elsewhere, but also anomalous in an emergent, if still regulated, market economy 'with Chinese characteristics'. Previously, this sector had not been appreciably open to market forces. By spring 1992, the government had decided on the basis of policies formulated in May and September of the previous year to steer these enterprises into the market, holding them responsible for their profits and losses, even to the point of bankruptcy. A reform of the labour and personnel system was announced at the same time, for 60,000 enterprises out of a total of over one million in the state industrial sector, potentially involving as many as 30 million workers. Such changes would thus affect nearly one-third of all state owned enterprises' workers and staff.

The Commission for Restructuring the Economy, the Ministry of Personnel and the All-China Federation of Trade Unions put forward a 12-point proposal for deepening the reform of the system of administration of labour and personnel, wage distribution and social insurance in enterprises in early 1992. The gist of this document was as follows:

1 To follow earnestly the guidelines of the State Council circular on stopping unnecessary inspection and appraisal of enterprises, and non-interference in the internal structure of enterprises. A comprehensive review of the various regulations and policies governing enterprises, formulated in recent years, should be conducted. Any contents which do not conform to the enterprise law and other relevant state provisions concerning improving enterprises should be revised or abolished.

It is necessary to take effective measures to do away resolutely with unnecessary activities on inspection, appraisal, target fulfilment, promotion and examinations; thus enabling enterprises to devote their undivided attention and efforts to improving production and operation.

2 To strengthen in a practical way the internal economic responsibility system in enterprises, and strive to establish and perfect various rules and regulations.

3 To carry out reform of the personnel system in enterprises, and gradually implement an appointment system for management and technical personnel.

4 To consolidate and improve the labour contract system.

5 To gradually implement a full-time labour contract system.

6 To strengthen wage management and improve the method of linking total wages to economic efficiency, and gradually switch linking wages with a single target performance to multiple-target performance. It is necessary to pay attention to maintaining and enhancing the values of state owned assets, technological advancement and productivity, as well as to improving other comprehensive economic performance indices including the ratio between capital invested and profits delivered, and taxes paid to the state.

7 To implement an independent distribution system with distribution according to work, and overcome egalitarianism. It is necessary to gradually practise a wage system based on the skills of a certain section on a production line, provided it is within the limit of the total wages determined by the state, and carried out on a voluntary basis among enterprises.

8 To make strenuous efforts to improve the quality of labour contingents in enterprises, and adhere to the principle of training before employment and training before promotion. Newly-recruited technical workers should undergo professional training and strict assessment.

9 To continue to implement the reform of pension and social insurance systems and gradually establish a multi-tier insurance system, integrating basic insurance provided by the state and supplementary insurance provided by enterprises with personal savings in insurance.

10 To continue to expand the scope of existing insurance and improve the system of on-the-job insurance.

11 To speed up reform of the labour planning system and implement autonomy in personnel appointments and wage distribution among enterprises.

12 To strengthen democratic management among enterprises and bring the role of the workers' congress into play.

(Summary of World Broadcasts 15 February 1992)

In short, in order to deal with problems in the state industrial sector, an initial reduction of the workforce was announced in early 1992, with the establishment of a new social security system (that is, incorporating unemployment insurance) to cushion the blow to those workers displaced. The state would at the same time develop employment in the service industries to absorb surplus labour and raise wages for both workers and government employees. The goal of these cuts was to deal with the low levels of economic efficiency, excessive over-manning and unduly high indirect employment costs due to the generous welfare provisions provided in state industrial enterprises, referred to, as noted earlier, as the iron rice-bowl. In order to deal with the human costs of bankruptcy, extensive retraining was proposed. Greater competition was to be introduced and life-time tenure for cadres abolished to encourage freer transfer of personnel. Performance-based remuneration was also to be implemented. Many enterprises, particularly in the north-east, were subsequently designated as experimental sites for this purpose.

The new regulations were intended to enable state enterprises to decide 'the time, conditions, methods and numbers when hiring new employees' and to adopt 'the contracted management or all-personnel labour contract system' (see *Beijing Review* 1992). Firms would have to recruit through examinations, senior staff who fail the tests would be assigned menial jobs, and junior employees would be promoted.

THE FIELD INVESTIGATION

Introduction

In order to understand the labour reforms in China in depth, we need to look at their implementation in greater detail. Data collected at first hand will be set out as follows. First, the enterprise characteristics will be outlined. Second, the specific three-system reforms will be set out. Third, the implications of the changes will be discussed.

The field investigation was carried out in Beijing and the north-east of China (in Heilongjiang and Liaoning provinces). It covered 10 large to medium sized state industrial enterprises (SOEs) as the main focus of the study (see Table 10.2). The firms were located in the cities of Beijing, Dalian, Harbin and Shenyang. In addition, background data was collected from discussions with experts at the Chinese Academy of Social Sciences (CASS), and three provincial academies, four major municipal and provincial labour bureaux, five university management studies departments, six economic and social science research institutes, as well as one economic development zone and one trade union federation headquarters, were visited. Structured interviews were undertaken with senior managers, labour bureaux personnel, researchers, and union officials, using colleagues from the CASS Institute of Industrial Economics as interpreters. Documents and statistics were also collected and translated by the latter. The field work was completed during July and August 1993.

The sample was selected by myself and colleagues at the CASS Institute of Industrial Economics as typical of large state enterprises chosen to be at the leading edge of the economic reforms, and mostly as pilot experimental sites in the north-east. Out of the 10 enterprises investigated, it is interesting to note that two were in the original World Bank/CASS study undertaken in the late 1980s (see Tidrick and Chen 1987).

Main characteristics of SOEs studied

The extent of the comprehensive labour reforms implemented within the cities visited in the investigation, we must note, is relatively important in terms of the number of large state firms located there. The pilot enterprises play a critical role in the economies of the cities in question (see Leeming 1992) and are intended to constitute role models for the rest of the state sector.

The main features of the sample of enterprises can be seen at a glance in Table 10.2. Although they were a pre-selected group of enterprises chosen by myself and social scientists who collaborated with the research investigation via CASS, they were well-known locally as being at the leading-edge of the enterprise reforms.

First, the variation in age of the organizations was interesting. Four were founded pre-1914 by the Russians and then run by the Japanese in the north-east, two founded by the Japanese in the 1930s; and four after the liberation, in the late 1940s or in the 1950s. They were all, therefore, well-established organizational entities, with the iron rice-bowl well institutionalized.

Second, all the enterprises investigated were state owned enterprises and were previously either run directly by ministries or bureaux. Even today, one of them, Harbin Power Equipment, is still formally under provincial level industrial bureau direction. Dalian Port was run by the Ministry of Transportation and the city government, while the others were corporations or parts of similar groupings.

Third, although a good proportion of state enterprises operate at a loss

Table 10.2 Enterprises in sample (in alphabetical order)

Beijing Iron and Steel Corporation (*Shougang*)
Dalian Port Authority
Dalian Locomotive and Rolling-Stock Works
Dalian Shipyard
Harbin Pharmaceutical Factory
Harbin Power-Equipment Company
Shenyang Area/Anshan Iron and Steel Complex (*Angang*)
Shenyang Gold-Cup (*Jin-Bei*) Auto Company
Shenyang Smelting Works
Shenyang Transformer Works

(it was claimed for example that four out of every 10 enterprises in Shenyang were 'in the red' roughly corresponding to the national average at the time) most of the sample made a profit. The average sales turnover in 1992 was just over 9 billion RMB, and the average profits plus tax were just under 0.90 billion RMB, a ratio of 1:10 approximately.

Fourth, the range of enterprises' products was also relatively wide, ranging from iron and steel to pharmaceuticals, but most were in the heavy industrial sector. Seven out of the 10 were located in the metallurgy-based sector. Only one was exceptional, namely Dalian Port, as it provided a service rather than a product, although very heavily capitalized.

Fifth, the variation in employee size deserves noting, as the enterprises ranged from 1,300 to 60,000 (and 220,000 if the entire Anshan Iron and Steel complex, known as *Angang*, was taken into consideration). The average size of the nine was just under 20,000 (it would of course rise considerably if the latter was included).

Last, the data on the enterprises and labour reforms is summarized in Table 10.3, showing the range of the three-system reforms, etc. To recapitulate, six out of 10 enterprises have all their employees on labour contracts and six out of 10 have fully adopted the 'post plus skills' wage system, for example. All had implemented the social insurance reforms. We shall now discuss these case studies in greater detail.

THE THREE-SYSTEM REFORMS

Labour and personnel reforms: introduction

This section deals in detail with the implementation of the three-system reforms in the (mostly) north-east, state owned enterprises investigated. For example, it describes the scope of contracts, how many employees were covered and so on. We then examine changes in the wages system and rewards to employees. Next, we look at changes in personnel policy including promotions (and dismissals). Lastly, we turn to the changes in welfare benefits and the implementation of a reformed social insurance scheme. (An extended, more detailed version of these findings is reported in Warner 1995.)

Beijing/Capital Iron and Steel

The labour contract system in Capital (Shoudu) Iron and Steel in Beijing (known in brief as Shougang) rather surprisingly is not very extensively developed and only 10 per cent of the employees have such contracts and then only newcomers. The view of the personnel department was that the new system was 'not a good idea' because there was 'no proper social insurance yet in China' and 'the new labour laws were not yet fully implemented'. When there was such insurance, they would change but are 'not

Table 10.3 Summary of case studies

	Case study no.									
	1	2	3	4	5	6	7	8	9	10
Enterprise	Capital Iron and Steel	Dalian Port Authority	Dalian Loco	Dalian Shipyard	Harbin Pharm.	Harbin Power	Shenyang (Anshan)	Shenyang Gold Cup	Shenyang Smelting	Shenyang Transformer
Product(s)	Iron and steel	Goods handling	Rolling stock	Tankers	Penicillin	Transformers etc.	Iron and steel	Auto	Non-ferrous metals	Transformers
Sales (RMB) (1992)	12.6 bill.	60 mill. tons	0.5 bill.	45 bill.	0.5 bill.	20 mill.	20 bill.	3.6 bill.	1.2 bill.	0.5 bill.
Profits and tax (RMB) (1992)	5.25 bill.	N.A.	60 mill.	6 mill.	38 mill.	—	2 bill.	0.3 bill.	0.1 bill.	40 mill.
Workforce (RMB) (1992)	60,000*	25,000	12,000	17,000	5,000	1,300	220,000	39,000	7,000	12,500
Av. yearly empl. income (RMB) (1992)	5,000	3,600	3,800	4,700	3,800	3,200	4,200	3,800	3,700	4,500
Labour contract system	10%	100%	10%	20%	100%	100%	10%	100%	100%	100%
Wage system	Post-skills + bonus	Basic + hourly + bonus	Post-skills	Post-skills	Post-skills	Partial post-skills	Post-skills	Basic + hourly + bonus	Post-skills	16 grades
Social insurance system	New	New	New	New	New	New	New	New	New	New

Note: *120,000 employees in city; 220,000 nationally

in a hurry'. They claimed that they never hindered people from leaving their job to work elsewhere. They had fired some of the workforce, but very few. The company policy according to the personnel department was to make the workers feel they are 'masters of the house' – a phrase resonant of the older (high Stalinist) rhetoric, originating in 1950s text-books translated long ago from Russian into Chinese (see Kaple 1994: 87–88).

In order to implement the labour and personnel reforms, the use of formal examinations in Capital Iron and Steel was extensive although this system was company-specific. There was an examinations committee that recommended which employees were to be promoted or demoted, based on committee opinions of employees' abilities after interviews and exam results. Individuals could not be promoted, demoted or dismissed by their immediate superior alone. The chairman of the committee was elected by the Workers' Congress and the other members elected from the different departments involved. Anybody, it was claimed, could apply to the committee to change their job or apply for a specific position.

Dalian Port Authority

The next state owned enterprise investigated operated on rather different principles. Every employee of the Dalian Port Authority now has to sign a labour contract and these range from one to 10 years. They may be classified in three categories: one-year, five-year, 10-year.

The contracts depend on the posts or positions filled by the employee. They do not say anything about payments, which is somewhat unusual according to 'model' contracts circulated by the Ministry of Labour. The rewards are now based on workers' individual responsibilities.

The labour force has been reduced by only a modest percentage, in fact less than 5 per cent since the economic reforms were introduced. The loading companies do not have autonomy to fire, unless workers are in serious breach of discipline. They have some discretion vis-à-vis hiring from the labour market but are not free to decide basic wage levels. If they wish to increase wages, they have to seek the approval of the city government. However, bonuses depend entirely on profits generated by the company.

Dalian Locomotive and Rolling-Stock Works

In 1990, Dalian Locomotive and Rolling-Stock, a long-established state owned enterprise, introduced a labour contract system for newcomers, including university graduates, which appears to be a little later than many others. Older workers remained under the previous arrangements. The renewable contract specifies the mutual responsibilities of the enterprise, period of employment (usually three years) and so on. The worker is free to leave after the contract expires, but it was said few do. The enterprise also signs a contract with the ministry, concerning profits, wages and productivity.

Since the early 1990s personnel reforms have been relatively widely introduced in Dalian Rolling-Stock across the board. The company is now free to hire as it sees fit. It mainly recruits new workers from its own technical school or from the labour market, the numbers depending on how many employees have retired. Apprenticeships vary in duration depending on the technology to be mastered; if unskilled, it is one year, with wages of at least 100 RMB per month. The rules on dismissals are as elsewhere, for example breaches of labour discipline, and so on. Promotion to technician or engineer rank now strictly depends on examination and other achievements like developing material-saving technologies or devising new technologies. For cadres, promotion hinges on introducing significant improvements in the organization of their departments. Workers too can be upgraded according to the state regulations.

Dalian Shipyard

Two types of employment statuses now co-exist in the shipyard. Workers recruited under the older system have fixed employment status, but after 1984 newcomers had to sign labour contracts as in many firms elsewhere. These could be for 10 years, between three and 10 years, or under three years. Over 2,000 workers have contracts, and 8,000 have fixed status. The goal was to have all-round contract reform by 1995, with everyone under the same system, covering responsibilities, duration of contract, rewards, sanctions and so on.

Although the personnel system in Dalian Shipyard has recently been reformed, recruitment is not yet drawn directly from the labour market. The firm has its own technical school, recruiting middle-school leavers for two or three years of study combined with an apprenticeship system. The latter lasts for up to three years' duration, with six months' probation, but this is not needed if the young workers have attained the level three technician grade. There are over 2,000 professionally qualified staff in the yard and over 100 university graduates are hired each year as trainees. Promotion for cadres is now through formal appraisal committees; for assistant engineers, there is an examination and appraisal; for workers, examinations and review of work performance are required. Dismissals are relatively few and according to state regulations, for example for unauthorized absence longer than two weeks or for running a business on the side.

Harbin Pharmaceuticals

Personnel reforms have been recently introduced in Harbin Pharmaceuticals and all employees are reportedly on contracts (even the directors). As the enterprise is expanding, it has sought another 800 workers, mostly female, a clear contrast with most other state firms in the city. The contracts cover the required items such as labour protection, responsibilities of workers, duration of contract, wages and so on. There is a standard contract as approved by the local labour bureau. Promotion is based on achievement, skill, and attitude. Dismissals are on the lines described for other state firms, and are relatively limited.

Fringe benefits are still an important factor in remuneration, with housing, education, health and welfare covered. Rents are very cheap, with less than one per cent of workers' incomes spent on housing. All levels of schools are provided from kindergarten to technical level. The director said his job was 'like that of running a small city'.

Harbin Power Equipment

A set of new comprehensive reforms were introduced in Harbin Power Equipment in 1991. Income distribution was to be linked to profitability and all employees were to go onto contracts. State employees were placed on five- to 10-year contracts (and can move to other such enterprises if they want), state contract workers are on one-year arrangements and temporary contract workers are on a six-month to one-year basis. There are also separate contracts for cadres and workers, and university graduates have to sign up too. Promotion for cadres depends on educational achievement and attitude; for workers, level of output, quality of work, discipline and training are important. Dismissals follow a probationary period if there is a breach of labour discipline. In 1992, only nine workers were dismissed, however.

Shenyang Area/Anshan Iron and Steel

Limited implementation of the labour contract system in Angang was apparent. Older workers did not need contracts it was said, but most newcomers had to have them. About 2,000 contracts a year are offered. About one in 10 workers are on a contract, although the 1,500 or so graduates hired each year do not require them. The contracts cover the customary areas such as responsibilities, rewards and benefits, social insurance and so on. The management now have greater power to fire workers for matters like disobeying safety regulations, absences and damage to plant or materials. In the final analysis, very few are fired, most being supposedly 're-educated' and 're-employed'. In 1992, a policy of labour reorganization was introduced with the goal of an overall cut of 20 per cent in the workforce and 40 per cent of administrative staff. Two out of 10 workers have been made redundant in several steel plants, and most were said to have found new jobs in the service sector, although there was no way this could be confirmed.

Shenyang Gold Cup Auto Company

All employees of the Gold Cup Auto enterprises were on contracts, including university graduates. The company contract covers:

- length of employment;
- wages and salaries;
- responsibilities of the job;
- termination of contract;
- welfare arrangements, such as housing, education, medical, etc.

With the reforms, several benefits will in future be paid for by the state rather than the company, such as pensions and, in due course, medical care. In Gold Cup Auto, very few workers have been dismissed or made redundant. They are reluctant to fire people because of the difficulty for them of finding other jobs. However, contravention of production operations regulations constitutes definite grounds for dismissal.

Shenyang Smelting Works

Almost all the workers and cadres at Shenyang Smelting Works were on contracts by 1992; only a small percentage transferred from the army were on temporary arrangements. Selection was based on an entrance examination and interviews. Successful workers were then offered a contract, detailing its duration (normally two years), the terms of employment, nature of the job, salary and conditions of work, and so on. If employees' performance was satisfactory, the contracts were renewed. Problems have been reported in only 0.3 to 0.5 per cent of cases.

Since the beginning of 1992, over 30 per cent of the workforce has been displaced. Most of these have gone into the service industries or left employment because of retirement or poor health. Around 350 have been put on a retraining programme. For the first three months, they receive 100 per cent of their previous salary, for the next three months 75 per cent, then after that 75 RMB per month. If they perform well, they can replace a non-performing worker. The following grounds were cited as causes for dismissal:

- breaches of labour discipline;
- contravention of operating regulations;
- poor performance;
- rejection of job transfer;
- corruption and theft;
- bad behaviour.

Shenyang Transformer Works

Every employee in Shenyang Transformers now has a labour contract, of varying length. Engineers hold five- or 10-year contracts. Cadres may not be re-appointed, and workers can be made cadres. Contracts have to specify the nature of the job requirements, rewards, conditions of work, welfare, social insurance and so on.

The normal reasons for dismissal apply, whether employees are male or female, such as labour indiscipline and unauthorized absence. If people want to leave voluntarily, this is permitted. Some are paid to leave, or found another job. If they cannot get another within three weeks, they continue to receive their former salary but without the bonus. After a year, they would be paid 70 per cent of this.

Wage-system reform: introduction

This section deals with the wage-system reforms introduced in the early 1990s. It examines how far the old eight-grade system inherited from the Soviet system has been replaced by a more flexible, efficiency-based one, and the weighting factors like post (responsibilities) and skills are balanced with other elements such as individual bonuses.

Beijing/Capital Iron and Steel

The wage system in Capital Iron and Steel has been significantly reformed since 1985 (see Ji Li, in Wedley 1992: 175 ff). Rewards became more performance related, so a worker on a given grade could earn more money. Over a third of the workforce are paid on this 'floating' system. If workers perform well they can go up a few grades; if they make mistakes, they can be demoted to a lower grade. If they achieve targets, they can get 11 per cent more. Bonuses are related to the worker's monthly performance record, using a points system. There is now a unified 16-grade system, with graduates starting on the sixth. The old eight-grade one was phased out in 1984. The new system produced a greater variation in income: if workers worked well, they could be rewarded. If the company made more profits, wages would go up.

The average annual level of wages (plus bonuses) in 1992 was over 5,000 RMB, rising to 7,000 in the subsequent year. (The term RMB – Renminbi – is used throughout this chapter to refer to the official Chinese currency unit, the yuan, as used by ordinary citizens rather than the version previously only available to tourists.) The wage system set managers' pay at around 10 per cent above the average level of incomes, but a production worker could earn more than that if being paid danger money and the like. *Shougong*'s policy was to break down the barrier between cadres and workers ('workers can be cadres, cadres can be workers' was the slogan invoked). Employees generally now work on a points system, and can aim to get more than their norm. Examinations are held each year for promotion to a higher grade. Rewards are closely related to the responsibilities of the post and the individual's performance level. The above wage totals for *Shougong* included bonuses and the overall figure cited subsequently for the other enterprises includes the final total paid out to the workers.

Dalian Port Authority

There are eight grades in DPA, as in the old system, but they are now based on:

- a basic income (of about 200 RMB average);
- an hourly rate;
- a period of service payment;
- a welfare provision (housing, education, etc.);
- an individual bonus.

The average wage (1992) is about 3,600 RMB a year – 300 RMB a month – with cadres said to earn about 50 RMB less.

Dalian Locomotive and Rolling Stock

Workers and staff in Dalian Locomotive and Rolling Stock were paid above the average level for state employees in the city, with average wages plus bonus of over 320 RMB per month (3,840 RMB a year). The old wage grade system had been displaced. Although special workers are on 1–8 grades, most are 1–6, with earnings depending on the following factors:

- post;
- skills;
- period of service;
- individual bonus.

Retirement is normally at 60 for men and 55 for women.

Dalian Shipyard

Wages in the Dalian Shipyard were relatively higher than elsewhere in the city. Average annual worker incomes in 1992 were around 4,700 RMB (400 RMB per month), due to profit-related pay. The determination of rewards per month was linked to the following factors:

- post (70 RMB);
- technical skill (160 RMB);
- plant efficiency (8 RMB);
- years of service (average 40 RMB);
- individual bonus, plus extras (up to 800 RMB).

The old eight-grade system was discontinued in mid-1993. The highest salaries (managerial or production workers) were then around 1,000 RMB per month, although the average director's pay is in the region of 600 RMB. There is normally a six-day week, except in the summer months.

Harbin Pharmaceuticals

The average wage in Harbin Pharmaceuticals is relatively high, approximately 3,800 RMB per annum, with directors getting up to three times as much. Some production workers can earn more than this under the new incentive system, however. The eight-grade wage ladder has been abandoned, and the new one is based on 'post plus skills', each carrying an equal weight, with years of service and bonus determining the final level of rewards.

Harbin Power Equipment

The wages system in Harbin Power Equipment is dependent on the 'post plus skills' system which was being introduced when the field work was done. The 'post plus skills' factor has a 40 per cent loading, with individual productivity having 30 per cent, the residual relating to welfare benefits allocated. Annual average wages are over 3,200 RMB. The bonus is based on the output of the workshop as a whole. Pensions are contributory with the individual paying 5 per cent, with a similar sum from the enterprise and again from the responsible ministry. Employees can also retire on 75–80 per cent of their original income.

Shenyang Area/Anshan Iron and Steel

The introduction of the economic reforms into *Angang* have led to a closer relationship between rewards and performance. Formerly, the incomes of workers were set by the Ministry of Metallurgy. After 1988, they had to be related to the efficiency of the steel complex. Enterprises there have the autonomy to increase their employees' incomes by 0.8 per cent for each 1 per cent increase of profits.

Anshan Iron and Steel has adopted its own version of the 'post plus skill' reward system. There are five elements: post, technical skill, enterprise efficiency, years of service, and individual bonus. In 1992, the 'post' element ranged from 4 RMB per month to 40. Technical skills ranged from 47–346 RMB per month. An enterprise efficiency bonus ranged from 4 RMB per month for white collar staff to 40 RMB for blue-collar workers. Years of service varied accordingly. Individual or competitive bonuses were between 35–40 RMB per month. The average income per worker was approximately 4,200 RMB per annum in 1992.

Shenyang Gold Cup Auto

The rewards system for Gold Cup Auto for production workers was determined by output and the number of hours worked. The range of wages went from 200–1,000 RMB a month, with exceptional payments to those involved in dirty jobs, like paint spraying. The average worker's income was 3,800 RMB in 1992. The cadres were paid on the 'post plus skills' basis. There were five post grades (100–50 RMB per month) with five grades of skills (100–240 RMB per month) plus an individual bonus (50–100 RMB per month).

Shenyang Smelting Works

The average gross wage in Shenyang Smelting in the first half of 1993 was in the region of 350 RMB including bonuses. In the second half, they were to be allowed to pay more (between 80–100 RMB) if profits rise. The average is set to increase to around 5,000 RMB (in 1992, it was 3,700 RMB). The level of wages was related to levels of efficiency and effort. If profits and tax grew by 1 per cent, wages grew by 0.87 per cent (before 1992). With the new system, such increases were to be equally dependent on rises in efficiency, foreign-exchange earnings and growth of output. In the metallurgy sector, Shenyang Smelting is the only one of three firms with the above system. It has worked successfully since it was introduced, and last year wages in aggregate grew by 5 million RMB.

Before the economic reforms, Shenyang Smelting had the old eight-grade system like the other large state owned enterprises. Since 1992, they have implemented the new 'post plus skill' system. This related rewards mainly to the responsibilities of the post and the technical skills of the worker. If workers perform well, they can earn appropriate rewards. Each year, the heads of departments select their best 10 workers for promotion to a higher level of wages in their department.

Shenyang Smelting has a flexible system of rewards with a higher wage and a lower bonus. In the main workshop, for those under the contract system, the bonus is 35–40 RMB for direct workers and 30–35 RMB for indirect workers (but only 25 RMB for non-contract workers). The bonus depends on production levels, quality, costs, etc. If the worker has a second child or an accident, the bonus is not paid. If a worker performs well, they can earn up to 65 RMB. Administrative staff receive the lowest bonus, only 7 RMB per month. The minimum of such staff are now employed since the reforms gave the enterprise the right to slim down the labour force.

Shenyang Transformer Works

Wages are now based on a 10-grade system for post responsibilities in Shenyang Transformers, with a range of 5 RMB to 44 RMB, and an average of 20 for this factor. Cadres' salaries are allocated on 11 grades (actually 12, but the lowest level was not used). The range in wages was broadly similar to that in salaries, except that the top (general director) post component of salary was 56 RMB. The average overall income in the enterprise in 1992 was in the region of 5,100 RMB. If profits increased by 1 per cent, workers' incomes could rise by 0.86%. The average bonus in Shenyang Transformers in 1992 was over 65 RMB per month, but could be as high as 200 RMB, which was higher than in the Smelting Works. The individual bonus depended on performance, such as completing work ahead of schedule.

Social insurance reform

This section deals with the last element of the three-system reforms introduced in the early 1990s. Basically, the national scheme sets out a macro-framework to replace the micro- one which previously existed under the iron rice-bowl arrangements in each enterprise. The scheme aspires to be national in its coverage, initially starting in urban areas in the state owned enterprise sector.

All of the 10 enterprises visited reported that they had implemented the new social insurance system reforms. Contributions to the new social and unemployment insurance schemes were now to be paid by the individuals as well as by the enterprise and by the State. Most state owned enterprises continued to provide welfare benefits as before, although the arrangements in Capital Iron and Steel had undergone reform according to national policy. Pensions, health care and housing were provided as before. If workers had worked for more than eight years for the company, Capital Iron and Steel paid all medical bills and invalidity benefit was set at 100 per cent of wages. As it made more profit, it provided better fringe benefits than other companies.

There are over 100,000 retired employees dependent on Anshan Steel (including cadres and workers) receiving benefits from the enterprise, according to their years of service. Cadres retired at 60; workers at 55 (50 for women). There was a special pensions and welfare department. Part-time work was sometimes offered to retirees. Service companies have been set up to help them, and provide additional income, such as The Old People's Bus Company. Retirement in Shenyang Smelting also normally takes place at 60 for men and 55 for women (the State specifies 60 for both but there is a surplus of female employees). If jobs are hazardous, early retirement at 45 is permitted. Before the enterprise reforms, the company could not ask invalids to leave; now they can do so. It is likely that it will take some years before national comprehensive social insurance coverage becomes effective.

DISCUSSION

Labour and personnel system reform

Whilst six of the 10 firms investigated had moved to labour system contracts, it was interesting that several major SOEs had not (see Table 10.3). If those at the leading edge of reform were conforming to the experimental initiative encouraged from above, the recalcitrants most likely had the political clout to resist such pressures (see Chan 1993). It was probably in industrial concentrations where political 'conservatives' (in Chinese terms) were strong and where enterprise/party/union factions were resilient. One may also surmise that it would be in the older enterprises and industries that such tendencies would be strongest, such as iron and steel, etc. Yet it is puzzling to note that if this reform was not fully introduced, other changes were implemented in the same SOE in the fields of wages and social insurance. Moreover, it was true to say that all newcomers in the recalcitrant SOEs had previously been on labour contracts since the mid-1980s.

It was also evident that one of the enterprises (Dalian Locomotive and Rolling Stock) did not even adopt the 'newcomer' labour system contracts until 1990, several years after the regulations were changed, and six years later than the Port Authority had conformed to the change in regulations there. Both Iron and Steel companies, *Angang* as well as *Shougang*, it should be noted, were still resistant to comprehensive contract system reforms.

Wage-system reform: summary

The north-east SOEs mostly reflected the post plus skills (plus bonus) model (see Table 10.3). Nearly all of them had displaced the old eight-grade ladder. Enterprises now had more autonomy to implement reward systems and there was now more interenterprise variation (see Child 1994). Differentials varied from 5:1 to 2:1 depending on economic circumstances. On the other hand, there was the 'national' reform model of a basic core of rewards topped up with collective and individual bonuses. Two of the SOEs (Dalian Port and Shenyang Gold Cup) even had a major hourly wage element in their rewards equation.

Workers' average annual incomes (for 1992) ranged from 3,200 RMB to 5,000 RMB, with an average of 4,030 RMB over the 10 organisations. These were higher than the annual average of 3,240 RMB cited for Dalian state enterprise workers in 1993 but much less than the 6,000 RMB estimated for rural industry employees, let alone the 9,600 RMB for those working in joint ventures in that area in 1993 (the latter groups not protected by the iron rice-bowl). At the time of the investigation, the now abandoned tourist exchange rate was just under 6 yuan FEC (Foreign

Exchange Certificate) for one US dollar, whereas the free rate was around 9 yuan RMB. The purchasing power parity equivalent was many times this, with some economists estimating it as up to six times greater (see Gordon *et al.* 1992).

Given the economic growth in the PRC generally in the last few years, and especially that of the fast-growing sectors, the earnings of those in SOEs were not as high in terms of relativities as they had been in the past. Many workers had 'voted with their feet' and sought work outside the state owned firms; others were displaced on the grounds that they could earn more elsewhere in the service sector or in the labour-market.

In contrast to labour contracts, wage-system reform in Capital Iron and Steel in Beijing had been a model for SOEs since it was introduced in the mid-1980s. It has been described as a form of MBO (management by objectives) by Ji Li (in Wedley 1992: 176). He notes that the absence of contracts for life-time workers mirrors Japanese experience, where he claims that only temporary employees have contracts.

Social insurance reform

Between 1978 and 1992, the numbers of workers in urban and rural industries covered by basic social insurance (for sickness, pensions, etc.) rose from 87 million to 204 million. Around 70 million employees in over 430,000 work units in the industrial sector were covered by specific unemployment insurance. Further, unemployment insurance benefit was paid out to 400,000 persons on a monthly basis in early 1993 (see *Chinese Trade Unions* April 1993: 6). Unemployment benefit was related to period of service and the original wage of the worker. It varied from 40 to 80 RMB a month. Currently, plans are being discussed to extend the scheme from the state owned enterprise sector to workers in all factories, but it is still early days in this respect. Funds are also available for the un-employed to set up as self-employed individuals or as small business collectives.

Apart from the national scheme, there are local arrangements. For example, the municipal authorities in Beijing initiated a new old-age pension scheme. It covers workers in state owned, collective and foreign funded enterprises in the city area. Workers pay 2 per cent of their average monthly wage of the previous year. To compensate for this cost, wages will be increased proportionally.

Trade unions in China have for a long time offered mutual aid insur-ance, as elsewhere. This had started in the early 1950s on a limited scale. More recently, it was extended to cover areas like old age, medical care, child-bearing, injuries, funerals and so on. There are said to be currently over 40,000 mutual aid insurance organisations, run by trade unions, involving over 7.6 million people, but this represents only a rather small percentage of the urban working class.

CONCLUSION

To sum up, although enterprise reforms were successively introduced throughout the 1980s, the iron rice-bowl proved rather resilient and still characterised the SOEs by the early 1990s. A socialist market economy had however slowly emerged and there was discernible if limited progress towards what is now called a labour force market. By the mid-1980s for example, jobs for life were still *de rigueur* in the typical large state firm, if eventually to be phased out, and seniority-based promotion systems were very common (see Warner 1993). In other words, it was only after 1985/6 that attempts to introduce labour contracts and efficiency wages were seriously placed on the economic agenda.

Even after state regulations were implemented to achieve employment and wage reforms in the mid-1980s (see Korzec 1992: 26–50) such reforms could be described by leading Western writers on Chinese economics as 'ineffectual' (Howe, Foreword to Korzec 1992: ix). Describing the reforms of the decade, he asserts that:-

[n]o significant dismissals have taken place, and in any case, the new regulations only allow worker dismissal in terms of infringement of regulations or imminent bankruptcy. Dismissal to cut costs remains illegal. Moreover, from the worker's point of view, the reform has not given him the right to quit work or take a better job elsewhere. Thus neither employer nor employee is in a position to strike a market-style wage-employment bargain.

(Howe 1992: ix)

After the 1992 reforms, it was evident that some headway had possibly been made. In the 10 SOEs investigated (see Table 10.3) labour contracts covering all employees were still restricted to seven out of the 10 sites, however. Wage reform was, on the other hand, fairly generally implemented and social insurance was comprehensively introduced. The upshot was that Western-style practices in the areas of personnel, rewards and social insurance had been grafted on to status quo characteristics, producing a hybrid form of labour–management relations (see Warner 1995, in press). The official goal was to 'corporatize' all state owned sector enterprises in the next few years. However, it is clear that in China there is frequently a gap between intent and practice. The (mainly) north-eastern state owned enterprises, although pilot sites for the three-systems reforms experiments, still provide evidence of organisational inertia. Even so, given the losses made by so many state owned firms – as many as one in two were 'in the red' by mid 1994 – the Chinese authorities are under pressure to extend the reforms to all such enterprises. To make firms fully responsible for their profits and losses by corporatizing if not wholly privatizing them, is seen as one way out of the double-bind of fiscal deficits and distorted resource allocation. If the pace of reform continues, there is some chance – if only a modest one – that this can be achieved in the short term.

ACKNOWLEDGEMENTS

The field work reported in this article is based on research in north-east China which was sponsored by the British Academy/ESRC/CASS exchange scheme, whose generous support was appreciated. I must acknowledge the contribution of Ms Ding Yi and Ms Wang Wei, who acted as interpreters and translators during the visits to enterprises and the Institute of Industrial Economics, Beijing, for their collaboration and help.

REFERENCES

Beijing Review (1992) 16 November: 14, Beijing.
Chan, A. (1993) 'Revolution or corporatism? Workers and unions in post-Mao China', *Australian Journal of Chinese Affairs* 29, January: 31–61.
Chinese Trade Unions (1993) April: 6, Beijing.
Child, J. (1994) *Management in China in the Age of Reform*, Cambridge: Cambridge University Press.
Dong, F. (1986) 'On the labour system and whether labour is a commodity', *Guangming Ribao* 4: 4 October, Beijing.
Gordon, M. J., Luo, F. and Wang, Z. (1992) 'International comparisons of China's GNP', in W. C. Wedley (ed.) *Changes in the Iron Rice Bowl: The Reformation of Chinese Management, Advances in Chinese Industrial Studies* 3: 5–20, Greenwich, Conn. and London: JAI Press.
Granick, D. (1991) 'Multiple labour markets in the industrial state enterprise', *China Quarterly* 126, June: 269–289.
Howe, C. (1992) 'Foreword', in M. Korzec (ed.) *Labour and the Failure of Reform in China*: vii–x, London: Macmillan and St Martin's Press.
Hsu, R. C. (1991) *Economic Theories in China 1979–1988*, Cambridge: Cambridge University Press.
Ji, L. (1992) 'Management by objectives and China's reform of the employment system', in W. C. Wedley (ed.) *Changes in the Iron Rice Bowl: The Reformation of Chinese Management, Advances in Chinese Industrial Studies* 3: 169–181, Greenwich, Conn. and London: JAI Press.
Kaple, D. A. (1994) *Dream of a Red Factory: The Legacy of High Stalinism in China*, Oxford: Oxford University Press.
Korzec, M. (1992) *Labour and the Failure of Reform in China*, London: Macmillan and St Martin's Press.
Lee, P. K. (1988) *Industrial Management and Economic Reform in China, 1949–1984*, Oxford: OUP.
Leeming, F. (1992) *The Changing Geography of China*, Oxford: Basil Blackwell.
Leung, W. Y. (1988) *Smashing the Iron Rice-Pot: Workers and Unions in China's Market Socialism*, Hong Kong: Asia Monitor Resource Centre.
Schurmann, F. (1966) *Ideology and Organisation in Communist China*, Berkeley, Cal.: University of California Press.
Summary of World Broadcasts (SWB) (1992) London: British Broadcasting Corporation, 15 February.
Takahara, A. (1992) *The Politics of Wage Policy in Post Revolutionary China*, London: Macmillan.

Tidrick, G. and Chen, J. (eds) (1987) *China's Industrial Reforms*, Oxford: Oxford University Press.

Warner, M. (1986) 'Managing human resources in China', *Organisation Studies* 7(4): 353–366.

—— (1991) 'Labour management relations in the PRC: the role of trade unions', *International Journal of Human Resource Management* 2: 205–220.

—— (1992) *How Chinese Managers Learn: Management and Industrial Training in the PRC*, London: Macmillan.

—— (1993) 'Human resources management with Chinese characteristics', *International Journal of Human Resource Management* 4(1): 45–65.

—— (1995) *The Management of Human Resources in Chinese Industry*, London: Macmillan.

Wedley, W. C. (ed.) (1992) *Changes in the Iron Rice Bowl: The Reformation of Chinese Management*, Greenwich, Conn.: JAI Press.

White, G. (1986) 'Labour market reform in Chinese industry', in M. Warner, (ed.) *Management Reforms in China* 113–126, London: Pinter.

—— (ed.) (1991) *The Chinese State in the Era of Economic Reform*, London: Macmillan.

11 Management education in the People's Republic of China

M. W. Luke Chan

ABSTRACT

With the upsurge in economic activities in the People's Republic of China, there is a growing need for people to manage such activities. This chapter summarizes the status of management education in China and its relationship to the economic reform process. Included in this chapter is a detailed discussion of the foreign assisted management education programmes as well as programmes offered by Chinese universities and colleges. In the main the potential benefits of management education are now thought to be appearing but the activity needs further expansion. This will be difficult since funding in tertiary institutes – the traditional provider of management education – is limited.

INTRODUCTION

It has been 15 years since China started its economic reform process. During these past 15 years, economic development in China has gone through changes that are so deep and widespread it is most unlikely that China will ever go back to the old style centrally planned economic system. With the current up-surge in privatizing many of the government enterprises the economic reform movement will continue to be a major force in decades to come.

One of the by-products of economic reform is the growing need for people to manage the reform process as well as the products of reform, which include the increasing number of joint ventures with foreign companies, the newly created contracted firms organized by private citizens, groups, and old production units, the ever expanding dimensions in foreign trade and international business, as well as the new phenomenon of privatization. All these have created a tremendous need for a new generation of managers who can understand the principles of marketing, advertising, finance (both corporate and international), accounting, inventory control, human resource planning and development, and international laws and regulations. It is, therefore, not surprising to note that the emphasis placed on management education by the Chinese government has been high. Accordingly, this chapter examines the status of management education in China. This is very important in understanding and predicting the process and the future success or failure of the economic reform movements in China. To many Sinologists, the success of the economic reform programme will be one of the key necessary conditions for a successful political reform. And yet very little research or discussions have been conducted in this area of vital importance.[1]

ECONOMIC REFORM AND MANAGEMENT EDUCATION

When the People's Republic of China was formed in 1949, economic reform did not immediately follow. In fact, the major task facing the government at that time was the process of recovery from the civil war. For almost three years, all the industrialists in China were allowed to maintain their enterprises. The biggest social change at that time was land reform. Land was redistributed from the rich land owners to farmers. It was 1953 when China introduced its First Five-Year Plan, thus creating a centrally planned economy. With a planned economy, all producer goods were allotted by the State Planning Commission based on state, ministerial or local government allocation. Outputs, on the other hand, were entirely purchased and marketed by the state. It is quite obvious that the need for market-oriented management personnel was virtually nonexistent. Apart from central economic planning, there were two other events that were detrimental to management education in China. The first was the College and Departmental Re-arrangement of 1952. Following the Soviet model of education, China embarked on a massive restructuring of its educational system. Many of the smaller colleges which offered management courses were closed or combined with the bigger universities. Courses in management were reduced, de-emphasized, or cancelled. Except for accounting, which can be viewed as bookkeeping, very few management courses were offered in universities and colleges. The second event that was detrimental to management education and for that reason education in general, is the Cultural Revolution. Between 1966 and 1976, many universities and colleges were closed and the entire educational process came to a complete halt.[2]

The current wave of economic reform started around 1976, right after the end of the Cultural Revolution. After the death of Mao Zedong in September 1976, and the downfall of the Gang of Four in October of the same year, China ran through a two-year period of economic and political adjustments which were very similar to the adjustments made during 1962–1965 after the Great Leap Forward launched by Chairman Mao in 1958. During the 1960s' adjustment, the focus was on re-alignment of all the exaggerated and unrealistic economic targets. For the 1970s' adjustment, the focus was to re-vitalize the slack economic conditions due to years of inactivity. To kick-start the process, China announced the Four Modernizations programme in 1978, providing some much needed impetus for the economy.³ The 1978 Four Modernizations programme was in fact suggested by the late Premier Zhou En-lai in 1964 but was not implemented at that time. One of the outcomes of the Four Modernizations programme was an increase in trade and business with the Western world. Between 1977 and 1979, the value of Chinese imports and exports grew at a rate of 17 per cent per year in real terms. With increased trade activities, investment activities also followed. These are direct results of the Four Modernizations programme and the Open Door Policy adopted by the Chinese government.

During the Third Plenum of the 11th Congress of the Communist Party (December 1978), two areas of focus were announced which re-defined policy from adjustment to active and rapid reform. These were particularly relevant to management education in China. To paraphrase these two announcements, the first one said that: 'one of the shortcomings in the structure of economic management in our country is over-concentration of authority ... [we must] boldly shift ... to lower levels ... [and give] local authorities ... greater power of decision ...'. The second one said that China should 'actively expand economic co-operation with other countries ...'. The implications of the first announcement are as follows. First, it was recognized that managing from the top had not been the most efficient way of managing the economy. Second, a shift towards decentralization of authority and responsibilities was deemed desirable. And, third, the decentralization process was not just to be confined to transferring authority from central government to municipal or local governments, but was to be extended to transferring authority from ministries to local enterprises and production units. This empowerment of decision making has created a tremendous need for management personnel at the lower levels, management personnel who are at the front line of the production and marketing levels, management personnel who are responsible for the efficient operation and profitability of their units, and management personnel who are responsible for strategic planning at the micro level.

The implications of the second announcement were even more profound in terms of management education in China. By expanding economic co-operation with other countries, China faced the need for a generation of management personnel who understood management principles, management styles and management practices in the West. After closing its doors to Western trade and investment for almost 40 years, China simply did not have the necessary number of management and business people to conduct business properly with the West. For instance, it took China almost two years after the announcement of the Open Door Policy on foreign business before the first set of joint venture laws were introduced. Then it took another year before China announced its regulations on labour management in joint ventures.⁴

With the push for decentralization and the desire to increase business and economic activities with the West, China announced the establishment of four Special Economic Zones in southern China in 1979. Each of the Special Economic Zones was given the authority and responsibility to develop and attract foreign investment. They were also given the mandate to '... absorb more management and production techniques', an indication of acute shortage of appropriate management personnel. This situation was further exacerbated by the opening of 14 coastal cities and Hainan Island to foreign investment in 1984.

To deal partially with this situation of increased demand for managerial personnel, the government responded by increasing the enrolment of management and business students. Table 11.1 outlines the number of new university and college students in management/business in China between 1976 and 1991. In the same table, we have included the numbers of new university and college students enrolled in engineering, medicine, education, humanities and sciences. Simple arithmetic reveals that while the overall intake of new college and university students increased by 28 per cent between 1976 and 1981 and nearly tripled between 1976 and 1991, the number of new college and university students enrolled in management and business programmes increased by more than five times between 1976 and 1981, and an astonishing 23 times between 1976 and 1991, reaching its peak in 1988. Undoubtedly, in 1976 the total new intake number of college and university students in management and business was very low, resulting in a low starting base number. However, in 1981 the total new intake of management and business students was very close to that in humanities and sciences, and the 1991 numbers reveal a phenomenal increase in new management and business students. In percentage terms, between 1981 and 1991, the number of management and business students increased by over 440 per cent. For humanities and sciences, the increases are 122 per cent and 30 per cent, respectively. It is quite evident from these numbers that the Chinese government has been putting a great deal of emphasis on management education as a means to complement the activities of economic reform. Of course, one can and should be mindful of the fact that new intake of college and university students in China does not happen by coincidence. It happens because of careful planning by the state at various levels.

This push to educate more students in the area of management and business does not stop at the university and college level. In China, to be admitted to university or college, students must complete 12 years of pre-university schooling, the equivalent of a North American high school education. However, a student who desires to enrol in a vocational school needs to complete only nine of the first 12 years of schooling. Table 11.2 summarizes the new intake of vocational students in management and business, engineering, medical and teachers' colleges between 1976 and 1991. Again, it is not surprising to note that of all the disciplines included

Table 11.1 Enrolment of new college and university students in selective disciplines[a]

Year	Total[b]	Management and business	Engineering	Medicine	Education	Humanities	Sciences
1976	217,048	2,453	71,618	35,324	44,167	15,961	13,846
1977	272,971	3,389	79,619	34,923	94,586	14,781	19,838
1978	401,521	11,960	135,741	47,320	123,996	21,765	30,261
1979	275,099	8,143	91,869	31,569	87,481	14,984	18,053
1980	281,230	11,973	92,387	31,277	89,046	12,863	18,539
1981	278,777	12,405	91,261	29,241	88,207	12,763	18,914
1982	315,135	18,274	102,825	29,486	97,177	16,048	20,573
1983	390,800	29,385	131,331	31,831	113,889	24,537	21,880
1984	475,171	39,702	158,925	35,863	134,494	34,715	25,661
1985	619,235	67,017	201,004	42,919	162,549	53,289	30,833
1986	572,055	58,112	184,958	40,647	170,071	35,983	27,778
1987	616,822	63,444	200,542	43,699	189,454	34,747	29,185
1988	669,731	76,041	219,532	48,135	203,446	34,687	29,485
1989	597,113	68,519	201,425	46,245	183,797	25,977	21,313
1990	608,850	67,446	208,285	46,772	182,467	27,756	24,034
1991	619,874	67,118	214,532	48,943	183,715	28,336	24,501

Notes:
a Information is derived from various issues of the *Statistical Yearbook of China*
b Not included in this total figure are new students enrolled in politics and law, physical education, fine art, agriculture and forestry

in Table 11.2, management and business experienced the highest increase in both absolute and percentage terms. Between 1976 and 1981, the number of new management and business students in vocational schools more than doubled. This phenomenon is not observed in any other disciplines during the same period. Between 1976 and 1991, the same number is even more pronounced, as an increase of new intake management and business students of nearly five times was experienced, whereas for all vocational schools in China the increase only doubled. The overall increase in intake of vocational students in management and business, however, is less impressive than the increase at the university and college level. This is largely due to the fact that at the vocational school level, foreign language training for such students has been quite minimal, so job opportunities for such graduates are by and large confined to domestic corporations where demand and therefore supply have not experienced the same degree of changes.

MANAGEMENT EDUCATION IN CHINA TODAY

Since 1980 there have been over 150,000 students recruited in the undergraduate programme in management education in China. During the same

Table 11.2 Enrolment of new vocational school students in selected disciplines[a]

Year	Total[b]	Management and business	Engineering	Medical	Teachers' college
1976	348,125	23,884	56,011	67,420	155,013
1977	366,312	30,321	69,172	67,443	157,548
1978	447,039	38,936	93,386	75,377	179,086
1979	491,551	43,596	83,806	79,125	226,165
1980	467,624	48,223	83,298	65,719	214,724
1981	433,179	49,582	85,303	54,128	195,081
1982	419,476	54,063	85,044	50,728	178,655
1983	477,763	76,559	91,203	61,684	191,380
1984	546,077	93,445	112,233	69,680	195,171
1985	668,271	127,906	144,829	87,925	216,343
1986	676,500	117,832	149,843	86,854	226,960
1987	715,227	133,108	161,333	96,818	230,251
1988	776,382	152,090	178,189	109,504	235,856
1989	734,861	147,043	170,239	93,142	227,199
1990	730,097	141,005	168,786	91,818	227,295
1991	779,955	151,349	189,400	94,745	229,275

Notes:
a Information is derived from issues of the *Statstical Yearbook of China*
b Not included in this total figure are new students enrolled in technical
  schools, in agriculture, forestry, politics and law, physical education, fine arts
  and teachers' colleges

period, the number of master's level students recruited was well over 7,000 and close to 300 doctoral students have enrolled in the management field. Currently, there are only 20 universities and colleges in China that offer doctoral programmes in management. Since there are over 1,000 universities and colleges in China, these 20 represent a very small fraction of the total number. One of the main reasons for such a small fraction of universities and colleges offering doctoral programmes in management is the tremendous lack of qualified supervisors. This is one of the bottlenecks in the overall development of management education in China. Table 11.3 outlines the number of faculty members by rank and by discipline in China in 1986 and 1991.

It is quite clear that apart from education, management and business has the lowest number of total faculty members and full professors. As of 1991, there were only 640 full professors in management in China. Furthermore, of the 640 full professors, only a small fraction are qualified to supervise doctoral students. If we compare the total number of faculty members in management and business to that in engineering, humanities and science, the shortage of good qualified instructors in Chinese universities and colleges becomes very apparent. Unfortunately, this shortage is not going to improve in the foreseeable future. Traditionally, the best graduates from each class are usually persuaded to stay at their alma

Table 11.3 Number of faculty members by rank and discipline in colleges and universities in China,[a] 1986 and 1991[b]

	Professors	Associate professors	Lecturers	Instructors	Teaching assistants	Total
Engineering	104,408	2,372	12,668	40,618	8,261	40,489
	(107,271)	(5,125)	(26,142)	(44,636)	(5,782)	(25,586)
Medicine	31,877	1,350	4,395	9,432	3,152	13,548
	(34,377)	(2,937)	(6,974)	(11,895)	(2,748)	(9,823)
Education	3,852	96	380	1,152	572	1,652
	(5,244)	(115)	(698)	(1,440)	(468)	(2,523)
Humanities	81,832	1,171	7,538	26,133	12,142	34,848
	(88,413)	(2,343)	(16,560)	(32,337)	(6,152)	(31,021)
Sciences	82,852	11,630	8,757	31,787	8,070	32,608
	(80,746)	(2,927)	(19,967)	(32,754)	(3,527)	(21,573)
Management and business	15,624	282	1,181	3,471	2,765	7,925
	(19,334)	(620)	(2,882)	(6,643)	(1,377)	(7,812)

Notes:
a Information is derived from various issues of the *Statistical Yearbook of China*
b The 1991 figures are in brackets

mater to become teaching assistants. With the passage of time, good teaching and research, teaching assistants are promoted to become instructors, then to associate professors and finally professors. Given the long Chinese tradition of valuing intellectuals, some students consider that an invitation to stay at their own alma mater as a teaching assistant is a family honour.

However, things have changed, particularly for management and business graduates. The attraction to work for joint venture corporations in China, or Chinese corporations with good international business networks is so strong that the very best graduates often refuse to stay in academia upon graduation. The opportunity to work for joint venture corporations or Chinese corporations with strong international business networks translates into a much better salary as well as opportunities to travel abroad. It is not uncommon to find a well placed graduate with a bachelor's degree in business earning far more during his/her first year of joining the workforce than a full professor. This is discouraging for professors and detrimental to management education development in China. Solutions have been suggested recently. First, a market-driven university education system is being promoted. Under this proposed system, students will be required to pay tuition fees for selected disciplines. Second, the salaries of faculty members will be allowed to increase to partially reflect market value. Nanjing University, for instance, has proposed to increase the monthly salary of its full professors in management from its current level of around 350 yuan to 800 yuan.[5] The salary level of all other ranks will also be allowed to increase proportionally. The timing of these proposed changes is critical to management education and university education at large.

At the master's level, there were 78 universities that offered master's degrees in management in 1992. This represents a fairly substantial and steady increase in the number of universities offering such a degree. There were only 39 such universities in China in 1984 and 49 in 1986. To put these numbers in a slightly different perspective, one can easily calculate that the number of universities that offer master's degrees in management has doubled between 1984 and 1992. The total number of universities in China during the same time period was recorded at around 850 and 1,075, respectively, an overall increase of 24 per cent. Using the same information, one can also conclude that in 1984, only 4.5 per cent of all universities in China offered a master's degree in management. This number increased to over 7 per cent in 1992.

For undergraduate management education, there are now over 270 universities and colleges that offer undergraduate degree programmes. Included in this total are 41 financial colleges, 49 comprehensive universities, 114 technical and engineering colleges, 38 agricultural colleges, eight medical colleges and over 20 other colleges and universities across China. The programmes offered by the universities and colleges tend to be very specialized and narrowly focused, and generally reflect the strength of the existing faculty members. For reasons outlined in the previous discussions, one can envisage that the majority of undergraduate programmes are concentrated in the more technical and quantitative areas of management. So it is not surprising to note that out of the 270 universities and colleges that offer undergraduate degrees in management, 114 of them are offered by technical and engineering colleges. Given the historical link between such colleges and the industrial sectors (e.g. the Chinese Ministry of Metallurgical Industry has 16 engineering universities and colleges across China), industrial enterprise management is the most popular management specialization offered by colleges and universities. This is followed by commercial enterprise management and then by management science. Included in the curriculum design of these specializations are courses which rely heavily on quantitative approaches in management disciplines. Also, one should recognize that the same specialization could mean very different course contents and overall course requirements across China. This situation reflects the very nature of the problems of management education in China. First, faculty members teaching management are mainly from quantitative and engineering backgrounds and often have very little management training. Second, the content and requirement for different specializations offered by different colleges and universities reveal a general lack of cohesive planning and organization of management education in China. Courses are based more on the availability of faculty and their know-how than on need.

It was not until the autumn 1990 intake of new graduate students that China offered a Western style MBA programme. Currently there are nine universities in China that offer Western style MBA degree programmes. The universities include (in alphabetical order): Fudan University, Harbin Polytechnical University, Nankai University, People's University, Shanghai University of Finance and Economics, Tianjin University, Tsinghua University, Xiaman University and Xian Jiaotong University. Except for Shanghai University of Finance and Economics which is under the jurisdiction of the Chinese Ministry of Finance, all the other eight universities are under the direct jurisdiction of the Chinese State Education Commission, a not unimportant indication of the focus and emphasis placed by the government on management education in China.[6] Under this new Western style MBA programme offered by these nine universities, not only will the degree designation be MBA (Master of Business Administration) instead of MA (Master of Arts), but the students will learn during the course of their studies the different functional areas of business (i.e. accounting, finance, international business, etc.).

In terms of doctoral education training, China has not been progressing as rapidly as at the master's level, which is indicative of the severe lack of qualified professors and supervisors in the field. For example, one of the nine universities that is currently offering an MBA degree has only one faculty member who is qualified and accredited by the state to act as doctoral thesis supervisor. Obviously, this is one of the bottlenecks for any future development of a management education programme in China. Because of this lack of qualified professors to supervise doctoral students, the level of government funding in this area has been quite limited as well. In 1991, there were only five doctoral projects funded by the government with a total budgetary commitment of 138,000 yuan. In 1991, there were only four projects and 101,000 yuan committed to doctoral education. This is indeed a very small financial commitment by the government.

Before leaving this section, we should also take a glance at management education for executives. Starting from the beginning of 1992, there has been a tremendous push to introduce management education to all the senior managers in state owned enterprises. The focus is to renew and revitalize management principles and practices at the senior level. This is a reflection of the government's effort to introduce the concept of life-long learning as well as a means to introduce new management principles to senior management. This second effort is critical if such principles are to be accepted at all levels of management. As part of the Eighth Five-Year Plan, the government is committed to implement full scale management training for all senior managers working in large and medium size state owned enterprises. For smaller enterprises, there is also a plan to push for management skill development and renewal. This plan covers a period of five to six years. Furthermore, the state also intends to promote management education for bright mid-level managers and younger workers who have good practical experience, to receive college and university education in management.[7]

FOREIGN ASSISTED MANAGEMENT EDUCATION PROGRAMMES IN CHINA

In terms of management education, China has, since 1978, sought and received many foreign assisted management education programmes. For the donor countries and organizations involvement in such programmes, objectives can differ. However, it is clear that each one of these programmes shares a common belief that by improving management education in China it is helping the process of economic reform. For the Chinese, the primary reasons for engaging in such foreign assisted programmes can be grouped into the following four main categories. First, through such foreign assisted programmes, the Chinese will be able to provide students and faculty members more opportunities to study management abroad. Second, the programmes will enable the Chinese to improve the knowledge of faculty members and thus improve the quality and standard of its curriculum in management theory and practice. Third, through these foreign assisted programmes, it is hoped that research in management will be improved and enhanced. And finally, because of chronic lack of emphasis on management education, the Chinese hope to be able to acquire some much needed teaching equipment, library material and other related information through these programmes.

In what follows, we try to outline some of the bilateral and multilateral foreign assisted programmes on management education in China since 1979. This, of course, is not an exhaustive list, but it does outline some of the more prominent programmes and their special features.

The first foreign assisted management education programme and one of the most visible was the National Centre for Industrial Science and Technology Management Development in Dalian, often referred to as the Dalian Centre. It started in 1980 as an outgrowth of bilateral agreements on co-operation in science and technology at the initiative of the US Department of Commerce, Office of Productivity, Technology and Innovation. The initial 18-week intensive programme for managers, officials and academics was set up by the Chinese State Economic Commission, the Chinese Science and Technology Commission, and the Chinese Ministry of Education with the US Department of Commerce as a centre for management of science and technology. After two years, the programme evolved into a general two-year MBA programme based on the MBA curriculum of the State University of New York (SUNY) in Buffalo. Five groups of 40 students have finished the programme. Prior to 1989, students spent half of the time at the Dalian Centre and the other half at SUNY Buffalo. After 1989, the SUNY Buffalo portion was replaced by internship in China with

American joint venture corporations. One important feature of this programme is that all the students who complete the degree programme receive a SUNY Buffalo MBA degree. The Dalian Centre was a successful and high profile programme but its prominence derives mostly from its executive training programme and not from the MBA programme. Since its inception, the Americans have insisted that a high proportion of participants be actual factory managers and (initially) officials of the Chinese Science and Technology Commission and the Chinese State Economic Commission. As it was one of the earliest executive education programmes in China, it attracted many senior and influential executives to attend its training courses. The centre also provides consulting services to Chinese industry and joint venture enterprises in China on a fee for service basis. Apart from the Dalian Centre, there has been no other official educational aid programme for China organized by the US government. There are programmes organized on an individual exchange basis such as the Fulbright programme, the Fulbright–Hay grant and the International Visitors Programme. These are not discipline specific programmes, but a fair number of management students and educators have been involved in them.

In terms of scope and scale of foreign assisted programmes in management education in China, Canada is definitely one of the most prominent countries. As early as 1981, Canada decided to focus on management education as a key area of development assistance in China. At the university level, a Canada–China Management Programme was established involving eight key universities in both countries to engage in exchange activities in 1983. The programme has four important elements: an in-China MBA programme, a graduate studies programme in Canada, a visiting scholar's programme and an equipment and library acquisition programme. Unlike the Dalian programme, the in-China MBA focuses on the MBA curriculum in China taught by Canadian faculty. Students will receive a Chinese graduate degree. The graduate studies programme in Canada involved both MBA and PhD studies in Canada. A total of 105 students were sent to Canada to pursue MBA degrees in Canadian universities between 1983 to 1987. During the same period a total of 20 doctoral students were sent to study in Canada under the programme. There was a total of 44 visiting scholars at a number of different Canadian universities. Their visits ranged from six months to two years. The total budget for this programme was Canadian $12 million, of which C$858,840 was also spent on equipment and library purchases.

At the time when the university level exchange programme was set up, Canada also established the Canada–China Enterprise Management Training Centre in Chengdu. This programme was implemented by the Association of Canadian Community Colleges. For this reason, the centre tends to teach more practical know-how in management to enterprise managers and government cadres. During the initial phase of the programme which ran from 1983–1987, a total of Canadian $3.1 million was committed. The programme has since been extended twice, once in 1986 to cover a period of 1986–1991 and more recently in 1991 for the 1991–1996 period. Under the first extension, a total of Canadian $4.8 million was committed by the Canadian government while a further Canadian $5.0 million was committed in the second extension. The university level management education programme was also extended for a second phase to cover the period from 1989–1994 with a further financial contribution of Canadian $26.3 million by the Canadian government.[8] Under the second phase of this university level programme, the original eight key Chinese universities were expanded to nine. A new network of 44 associate universities in different parts of China also joined the programme. On the Canadian side, the linkage was expanded to include a national executive development programme and an in-China PhD programme.

Canada's effort to improve management education in China did not stop at the university and college level. In Anhui province, a relatively poor and backward province in China, the Anhui Enterprise Management Training was established in 1986 to strengthen the curriculum and organizational structure of the Anhui Economic Management Cadre Institute. Total financial commitment was Canadian $2.53 million. To help speed up economic reform amongst the coastal cities, a Coastal Cities and Open Areas Project was established by the Canadian government in Tianjin. The main objective of this project is to upgrade the management and planning skills of the government cadres involved in the 14 coastal cities, the four special economic zones and the three delta areas. Total financial contribution by the Canadian government was Canadian $7.9 million between 1986 and 1992.

Japan has also been quite involved in management education in China. In 1983, an Enterprise Management Centre was established in Tianjin. The objective was to train senior and mid-level managers in Japanese management practices. Two interesting features about the centre are worth noting here. First, teaching is by and large staffed by Japanese retired executives. Second, while the total contribution towards the establishment of the centre was quite substantial, amounting to US $50 million, about 45 per cent of the total contribution was earmarked for the purchase of Japanese equipment.

Australia started its aid programme in China in 1981 by signing the Technical Agreement between Australia and China which involved a financial commitment of approximately Australian $160 million. Under this agreement, there was a component related to education, particularly management education. However, most of the management related programmes were targeted at short-term visits to Australia for managers and short management courses offered by Australian management consultants.

The European bilateral programmes in management education in China have come mainly from three countries, France, the Federal Republic of Germany and the United Kingdom. The French initiated two major programmes, an MBA degree programme and an executive training programme. The MBA degree programme began in 1987 at Nankai University in Tianjin, and was subsequently moved to the University of International Business and Economics in Beijing in 1988. The main objectives of the programme are two-fold: first, to train French speaking managers for Chinese enterprises and Sino–French joint ventures; second, to train a group of French speaking management faculty. The Sino–French MBA is a two-year programme. Students who have completed the second year of the degree programme also travel to France for a three-month internship in a French company. The degrees granted to the students are from a French university. The executive training programme is jointly funded by the French and Chinese governments. The Foundation National pour L'Enseignement de Gestion des Enterprises which began in 1991 is a programme designed to introduce French style management to senior Chinese managers. Three-month courses are taught in Beijing in English to Chinese managers. This is followed by a three-month visit to French companies in France.

The Germans approached their assistance in management education in China quite differently. In 1989, the Federal Republic of Germany established a German Management Training Centre in Shanghai to train managers in very specific industries which are linked to industries in Germany. This is a six-year project with a financial commitment of US $5.5 million. There are also university exchange and scholarship programmes which relate to management education but on a more *ad hoc* basis.

United Kingdom initiatives on management education in China came under one of the Technical Co-operation Programmes sponsored by the UK government. Lancaster University and Xian University set up an MBA programme for Chinese students to attend Lancaster University. However, since 1989 the programme has been suspended due to the non-returnee problem. There are, of course, many governmental sponsored scholarship and fellowship programmes whereby students can apply to visit or study in the UK for management related programmes and subjects.

At the multilateral level, management education training comes mainly from the United Nations Development Programme and from the Commission of the European Communities. The World Bank has been a big contributor towards education reform in China. Most of the World Bank money, however, has not been earmarked for management education. Under Phases I and II of the World Bank University Development Programme, a total of 75 Chinese universities have benefited from equipment and library acquisition. This undoubtedly has created direct and indirect benefits towards management education in China.

United Nations Development Programmes (UNDP) offers a very broadly based management training programme in China. In Changzhou, for instance, it set up a Management for Rural Enterprises training centre in 1990. The main focus of the centre is to offer consulting advice to local entrepreneurs. Along the same lines, the UNDP has utilized US $2.4 million to set up four regional centres, one in Lanzhou, one in Chengdu, one in Beijing and one in Nanning to train managers for the poor and remote areas of China. The objective is to train 1 000 managers in four years who will assist in the development of the poor areas. The UNDP are not confined to rural enterprises alone. The programmes operate a very successful foreign trade management training programme for the Chinese Ministry of Foreign Economic Relations and Trade (MOFERT). Under this programme MOFERT has identified four of the universities that are under its direct jurisdiction to conduct research on trade policy and to develop a new curriculum for the four universities. Other UNDP management training programmes have involved the training of bank managers who are responsible for international banking management, and the training of high level civil service officers in dealing with human resource management. The UNDP also ran a successful executive training programme from 1990–1993, in which senior managers in the key trading enterprises operating under MOFERT were trained by faculty members from the UK, Canada and the United States.

The Commission of the European Community set up the China–European Community Management Institute in Beijing in 1985 to train 40 MBA students a year to serve the European Community corporations operating in China. This is a two-year MBA programme taught by faculty members from many of the best known business schools in Europe. All the students enrolled in the MBA programme must have a minimum of five years work experience, be proficient in English, and pass the entrance examination and an interview. Learning is often project-based and is relevant to situations in China. Included in the MBA programme is a four-month internship with a company in Europe. The programme is highly successful and has attracted many good candidates. The institute also operates an executive training programme and carries a research agenda on management of joint ventures in China.

The above is not an exhaustive list of foreign assisted management education programmes in China. It does, however, outline many of the educational programmes provided by foreign countries to assist China in the management of its modernization and economic reform process. There are numerous institutional linkages and individual activities that are not included in this summary.

THE RELEVANCE OF MANAGEMENT EDUCATION AND ECONOMIC DEVELOPMENT IN CHINA

One interesting and important question that readers of this chapter and observers of economic development in China might ask is about the relationship between management education and current economic development in China. Any answer to this question can only be subjective and descriptive. To understand and appreciate the impact of management education on economic development, one has to understand the economic system in China prior to the economic reform era of 1976. The country as a whole was under one centrally controlled planning authority. The planning authority had the overall control and responsibility for the distribution and allocation of all productive resources including human resources. This means that the planning authority directly or indirectly controlled all enterprises, farms and factories in terms of inputs as well as production targets. The consumption of final products was also controlled by the planning authority. Rationed goods were distributed to consumers through the rationing system while the non-rationed goods were sold by stores controlled by the planning authority. The planning authority, of course, also determined the price as well as the quantity available for each store. It is quite obvious that the need for management of production and distribution at that time was limited to large scale resource allocations and balancing, rather than to micro optimization at the firm level. Accounting was reduced to simple bookkeeping, while rewards and incentives were reduced to T-shirts for model workers. Material incentives for meeting the plan were in place, but were enforced with a collective spirit which usually negated their effort.

The economic reform process introduced in 1976 has resulted in some very major changes in responsibilities. Not only was there was a push for decentralization of authority and responsibility as previously outlined, but many production units were given for the first time the responsibility of accounting for their own production mix, their own profitability and, more importantly, their own reward and incentive schemes. These changes may be seen as natural, inevitable and simple, but it required a great deal of knowledge and understanding to move from a centrally planned economic system to a market driven economy. To create a fair reward and incentive scheme required understanding and identifying the precise nature of each job category, its expectations and mandates. Only then could the achievement and performance of the workers be measured. This emphasis on individual accountability was a significant departure from the management style promoted during the Cultural Revolution (1965–1976). The potential impact of management education, and in this case learning about and understanding human resource planning and development, is quite obvious.[9]

It is true that in some Asian countries, noticeably Japan, the importance attached to formal management education is not as emphasized as in Western countries. There is therefore, a temptation to ask whether the cultural similarities between Japan and China, and perhaps even the geographical proximity, might mean that formal Western management education has no role to play in Chinese business practice. This issue should be carefully examined and addressed. First, unlike Japan, China was emerging from a planned economic system to a market driven economy, so the need to organize such a transition systematically became very critical. Second, this transition from planned economic system to market-driven economy was further complicated by the pre-reform closed economy to an economy more open to the outside world, making understanding about Western management education both necessary and important. When Taiwan began its economic development in the 1950s and the early 1960s, formal management education at the university level was not taught by any of the major universities. However, in recent years, in order to advance the economy further and faster, management education at both college and university level has been emphasized. Today, all the major universities in Taiwan have management faculties or departments.[10]

The delivery of management education has also gone through some interesting and not insignificant changes in China. In the early days of management training in programmes such as the Dalian programme described in the earlier section, teaching materials were essentially North American-based. North American instructors using existing teaching material and methodology conducted short- and medium-term management courses with the assistance of Chinese interpreters. Such teaching materials were often translated into Chinese for wider circulation. This included the very successful series published by the Dalian Centre. The current management education programme, which moved into a more structured degree programme in the mid- and early 1980s, now typically has two distinct components. One component is very North American in form and substance, and includes basic courses in micro- and macro-economics, finance, marketing and accounting. The other component is rather Chinese in character. It consists of courses in political economy, mathematics, some language and computer training and, depending on individual institutions, a collection of quantitative courses. This has resulted in a massive need for textbooks for the first component of the programme. Consequently there was an up-surge in translating existing standard North American texts into Chinese. A typical example of such a venture is the very popular translated version of *Price Theory and Its Uses* by Watson and Holman.[11]

The dichotomy of a North American component and a Chinese component is very typical to all Chinese management degree programmes both at the undergraduate and graduate level. The only difference in recent years is the increased proliferation of management textbooks with Chinese cases, examples and characteristics. There are now books written in

Chinese in different functional areas of management with strong Chinese characteristics. A good example is the book on *Chinese Financial Institution and Management* by Zhang, Dipchand and Ma. Cases of Chinese industries are now also available for graduate curriculum.[12]

The last issue that we will touch upon in this section is on management education and its benefit on individual job related performance. It is, of course, very difficult to assess directly how individual management graduates have benefited from management education in terms of their job performance and job promotion. Putting the same question slightly differently, one wonders how these management graduates have benefited their respective corporations. In many ways, the jurors are still out as the history of management education is relatively short when it comes to making a meaningful analysis. However, at the executive management training level, the impact is more direct. In a follow-up summary and analysis conducted by a monitor of a Canadian government sponsored management education programme, the monitor concluded that,

> In each case, the programme [executive training programme] was considered [by the participants] extremely valuable, in that it provided new ways of thinking, new concepts and ideas . . . reshaped [the participants'] understanding of quality control and costing, and their relation to market needs. . . .

It is quite evident from this survey that management education does provide a useful foundation for managing Chinese corporations and enterprises at the senior level.[13]

SUMMARY AND CONCLUSION

From our previous discussion it is quite evident that China has received a great deal of assistance in management education from foreign countries. In this section, we will outline some of the problems facing China in this field, its future outlook and some suggestions for change.

Without doubt if China wants to be successful in its economic reform process, it needs a generation of people, young and old, to manage the reform. Unlike their Soviet counterparts, the Chinese are generally more entrepreneurial by nature and the period during which a planned economic system has been in place is shorter than was the Soviet experience. People with management know-how and entrepreneurial experience are still around to pass their spirit, their knowledge and their enthusiasm to the current generation. As long as the economic reform continues, the need for management personnel will soar. The central question is whether the influx of support from foreign governments and agencies has had any impact on management education and the supply of qualified managers and instructors in China. Along the same line, one might also ask about the impact on economic reform due to these foreign assisted management programmes. The answer to the second question is an important one but obviously very speculative. One would be hard pressed to argue that management training and management education have not assisted China in the economic reform process. A new generation of management students has graduated from universities and colleges across China. Many factory and enterprise managers have gone through modern management training. Some are now working in joint venture corporations and state owned corporations that are issuing or have issued stocks in the two emerging stock exchanges in China. The impact may be difficult to quantify, but even the sceptics must acknowledge that management education has helped in advancing economic reform in China.

To answer the first question, it is quite evident that comparing the pre-1979 management education situation to the current management education situation, China has made important and significant advances. China now has nine universities that offer Western style MBA programmes, over 270 universities that offer undergraduate programmes in management and related specialities, 78 universities and colleges that offer graduate programmes in management and 21 universities that offer doctoral programmes. However, with the current speed and momentum of reform, the demand for such personnel is even greater than the supply. This excess demand is compounded by three other road blocks.

The first road block is the issues of non-returnees. China has sent its best and brightest students to study abroad, either in one of the previously mentioned foreign assisted programmes or through scholarships or private sponsorship. Privately sponsored Chinese students studying abroad have tended to remain abroad if they could find work upon graduation. In the aftermath of the 4 June 1989 incident (Tiananmen Square) many of those on official programmes also elected not to return to China. This represents a tremendous brain drain to the system. Recently, efforts have been made by the Chinese government to attract some of these students back to China, but the success of these efforts is not yet known.

The second road block is the chronic lack of funding in the education system together with the high salaries offered by joint ventures or profitable enterprises. These forces lure away some of the best graduates from the education system. Very often, one will find the same faculty members teaching in a university as they were five or 10 years ago with no new members to take over from those ageing professors who were educated prior to the Cultural Revolution, or even prior to the Communist Revolution of 1948. This situation can only be dealt with at the national policy level. Fortunately, some movement towards adjusting faculty salary, in particular among the business schools is beginning to occur.[14]

The third road block is the current speed of economic development. With the economy growing at a rate of over 10 per cent a year in the past few years as well as in the foreseeable future, there has been greater demand for young people to work in the trading and business sector. This demand is translated into the temptation either to abandon formal management training or be reluctant to receive advance training in management. Hopefully, this phenomenon is only short-term and the value of a formal and well structured management education will be considered by both employers and employees to be a value added to the operation of a successful corporation.

At the macro level, management education in China should advance in the following areas and directions. In order for the masses to understand, appreciate and use modern management practices, China should engage in management training and education at the broader level and at a more senior level. This can be accomplished by introducing the concept of advance executive training programmes and executive MBA programmes. Only as management at the top come to understand and appreciate the benefits of modern management practices can the same practices be accepted and implemented. China should also develop teaching materials that are relevant to the Chinese system, culture and practices. The proposed establishment of the three centres in China to develop Chinese case material is long overdue. Finally, the bottleneck in doctoral training is a most serious situation and China should seriously consider relaxing of its rule on using Chinese only supervisors. There are many qualified Western professors who would be willing to help in supervising bright Chinese doctoral students in China.

ACKNOWLEDGEMENTS

Comments provided by Hugh Thomas and Mike Gordon on an earlier version of this chapter are greatly appreciated. Information and discussions provided by Professor Zhao Chunjun of Tsinghua University, Professor Chen Bingfu of Nankai University, Professor Guan Zhian of the University of Science and Technology, Beijing, Mr Liu Dianqin and Mr Li Shunxing of the Chinese State Education Commission have been most useful in forming the framework of this chapter. Comments by participants at the International Conference on Management Issues in China at St John's College, Cambridge, 23–25 March 1994, and particularly the editors of this book, were most useful. The author alone, however, is responsible for any errors or omissions.

NOTES

1 In a 1990 conference of management which has a specific focus on China, there were 91 papers presented. However, only five papers were related to management education. Two of these five papers were authored by Chinese scholars and researchers, one had joint authorship: a Canadian and two Chinese professors on a specific MBA programme experience in China; one was by two American professors discussing North American Management Schools, and the other by a Western scholar of MBA programmes in China. What is more

surprising is that in the biographical and reference sections of the paper, there was no citation of published research in the subject matter.

2 A good general discussion of management education in China prior to the 1949 liberation can be found in Cheng and Hu (1990: 182–184). While management education in Beijing, Shanghai and Tianjin between 1979–1988 is best summarised by Warner (1990), a more recent survey of management education in China can be found in Borgonjon and Vanhonacker (1994: 327–355).

3 The Four Modernizations Programme includes the modernization of agriculture, industry, science and technology and defence.

4 For a detailed discussion of laws and regulations pertaining to the early operation of joint ventures in China, see Chan and Guan (1986b).

5 At the end of 1991, the official exchange rate for one US dollar was equivalent to 5.7 yuan. In 1994, the official exchange rate for one US dollars was about 8.5 yuan.

6 Currently there are only 36 universities in China that are under the direct jurisdiction of the State Education Commission of China.

7 There have been some interesting empirical analyses focusing on how Chinese managers learn (see Warner 1991), as well as analysis on managerial competencies (see Bu 1994). Brown and Jackson (1991) also perform an interesting study on the changing Chinese environments in the requirement for management education.

8 This programme was recently extended to 1996 due to programme interruption after the 4 June 1989 incident.

9 One can expand this discussion to cover areas such as accounting, finance, marketing and other areas of management disciplines. For related points on human resource managment (HRM) see also the chapters by Warner and by Brown and Branine in this book.

10 In a recently held conference between the Chinese and Canadian university presidents in Canada (5–7 November 1993), the Chinese delegation identified the area of management education assistance from Canada as the number one area that China would like to strengthen and widen in terms of co-operation and assistance.

11 This book was so popular at one time that the price went from the list price of 1.75 yuan up to 6.20 yuan, then to 15.50 yuan. It is an excellent example of price theory in action.

12 An example of this can be found in Leenders and Erskine (1991).

13 A complete survey is available in Cairns *et al.* (1992).

14 Apart from salary adjustment, there has been a new trend developing that many bright young university graduates who have been working for joint venture corporations are now seeking employment at universities and colleges. This is part driven by the fact that most joint venture corporations do not provide housing arrangements for their employees. After having made an above average income and gained some valuable experience, graduates now find that universities with housing arrangements have become an attractive and viable alternative.

REFERENCES

Borgonjon, J. and Vanhonacker, W. R. (1994) 'Management training and education in the People's Republic of China', *The International Journal of Human Resource Management* 5(2): 327–355.

Brown, D. H. and Jackson, M. R. (1991) 'Meeting the challenge to provide effective managers in the changing Chinese environment: a systemically structured

analysis of the requirements for management education', in N. Campbell *et al.*
(eds) *Advances in Chinese Industrial Studies, The Changing Nature of
Management in China*, 2: 117–136, Greenwich, Conn.: JAI Press,.

Brown, W. N. (1990) 'Towards an indigenous MBA programme in China', in
Y. Wang and W. C.Wedley (eds) *Proceedings of the Canada–China International
Management Conference* 69–378, Xian.

Bu, N. (1994) 'Red cadres and specialists as modern managers: an empirical
assessment of managerial competencies in China', *The International Journal of
Human Resource Management* 5(2): 356–383.

Chan, M. W. L. and Guan, Z. (1986a) 'Management education in the People's
Republic of China, with special reference to recent support programmes by
foreign countries', *Management Education and Development* 17(3): 1181–1190.

—— (1986b) 'An overview of Chinese law and regulations relating to foreign
investment', *Quantitative Study of Economics and Population Research Report*
173, Hamilton, Ontario: McMaster University.

Cairns, J. C., Wedley, W. C., Zhao, C. and Bai, X. (1992) *Management Education
Analysis Mission: China – A Study Prepared for the Canadian International
Development Agency*, Ottawa.

Cheng, M. and Hu, H. (1990) 'Characteristics and prospects of the development
in higher education of management in China', in Y. Wang and W. C. Wedley
(eds) *Proceedings of the Canada–China International Management Conference*
326–328, Xian.

Chinese State Statistical Bureau Publishing (various years) *Statistical Yearbook of
China*, Beijing.

Chow, G. C. (1985) *The Chinese Economy* New York: Harper & Row.

Dipchand, C., Ge, J. and Liu, P. (1990) 'Development of management education
in China: The MBA Centre at Xiamen University', in Y. Wang and W. C.
Wedley (eds) *Proceedings of the Canada–China International Management
Conference* 360–365, Xian.

Li, S. (1992) 'The development of management education in China', speech delivered at the Canada–China Management Education Programme Co-ordinator's
Meeting, Hamilton, Ontario, 28 November.

Leenders, M. R. and Erskine, J. A. (1991) *Guanli Anli Bianxie Zhinan*, instruction for writing case material, Dalian: Dalian Pressing House.

Wang, Y. (1990) 'The development and reform of management education in
China', in Y. Wang and W. C. Wedley (eds) *Proceedings of the Canada–China
International Management Conference* 329–349, Xian.

Warner, M. (1990) 'Developing key human resources in China: An assessment of
university management schools in Beijing, Shanghai and Tianjin in the decade
1979–88', *International Journal of Human Resource Management* 1(1): 87–106.

—— (Summer 1991) 'How Chinese managers learn,' *Journal of General
Management* 16(4): 66–84.

Index

Abernathy, W.J. 153
Abramowitz, M. 22
abstraction, and modernization 43
accountability 251
administration, decentralization of *see* decentralization
agriculture: economies of scale 19–20; free market 1; growth in 14; 'lumpiness' of systems 32n.; modernization of 1, 87; role in national economic growth 22; and rural industry 131; Stalinist organization of 19–20; and township enterprises (TEs) 133
Albania, economic performance 17, 22
alliances: providing horizontal and vertical integration 48–9; of state enterprises and non-state sector 50
Andrew, K.R. 79
Anshan Iron and Steel complex 220, 221, 225, 229, 231, 232
apprenticeships 224
Armstrong, M. 193, 194
Aslund, A. 26, 28, 32n.
Astley, W. *et al.* 109
Aston Programme of organizational studies 66
Atkinson, J. 198
Atkinson, J. and Meager, N. 198
audio sector 64, 70, 71, 72
audio-visual sector 64, 65, 66, 67–8, 71, 72, 77
austerity schemes 71–2, 77, 78
Australia, and management education in China 248
authority, devolution of in state sector 1–2
automotive sector 64, 65–6, 67, 71–2, 146; decision making in 89–93; joint

ventures 91–3; state monopolized distribution 79
autonomy, factors affecting levels of 67–72; and lean production 157; of research organizations 182
awards, National Awards for Scientific and Technological Progress 176–81

banks 55n., 71; and joint ventures 152
Barwise, P. *et al.* 111
batch production 155, 156
Beer, M. *et al.* 197, 198
Beijing, reforms of state enterprises 65–7
Beijing Academy of Non-Ferrous Metallurgy 186
Beijing/Capital Iron and Steel 221–3, 227–8, 231, 233
Bennett, D.J. and Forrester, P.L. 156
Bennett, *et al.* 88
Bennett, D.J. and Wang Xing Ming 145
Bergere 21
'big bang' economic reforms 26, 27
Blecher, M. 98
Blyton, P. and Turnbull, P. 208
Boisot, M. 42
Boisot, M. and Child, J. 37–8, 48, 78, 79, 210
Bolton, P. 52
Bond, M.H. and Hwang, K.-K. 42
Borys, B. and Jemison, D. 52, 79
bounded rationality 107
Bower, J. 107, 113
brigade-run enterprises 130, 131; *see also* township enterprises (TEs)
Brit-Chem 107, 111, 114, 116, 117; MMA plant investment 120–1